TUNING IN TO THE AFTERLIFE

HOW TO STAY IN TUNE WITH THE FLIPSIDE

BY RICHARD MARTINI

Tuning In to the Afterlife: *How to stay in Tune with the Flipside*

Copyright © 2021 by Richard Martini. All Rights Reserved.

No part of this book may be reproduced by any mechanical, photographic, or electronic process, other than for "fair use" as brief quotations embodied in articles and review without prior written permission of the author and/or publisher.

The author of this book does not claim the individuals named in this book are the people themselves. There is no way to prove anyone is communicating from the afterlife, nor does author claim doing so.

Author makes no claims about the authenticity of the reports. He turns on the camera or recording device, turns off the camera or recording device, and transcribes those sessions. He does everything he can to ensure transcripts reflect the footage or tape. The fact that people claim to be talking to, hearing from, having a conversation with, answering questions from is not his claim, theory or belief. He films them doing so.

Author does not claim to offer medical advice or prescribe the use of any technique as a form of treatment for physical or medical problems without the advice of a physician, either directly or indirectly. The intent of the author is only to offer information of a general nature to help you in your quest for emotional and spiritual well-being. In the event you use any of the information in this book for yourself, which is your constitutional right, the author and the publisher assume no responsibility for your actions.

Homina Publishing PO Box 248 Santa Monica, CA 90406

Painting: "Angel Playing a Lute" by Rosso Fiorentino (1521) Uffizi Gallery

TABLE OF CONTENTS:

CHAPTER: PRELUDE: MUSIC OF THE SPHERES

CHAPTER ONE: BEYOND SOUND

CHAPTER TWO: MUSIC IS MATH

CHAPTER THREE: WHERE DOES MUSIC COME FROM?

CHAPTER FOUR: SOUL MUSIC

CHAPTER FIVE: A FIFTH OF BEETHOVEN

CHAPTER SIX: THE FREQUENCY OF LIFE

CHAPTER SEVEN: IT'S ALL FREQUENCY

CHAPTER EIGHT: WE'LL BE RIGHT BACK

CHAPTER NINE: MUSIC THAT HEALS

CHAPTER TEN: FEELS LIKE A THOUSAND YEARS

INTERMISSION: MUSICAL MUSINGS

CHAPTER ELEVEN: THEY'VE BEEN WAITING

CHAPTER TWELVE: ONCE MORE WITH FEELING

CHAPTER THIRTEEN: MUSICAL CONSCIOUSNESS

CHAPTER FOURTEEN: IDEE FIXES

CHAPTER FIFTEEN: CELESTIAL MUSIC

CHAPTER: REPRISE: ONCE MORE WITH FEELING

CHAPTER: ENCORE: LET IT BE

AUTHOR'S BIO AND THANKS

PRELUDE – "MUSIC OF THE SPHERES"

Concert Pianist mom Anthy Martini and her biggest fan

"There is geometry in the humming of the strings, there is music in the spacing of the spheres." Pythagoras

My first note was mom's.

I could hear her playing the piano while still in her womb. The sounds were muffled, distant, but there was a joy to the playing that I could hear.

Literally.

I didn't recall this sound until decades later, when doing my first of six deep hypnosis sessions with different hypnotherapists trained by the Newton Institute.

I had been asked "What's your first memory?" by Jimmy Quast, of Easton Hypnosis. Jimmy was the person at the Newton Institute who verified, licensed the people who submitted their taped recordings of hypnotherapy sessions for accreditation.

Jimmy was in the midst of conducting a four-hour session – which Michael Newton had suggested along with Paul Aurand, then President of the Newton Institute. They said;

"Why don't you try one Rich?"

I thought it a perfect opportunity to prove hypnotherapy false.

I hadn't come there to prove there was an afterlife – I hadn't believed that I had any past lives, and I didn't think that I could be "put under hypnosis" because of my generally active mind. Plus, I'm acutely aware of what the camera is seeing having written and or directed 8 theatrical feature films.

So, when Jimmy said, "What was your first memory?" I heard mom playing the piano. But because of the muffled tones, I realized where I was hearing them from.

Jimmy asked, "Do you feel comfortable with this choice of a lifetime?" I hadn't learned yet the process of choosing lifetimes, I was just answering his question. "Yes, I feel that this is going to be a lot of fun. Mom seems like she's happy to be having me."

I have met people who recall being born. It's one thing to read about someone saying "Yes, I recall being born" but another thing to recall that feeling of being pushed from dark to light, from warmth to cold, to that overwhelming light that comes inside the hospital room.

The look on the Doctor's face as he's holding me up, eyeballing me. Me seeing his hazel eyes and mask, and that funny metal circle above his head. He seemed concerned about the fact that I wasn't breathing. At least that's the only explanation I had for him smacking me and putting me into my mother's loving hands.

I can recall those loving hands.

The last day of her life she played the piano for an hour – classical pieces. I was holding her strong hands when she passed, strong from a lifetime playing until her last concerto: at age 88, appropriately enough for those who count piano keys.

Mom was a concert pianist, her father, US Navy Commander Edward A Hayes was invited to Washington DC to serve in FDR's cabinet. Former National Commander of the American Legion, he had the Legion of Honor award and many others in his career – and because he was the campaign manager for then Republican candidate Frank Knox in Chicago, when Knox was made Secretary of the Navy, he brought along Edward, and Edward brought along my mom.

Mom performed in many embassies in DC, but was also a dancer, and had a contract with the Shubert organization – a pretty big deal for actresses who wanted to work on Broadway. She was performing at the Watergate Theater in DC when my father, the future architect, Naval Officer, was working the lights backstage. Story goes that he threw a green light on her, as it made her red hair pop out while dancing… and at the cast party, she met this handsome Italian American who has teased her with his lighting skills.

But she was on her way to NYC and doing plays on Broadway for the Shubert organization. She was in New Haven when my father wrote to say he missed her, and she told the theater director she had to follow her heart. She was replaced in the show by Oona O'Neill (who went on to marry Charlie Chaplin.)

While mom hung up her dancing shoes, my father always made sure she had pianos to play no matter where they lived. Whether it was in Cairo, Houston, or Northbrook Illinois (where she had two) he always made sure she could play.

It was my uncle who bought a concert grand piano so she could play in their estate in Brecksville Ohio. I can recall many warm summer nights, the doors flung open, and mom entertaining not only the friends and family, but the deer, fox and other animals who would gather outside his backdoor for her concerts.

When it came time for my dad's passing, mom had me record music of her playing songs for his funeral as she knew she would be too emotional to play during that event. And so, when she passed a few years later, in the same church we had attended for so many years, gone to midnight mass on Christmas together, fidgeted in for my confirmation, used for my son's baptism – that music rang out over the pews and arches of St. Norbert's church, a church she had played in before many times before, and one last time...

How many musicians can say they've played their own funeral?

Music was the first thing I can remember hearing and it was before I was on the planet. Growing up, we were surrounded by music and musicians. We had two pianos so she could play duets, had the "first chairs" of the Chicago symphony stop by to play monthly. I used to stand at the edge of the piano, listening to them and would chirp when they made a mistake.

How did I know they were making mistakes? I have no clue – but I can remember being banished from their rehearsals for doing so.

I played in a rock band in high school – we did Rolling Stones covers and Chicago blues. That began a trip behind the keyboard that up to present day, sitting in with bands when I could, playing in nightclubs in far flung countries. When I had the chance, I'd play for an audience and sing some Chicago blues.

One of the first concerts I recall was Chuck Berry's. I was in high school, drinking beer illegally with my brothers at Southern Illinois University, the show was typical Chuck, playing with locals who didn't know all the tunes he called out. An uneven set to say the least. 25 years I later saw Chuck play at the Moscow Film Fest. and was not surprised the show was the same – musicians trying to catch up while Chuck did his own thing on stage. Johnny Be "not so Good."

I become a music critic at one point. My pal Bruce Haring, then music editor at Variety needed stringers to write reviews and asked if it was something I might do on the side when not writing and directing movies.

I loved it; free tickets to the best shows in LA, write a review and bring music to life in 250 words. It's how I got to review and meet Prince, Sting, Van Morrison, Dylan, Elton John. It's how I got slapped in the face by Johnny Mathis. (For saying my mom was his biggest fan – it was an age thing.)

I shook the hand of Carlos Santana backstage, and as I did so, recalled this was a boy who sold Chiclets on the border of Tijuana, and now here he was a transcendent musician with golden fingers.

I loaned Mick Jagger a bowtie in Cannes, he promised to give it back one day. (He once called on my parents' car phone – helping me with tickets to his film in Sundance, and my parents laughed as I said, "My old pal Mick returning my call.")

With Mick's dad Basil

I have tickled the ivories in bars and clubs from Mumbai to Soho House in London, the Ambassador's home in Shanghai, in college had a gig at the Excelsior Hotel in Rome. In Paris I had a standing invite for a gig at Monteverde restaurant in Odeon. In LA, we played in a band called "Imminent Disaster" which was composed of music critics led by Variety's Bruce Haring, Bob Bernstein, Craig Cole; we played gigs on Sunset Strip and the House of Blues.

Later Craig Cole and I played gigs at the trendy Les Deux café, where people sat in from Billy Zane to Don Everly.

Julian Lennon the original white feather.

I mention this because there has never been a time where I wasn't somehow involved with music.

In reflecting upon this, I realize I've seen musicians play, then somehow meet them in person. Seeing Elton John open for Derek and the Dominoes as a teen, then shaking his hand after his Leon Russell gig and thanking him for a lifetime of playing his tunes, learning Mick's songs then meeting him in Cannes and asking what "Crossfire Hurricane" meant ("Don't know mate; two words that went together") having Van Morrison grill me how I got backstage (licensing his song "Wild Night" in my film "You Can't Hurry Love") meeting Springsteen in Charley's Pub in Boston, then decades later at Sting's show, reviewing that show, then sharing a multi-airport chat with Sting on the way to Rome, seeing BB King as a teen then meeting him backstage at Johnny Carson where he gave me a pin… singing Ray Charles tunes in high school, then directing him in a feature film.

It's as if the "resonant frequency" of their music rattles around in my journey and I find myself in their field of view. I am also a card-carrying member of BMI and some of my film scores have paid more residuals than my directing gigs. I have tunes playing on Tik Tok that I didn't know about until the residual for two cents arrived.

I'm tying this all together, like pulling the random notes from a musical score and setting them into some semblance of order because my life has been musical from birth and prior.

Based on this decade of research accessing the afterlife via the flipside, I've become aware of how music and consciousness are apparently linked.

What does tune in *to the flipside mean?*

We're going to discuss how to do that – how to "tune into the flipside" –how consciousness has its own frequency, how each individual has their own version of a frequency like a thumbprint, how we can lower or raise that frequency in order to imagine, and later forensically prove we can communicate to our loved ones.

Also explore what tuning into the afterlife means for those on the flipside. What it's like for them to realize they are "no longer on the planet" and learn to adjust their awareness, like tuning a guitar, they tune themselves to become aware of how that process works over there.

Explore the limiters and filters on the brain – the ones that science tells us exist, as noted by UVA's Dr. Bruce Greyson. Dr. Greyson was the first person I became aware of using the term "filters" to mean "how certain aspects of consciousness are not available to us." (See Dr. Greyson's "After" for references to "filters on the brain.")

Some children seem to lack filters up to the age of 8 ("I saw grandpa in the kitchen") some older people lose the filters prior to passing. Some mediums don't have those filters and some people can bypass them through hypnotherapy or meditation.

In short, in this book we're all going to be tuning into the afterlife.

In my three books with Jennifer Shaffer, a medium who works with law enforcement agencies nationwide on missing person cases, we've had many musicians have come forward from the flipside to talk about the process, to talk about their journey to talk about why they left when they left.

They all have opinions, thoughts, observations about how consciousness works, what it is to make music on the flipside, and how they "orchestrated" many of the events involved. Pun intended. This book contains musical excerpts of those six years of conversations with people on the flipside. It was Prince who during a session with Jennifer told me my "next book should be about music." This book is festival of music as well as a mental festival, it's a consciousness raising as well as a consciousness lowering exploration of how music is related to our journey on the planet.

A flipside Lollapalooza.

So, crank up the volume, sit back, and tune into the flipside with me. Allow me to explore the music of the spheres with you and learn how to access each other's frequencies.

CHAPTER ONE: BEYOND SOUND

"The universe is a symphony. And the mind of God, which Einstein eloquently wrote about, is cosmic music resonating through spacetime…

If we had a microscope powerful enough, we could see those electrons, quarks, neutrinos are vibrations on miniscule loops resembling rubber bands. If we pluck the rubber band enough times and different ways, we eventually create all the known subatomic particles in the universe.

This means that all the laws of physics can be reduced to the harmonies of these strings. Chemistry is the melodies one can play on them."

(Michio Kaku "The God Equation" (Doubleday 2021) Above "Song of the Angels" 1899 William Adolphe Bouguereau)

While at film school at USC, I was part of a project with a hearing-impaired filmmaker, helping write a grant for filmmaking opportunities. We called the grant "Beyond Sound."

Through Greg Brooks, a deaf filmmaker from AFI, I learned rudimentary signs in Ameslan, American sign language. It's a visual way of speaking. It demonstrates one doesn't need sound, and when one considers that Helen Keller couldn't see, hear or speak until later in life, yet she became someone who toured the world. Communication needs no words, nor pictures.

Ameslan came in handy recently. I was speaking with the medium Kimberly Ray Babcock, who was speaking directly to someone on the flipside describing how the afterlife worked. I asked him, "What's your opinion of this research?" She answered, "I don't know what this means but he's moving his hand from his mouth towards you in reply." I said "That means "Thank you" in sign language." She lit up. *"That's what he's saying!"* (It's in my documentary "Hacking the Afterlife")

In dreams we communicate telepathically, never using actual language, when we speak to animals we often speak in tones without language – with music, we speak with notes and emotion and without words.

When one thinks of what light is – both particle and wave, it's reminiscent of what music is. Both solid (the plink, the pull, the tap of the string, drum, piano, or use of vocal cords) and then the resonant wave that moves away from the instrument and hits our ear. Which is then translated into electrical signals that become sound when hitting the receiver of our brain. Depending on the emotion behind the note, we receive a message from the artist who wrote it or performed it.

As noted by Dr. Greyson in his book "After" or in his YouTube talk "Is consciousness produced by the brain?" scientists now consider "the brain functions like a receiver." Like the stereo receiver that gets unlimited band waves of information, the brain filters out what isn't related to survival.

Can we go beyond sound and bypass those filters?

We can with the help of hypnotherapy, mediumship or meditation. In each of my 8 books on the topic, I filmed people doing just that – bypassing filters, sometimes while under hypnosis, sometimes while accessing a loved one via a medium, sometimes through simple questions about an NDE that someone had years earlier. All yield the same hallmarks, the same results.

One could argue it was the tone of my voice, my questions, that bypass the access to the higher self. That would make sense except that I've filmed people doing the same without me speaking, with hypnotherapists asking questions or with mediums who are translating those answers directly.

Literally doing the same thing a musician does – taking an emotion, idea or concept and turning it into an expression that conveys meaning.

Having sold stereo equipment at Systems Warehouse at 60 Green Street in San Francisco in the 70's, I know how receivers work; with their limiters and filters that parse information from sound waves and turn them into electrical signals that make speakers jump.

They filter out extraneous information, undesired frequencies. However, the older speakers can pick up all kinds of sound, walkie talkies, cell phone calls. Odd radio stations running at a particular frequency that has a mathematical correlation (chromatics) to the speaker's reception. "Sound" or "music" would come from the speakers that weren't on, weren't hooked up – just randomly "announcing their existence."

In Italy, there was a fellow who had an old tube radio that was receiving more than just stereo. He was clearly getting "voices" (EVPs) and a number of people filmed interviews with this fellow and examined his old tube radio. For some reason, people would show up in his shop, and then a voice would come on the speakers (hooked up or not) and the person in the shop would say "That's my mother!" or "That's my brother's voice!" (Marcello Bacci of Grosseto, Italy began to dial in these "spirit voices" through his vacuum tube radio in the 1960s. Clips are on YouTube)

I watched a video of his device – since I speak Italian I could hear what people were saying. It was a bit like a scramble of noise – with a few words. The people who heard the voices claimed beyond a shadow of doubt they heard loved ones. Skeptics argue they're stray radio signals. If it was that easy to "dial in the flipside" we'd all be doing it, wouldn't we?

I had the experience of descrambling a "voice from the flipside" when I first met Dr. Elisa Medhus. From Houston, her son had passed from a self-inflicted gunshot. As an atheist and skeptic, as a scientist she did not believe in the "afterlife" until one day when her cellphone rang, she answered the "unknown caller" and heard her son's voice say "Mom. I'm okay."

Then she got a call from a medium in Atlanta – Jamie Butler. Jamie said, "Your son showed up in my living room and won't leave until I called you."

Since then, Dr. Medhus has had a number of mediums of differing abilities show up and hold conversations with her son on the flipside. With the help of Jamie Butler, her son wrote a book from the flipside "My Life After Death" – which at some point I tried to help her get interest from Hollywood. (None could comprehend what was being said.)

But I met Dr. Medhus when she said she was about to do an interview with someone, and that person was someone I had researched extensively, so I offered to supply the questions. I did, and that interview with Amelia Earhart is reproduced in the book "Hacking the Afterlife."

But when I was checking out Dr. Medhus' site, I came across an interview she had done with "Jesus." I have to include quotes, because there's no way to prove that this person on the flipside was him – other than by gauging his answers and examining them in light of others who might claim to be speaking to him.

In this interview, her son brought two people into Jamie Butler's living room. Dr. Medhus was on Skype in Texas, and Jamie in her office in Atlanta. Jamie said that "Erik is here, and he's brought a friend." She went on to describe the author of the "Naked Civil Servant" Quentin Crisp.

What made that detail mind bending was that neither the good doctor nor the medium Jamie Butler knew who Quentin Crisp was, or why he stopped by. But he said, "I'm just here to watch this interview like you two."

Jamie described his outfit to a tee, and anyone who knew who Quentin Crisp was, would know what kind of outfit he might wear. He made a few hilarious comments – the kind of comments an out and proud gay man might make during an interview – but neither knew who he was or that he had died in 1990.

So that began the interview with "Jesus."

As Jamie described him, she suddenly burst into tears and was not able to breathe. She said, red faced, tears coming down her cheeks, "I'm sorry I have to stop. He's standing too close to me and it's overwhelming." She asked him to "scoot back" a bit so she could continue the interview.

Then during the interview, a voice answered her question.

Jamie didn't hear it, nor did Dr. Medhus. I did.

Dr. Medhus asked if he had "reincarnated since then" and a male voice clearly says *"Yes"* a split second before Jamie says, *"He said "Yes."*

That made me sit up. He spoke a few more times, including correcting Jamie mid-sentence (she says, "useless effort" and he corrects her saying "wasted effort.") I clearly heard it, but neither of them did. Then later, at one point, two male voices can be heard whispering, *"Why don't you go on about selflessness?"* and the other person responds, *"We're done with (the topic) selflessness."*

I reached out to Dr. Medhus and Jamie. "Were you aware there are voices on the track?" Neither of them was. Both confirmed their recordings were done in quiet rooms with no one nearby.

I downloaded the track, slowed it down, sped it up, boosted the volume. There's a "click" sound that accompanies the "yes," and then later, the two whisperings – which were unintelligible at normal speed (the voices sounded slow or slurred) – by speeding them up 1.5 times, they sounded normal. Intelligible.

And there's a scientific phenomenon where if someone scrambles a phrase, and then reveals it, a person cannot "unhear" the phrase. It's no longer scrambled in their minds, but clear.

Hence the comment "Why don't you go on about selflessness" (as they were discussing being selfless) and the comment *"We are done with selflessness"* can be heard. Clearly audible.

Just as a phenomenon of sound recording, it's next to impossible to record two voices at the same time at different speeds. It would be possible if someone had recorded a conversation and then slowed it down – but it happens three times in the same tape. "Yes," "Wasted effort" and "We're done with selflessness" all sound normal when the sound is sped up. A physical impossibility when recording.

Which brings me to the idea of frequency.

During a dream my wife had, where she saw my friend Luana Anders telling her that our daughter's cold was temporary, that she would "be okay" – my wife, in her dream, said "but wait a second Luana. You died 20 years ago. How can you be here talking to me?"

She said, "**Think of 11:11. We meet at the decimals.**"

The next morning my wife asked what I thought it meant. To me it related to the speed of thought and frequency. I've heard it often – "We need to slow down in order to communicate with you. You need to speed up to communicate with us."

The slowing down is a way to slow down what they're experiencing – a different rate of speed, in order to communicate with us. And we need to "speed up" if we are asleep, meditating or using a medium to access this information. The medium doesn't need to "speed up" because their filters are already tuned to the flipside.

Apparently, the ability to communicate is related to speed and frequency.

When walking through Manhattan one day I passed a store on Fifth Avenue, then froze. I walked back and into the store and followed a bald tall fellow into another room. And then I heard his voice and recognized it instantly. He turned and it was my cousin Marty Callahan, tall, elegant fellow that I hadn't seen in decades. Had not seen since he lost his hair.

And yet, a glance into a storefront, at the back of his head made me think "I know that person."

On the flipside, people report that we can recognize loved ones instantly. Doesn't matter if we're seeing them young or old, or at an age we didn't know them – or in a lifetime that is previous to this one. "There's my dad." "I see my brother, but he's a girl in this lifetime." People report seeing their loved ones in other lifetimes – a bit like seeing a familiar actor in a movie where they're playing a completely different character.

We can recognize Meryl Streep, Daniel Day Lewis, Jim Carrey in whatever makeup or odd costume they're wearing. They might play different roles, or like Robin Williams, dramatic roles we barely recognize them in or even in drag, as Mrs. Doubtfire.

Same goes for the flipside. Doesn't matter what they show up as or costume they're wearing, we recognize their frequency.

Is that frequency?

The other night I had a dream about frequency. I became aware that I was in a conversation with someone – I don't know who precisely – but someone with knowledge about these things and was saying that "frequency is how you identify someone."

I often become aware of these profound conversations just prior to waking (and sometimes they show up in our podcast "Hacking the Afterlife with Jennifer Shaffer") but in this case, I asked for a term to remind me of the conversation. And I heard the word "I.D."

As in "ID card."

Our frequency is our ID card.

The best example I can give is one that occurred to me years ago. I was asleep in our apartment in Santa Monica, and became aware of an older woman crying, walking towards me, sobbing. "I can't find my husband." She was distraught, at her wits end.

I was aware of what she was wearing, she was like in her 80's and extremely upset. I stopped her. I said, "Can you show me him?" She looked at me and said, "I can't find him." I said, "But do you have a memory of him I can see?"

And she showed me a photograph of him – younger, happier.

I said, "Hold on a second." And I zoomed out into deep space, a bit like Superman just lifting off and zooming, and I was aware that I was traveling beyond light speed, because the light of the stars was melting around me, and I could see like a green pod of some kind in the distance, like a giant plant, and as I came closer (at lightning speed) I could see inside one of the pods, and there was this fellow, playing cards with his pals.

I mean literally sitting at a table with his blokes. And I said, "Someone's looking for you" and yanked him out of his chair, and we zipped together back "down" to the planet (up, down, sideways, no clue) and stopped in front of the woman.

"Is this who you're looking for?"

They embraced.

Now, after that dream I thought of what happened. It was like I "opened myself up to the entire universe" to find this fellow, and like a google search engine looking for unique digits, found him.

It reminded me of a session I filmed for "It's a Wonderful Afterlife" where the skeptical film producer who didn't think she would "get anywhere" was describing a game of "tag" with her "soul group" or the classmates she normally incarnates with. She was laughing and smiling while watching this. The hypnotherapist Scott De Tamble (lightbetweenlives.com) said "describe it to me."

She said "They're playing tag. At first, I was like, "what?" They wanted me to come with them to play this game. And I was saying to them, "Tag? Really?" And then they showed me this wasn't normal tag, because you could hide anywhere in the universe. And to complicate matters everyone is invisible, so they could hide anywhere in the universe, and then as an added incentive it could be in different time frames or in different realms. And to win, you had to capture all six simultaneously."

I was filming that episode. She was a skeptic, didn't believe in an afterlife, didn't believe she'd get anywhere and in a few minutes was recalling a lifetime in Arizona that I could verify on the internet – the name of the town in 1820 in old Arizona.

And now here she was watching her pals back home playing "Lightning tag" or "etheric tag" or some game that was mind bending.

But that came back to me after I "found this fellow" in deep space. It's like she showed me a mental image of him, I then took the information from the hologram, the photograph, put it into my "search engine" and found him, in a split second.

And I mean – a split second. Retrieving him and putting him in front of her took no longer than "hang on."

I haven't really spoken often about this incident, because it's mind bending, and puts me in some category as a kind of google engineer. But I'm not aware of that – and I can only assume that anyone can do the same.

And this was the memory that the person in my dream wanted me to talk about.

Identification. Frequency identification.

When you think of your grandmother, can you hear her voice? Can you see her face? Feel the touch of her hand? That's all a holographic memory of them. Those senses are part of your memory of them, but also part of their existence. So, when we talk about a person bringing a portion of their conscious energy to a lifetime, and the rest stays home – that home portion is accessible.

How to get someone to show up without knowing their exact frequency?

Ask.

So, as we report often – anyone can do the same.

1. *Say their name.*
2. *Ask them questions.*
3. *When you get an answer before you can ask the question, you'll know you've made a connection.*

It's knowing the frequency of the person – even in a casual way. How would their name be the key?

Because they've heard it before, they know it's being used. I often joke that poor Jesus has to show up all over the planet every time someone calls for him – and they call for him for the most minor of reasons. "Jesus!" "Jesus H. Christ!"

Imagine that for a moment. "What?" "Excuse me, who are you?" "You asked for me, I'm here. What?"

Would scare the bejesus out of some folks.

So, the idea is to identify them in your head – you can think of a photograph, painting, you can say their name aloud. Doesn't have to match the name they grew up with but you know your grannie's name, what she looked like, the feel of her hands, the smell of her perfume, the tone of her voice.

Ask her to come forward and answers some questions. Tell her I said hello.

So why can't we hear the music of the spheres that some other scan?

It's the filters.

Filters prevent us from accessing information that's not about survival. For some bees can see UV light and we can't. Dogs can smell cancer; elephants can hear sound from 20 miles away. Actually, humans are pretty dense.

I mean that in a positive way.

I've been filming people bypassing their filters for over a decade. Anyone can do it. Not many want to.

But some of us have different filters. Many report a "gut feeling" about someone, or we "recognize someone as if we've known them forever" or we experience "love at first sight." That profound recognition of someone we've never met. We experience it in déjà vu, or sometimes as Deja nu as I call it – some part of the blueprint of our life plan that is pointing us in a direction. (As noted in "Architecture of the Afterlife.")

Sometimes people who have an NDE experience hear "music of the heavens." People always thought this was aberrant behavior, Oliver Sachs wrote a book about hallucinatory music, but as noted, it may *not be imaginary* music. It may actually be music.

Take composer Robert Schumann's case for example:

His wife Clara in her diary her husband "complained of strong tormenting auditory disturbances last night." "He complained of always hearing the same tone (then) another interval as well," she recorded in her diary.

He would hear music "so glorious, with instruments sounding more wonderful than one ever hears on earth." **"Exquisite suffering," Schumann reported in his diary. "(I was) severely carried away by wondrously beautiful music."** The composer said, **"This is how it is in another life, after we've cast off our mortal coil."**

He told his friend **"Franz Schubert had appeared and sent him a magnificent melody, which he had written down and composed variations on."** (Schubert died in 1828, this was decades later.)

Not much later, he agreed to "check himself into an insane asylum because he could no longer control his mind." There was a suicide attempt, where he was fished out of the water, then sent to a private asylum under the "care of psychiatrist Dr. Franz Richaz." He never left the asylum, died in 1856.

(Excerpts from "Schumann: The Inner Voices of a Musical Genius" by Peter F Ostwald Northeastern University Press; revised edition (July 8, 2010)

What if the composer Schumann wasn't bipolar?

What if he was actually hearing music because his filters were down? Instead of institutionalizing him to make him "normal" – put him somewhere that he could write with abandon the music that was in his head?

What if music could be used as a healing tool?

Studies suggest that just listening to different frequencies can be healing. Some have claimed that the music of the Renaissance, chanting, can heal people tonally.

Perhaps one day instead of a trip into the MRI scan, people will enter a sonic chamber and spend an hour getting a "sonic bath" of different frequencies to help heal different parts of the body.

How does frequency come into play in terms of the universe?

As string theory offers, everything is vibrating at some level. As Michio Kaku PhD has noted – the "universe is music." We can add Rumi's observation, **"You are not a drop in the ocean; you are the entire ocean in a drop."**

If the universe is music, then we are music. If the "Kingdom of Heaven is within" then we are heaven. ***Veritas Libertas.*** If the truth can set one free, learning that we are both music and heaven is something worth knowing.

Some point to the "Golden Mean" of the Fibonacci sequence as examples of ordered consciousness. "The Fibonacci Sequence has been nicknamed 'nature's code', 'the divine proportion', 'the golden ratio'; some physical examples of it: The Nautilus shell. The Mona Lisa. The bass clef.

The five fingers of a hand represent the same math. Tree branches, storms, seashells, flower petals, galaxies, animal bodies, faces... DNA molecules all reflected in the Fibonacci sequence.

So while string theory can point to how everything in the universe vibrates, the Fibonacci sequence points to the orderliness of many things with regard to what we observe, see, feel, experience. Spirals and mathematical counterpoints in a semblance of order.

So how do fractals, geometric shapes, vibrating strings, Fibonacci sequences translate to life, become the music of our many lifetimes?

For the past six years Jennifer Shaffer, my pal the medium and I have met weekly to chat with people on the flipside. In those books "Backstage Pass to the Flipside" 1, 2 and 3 there are numerous interviews with anyone who shows up in our "class" and many of those interviews are with musicians, for whatever reason.

That includes musicians I've met who are no longer on the planet, musicians I reviewed while working as a music reviewer at Variety, musicians I've played with onstage with our band, musicians I've played with in nightclubs around the planet, musicians I've met over the years in my different hats as film director, music reviewer, etc.

And sometimes they are musicians I've never met, don't know, but someone on the flipside knows them and has invited them into our "classroom."

Putting together this flipside music book, I went over some of the previous interviews we've done with musicians on the flipside. Some of the listeners or readers have already read these – in "Backstage Pass to the Flipside" or "Hacking the Afterlife." But in putting together a book about "music on the flipside" I found that excerpting the interviews allowed me to revisit what they had to say and give context where it wasn't before.

Like taking out an old song and writing new lyrics and adding new thoughts.

What does "music" have to do with the afterlife?

Apparently, everything.

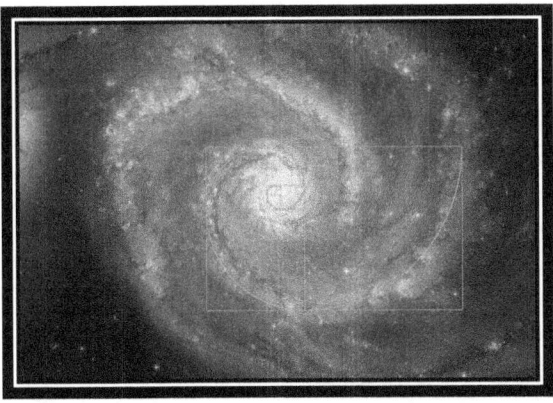

I feel like I've been here before... The Fibonacci Rodeo

CHAPTER TWO: "MUSIC IS MATH"

Hmm. Wonder who this could be?

Jennifer Shaffer introduced me to the concept that mediumship is like having a cell phone to the flipside. As noted, after hearing her departed son Erik's voice on her cell telling her he was okay, Dr. Medhus began conversing with him regularly with the help of mediums.

One day she asked if I might interview a new medium Raylene Nunes, someone she was going to be working with her on the channel. Raylene is featured in the documentary "Talking to Bill Paxton" on Gaia TV but this was our first conversation.

Raylene Nuanes from her home in Colorado.

Her answers are in **bold,** my questions in *italics.*

Raylene: Erik Medhus is coming through and says, "It's a process that has to be taught, we all have a knowing of it, but we have to learn how to communicate with them – the spirit lowering their vibration, the newly deceased aren't used to that vibration they have to learn how to do it. It's more like a therapy – he's talking about energy for people to lower their vibration."

Rich: How would you describe that to someone over there?

He's showing me the way they communicate is not with mouths – he's showing a (complete) visual to a person, like watching a tv show. He's putting images into their mind with his mind and is showing them over there how to do the same – not so much with words but showing them how to do it with their minds.

Just thinking it.

Yes, just thinking it. Prince comes through and says, "You are more at home than others." He says, "I'm connected to you," and he's also one of your guides. He likes the type of work you do – because you notice people and he's helping you to notice people. He says, "He's on your soul train – he's connected to you and says that you're home."

(Note: At this point in time, I had not published any of the interviews with him. Raylene could not be aware that I'd chatted with him a number of times.)

I know a few people that Prince helps communicate – like it's a frequency with musicians.

Exactly, that's a really good way to categorize it. People who work with art, theater, music; he says, "There is a connection to these souls these types of beings." But he's

correcting you, he's saying, "You channel him on a regular basis." He says "The way I communicate with you is your thought process. I'm talking about you creating music and not only movies; this is more, I would say (more) deep – instead of writing it out, it's what you're supposed to create."

Let me ask you Prince, they're going to be releasing some of your old work – anything you want to mention about that?

He says "Tell them to not alter my work. It's ok to release my work he wants it to be out there – but not altered."

You mean editing? Remixing?

"Yes," he says, "not to change the words or wording – he doesn't want it altered." He says, "He doesn't want them remixed because it's authentic to him – it's not a selfish thing he's very proud of the work that he did."

Okay. I mention one of the interviews he did with Kim Babcock, where he talked about a previous lifetime where he suffered from not being able to communicate. And this time around he wanted to communicate on a global scale.

He's saying, "Thank you for pointing that out – you're absolutely correct about that." He says "I still continue to work (on my music) from this side. People will still be saying "Prince inspired their music."

What would be the most authentic way to reach out to you?

He smiles, he's flipping his hair, getting really serious. He says, "Just say "Prince" and think of me and I'm there – think of me and I'm there – think about me and you're connected instantly – I have a knowing where you are."

He says, "He can visit people instantly by thinking about them."

So, why'd you check out early? You told Jennifer Shaffer that "dancing killed you" – meaning jumping off pianos hurt your ankles, which got you addicted to drugs.

He says, "Thank you for being supportive – his disability from piano and many other things did lead to a drug addiction because it was more of an addiction used for pain." He's telling me, "It wasn't smart of him, but it was easy for him to access it – he doesn't blame anyone for his transition, he was ready to go – he was tired."

Are you playing with anyone over there?

He says, "I play with other music artists – we don't get together like we did in life because we're all connected now – think about having family function and being connected to every person – he's more into being in spirit form at the moment, if that makes sense. He's not urgent for the human experiences, he's not urging for that anymore – I can go back into time into my Prince memory and live that time as a human if we want to."

Let's talk about music – are you aware of music over there you were not aware of over here?

"Yes, it's all vibration, very different over here – no words to it, it's all vibration and it's very beautiful colors are different too."

To give us reference – I understand it's more of a feeling, but can you give us a description – as an instrument?

He's going on about a guitar. He says, "Imagine a guitar, the string, when you push it and it makes the vibration and think about the color coming off the string, and the color *red* coming off the string."

Color is a vibration; red is a vibration – a wavelength. Are you saying if I play a note that corresponds to red – are the wavelengths similar?

He says, "It's very similar."

I want to ask you about the music that you can hear that you're not creating over there. It's not coming from you or created by you – what does that sound like?

He says he's trying to explain it in a simple way – he says that it is hearing but also feeling. "You know how we can feel wind but can't see it?" He says, "It's a vibration," he's comparing the vibration "to wind, to water. As to the density – it's like a love song would be love, a sad song carrying a soft vibration of music" – He's talking about "Wind, water, moisture."

And I'm thinking in reference to people who have heard music during their NDE (near death experience). Everyone that I've interviewed who experiences music over there – they don't hear one symphony or note, but etheric beautiful tones. I guess I'm trying to ask where does music come from?

He says "light."

Does it come from a particular person or place?

He says, "From source."

Can we identify that place – I know it's hard to use human words – but who or what is the source?

He says, "Well "God" is source – it goes onto your belief system." He says, "There's only one source so if you have or think of your sources as Jesus, that would be one source – you're connected to source so you could think of yourself as source as well."

I understand that God is an experience more than a person – related to love, and if you open your heart to everyone and all things you can experience God?

He says, "Yes. You could characterize that as walking through a garden. The garden is what god is, the religion is the flowers."

(Note: In the interviews we've had with Jesus, he's said the same thing, but not through this medium. But that "all religions point to the same garden.")

I'm asking about the celestial music. What are you hearing in the garden?

He says, "Each movement with the wind has a different tone if it goes down or up it makes different sounds – he says it's different tones."

So, when Beethoven talks about channeling the spheres to access music – was he channeling that musical wind?

He says, "That's a good way to think of it; channeling the wind." "But," he says, "It's on a broader band, more than wind." He's giving me a visual... "You can't see wind, imagine a tree moving back and forth – beaming down

from the high end, the air is not coming down in one chunk."

He says, "Think of musical notes; it's coming down in notes, in wind notes, in tones, and then it transfers to your head. You can hear it – the channelers of music – they can hear the beat, it's a channeling of communicating with higher beings."

*****

I didn't know Raylene, I've never met her in person, but we've done a few interviews together. This may have been the first one. There's a chapter where she accesses some animals in the book "Architecture of the Afterlife." She's quite talented at what she does, and every time we've spoken it was mind bending.

But Prince's discussion of how colors have wavelengths that coincide with the frequencies of sound, reminded me of a topic I visited a long time ago. How the wavelengths of color and music can be compared. How the wavelengths of music and color can be mixed up in the mind of someone with synesthesia.

About his comment on frequency and color:

(Isaac) Newton demonstrated that color is a quality of light... light has properties in common with both waves and particles. It can be thought of as a stream of minute energy packets radiated at varying frequencies in a wave... Light has specific values of frequency, wavelength, and energy associated with it" From Britannica: "The visible spectrum"

What is being reported is that music and colors carry the same vibrational qualities and creating visual color is related to music. Chromatics include both frequency and tone, as well as the colors associated with the wavelength. Pink or rose would have the same "chromatics" of red, the way a note five octaves away from the original would carry related waves of the frequency.

For example; there are cases of people with synesthesia, where people report they *hear* music as *color.*

In high school, the lead singer of our band, Abbie Adams revealed she could hear music as colors – if something was in tune, or in the right tune, she'd see a corresponding clearer color to that note played. *"Synesthetes might see colours when they hear sounds, for example or experience tastes in the mouth when reading or speaking... These sensations are explicitly experienced in that synesthetes are consciously aware of them in daily life."* "Defining synesthesia" British Journal of Psychology. London, England. Feb 2012)

In an interview with Jimmy Fallon on the Tonight Show, Billie Eilish revealed three members of her family have synesthesia, her father, brother Finneas and herself. "Synesthesia, (is) a brain condition in which a person associates colors and numbers to people and objects. For instance, she sees "Tuesday" as purple, while her father, who also has synesthesia, sees it as orange." (CNN 8-10-21)

Billie said they actually "argue about it."

As for Fallon, Eilish sees him as a "vertical brown rectangle," she associates the letter J and M as brown. She noted this all translates to a "vertical brown image" in her mind.

Instead of classifying it as a brain disorder *("Disorder? Where can I sign up for that Grammy wining talent?")* the three of them are leading the way into people discussing how consciousness works, how the brain associates colors with frequency, how the mind associates colors and frequency with content. In short, giving people insight into how musicians create.

She said that her previous album, tour – emerged from her visual sense of what the shows should be, colors and frequencies that "she associated with that music."

As to her latest album, "Happier Than Ever," *"I didn't know what I was going to do until when the album was over. I didn't know what it was going to be called, what the vibe was going to be, what the artwork should be. I knew I wanted it to feel very specific… have a real feeling and aesthetic to it."* And then, she said *"I (suddenly) got it." (Like a download.)*

As we'll hear later in this book, recently during a podcast, medium Jennifer Shaffer said **"Prince is here."**

I asked why, she said **"He wants to talk to you about tuning. I'm seeing guitar strings. He wants you to tune them."**

I thought of all the guitars in our place – and which one might need some new ones. But I asked, *"Wait a second, what's he physically showing you?"*

She said, "He's showing me that if you tune strings too tight, they'll break."

I asked, *"Is this a metaphor? Is he talking about our journey, our path, how we need to find the middle way, not too tight and not too slack?"*

Jennifer's eyes went wide and said **He says, "*Yes! That's it!*"**

I couldn't recall where I'd heard that before, it might have been in one of the chapters mentioned in this book. Find the middle way, not too tight and not too slack. Find the right frequency for you, find the right frequency to connect with loved ones on the other side. After all they're just chromatics of the notes we've already played before.

A musical excerpt from "Architecture of the Afterlife."

In this interview, my pal Iris runs into some music icons. The reason I include it is because there are some unusual concepts offered within. At this point in her session, she is accessing her guide, who is introducing her to the flipside.

In this recorded session, Iris and I are at Scott De Tamble's office in Claremont, California. Iris has flown in to do a hypnotherapy teaching session taught by Scott, a clinical hypnotherapist trained in many different modalities, including by Michael Newton.

In this case, I'm playing the role of hypnotherapist. While other students are using the playbook about past life hypnosis, I know that Iris has done hypnotherapy before, so it's simply me asking her questions while her eyes are closed.

Her voice goes up a half an octave in this state, so it's unusual to hear my friends voice, someone I've known since high school, speaking from outside her body. At this point in the session, we're speaking with her guide about her classmates.

Rich: Are you a member of Iris' soul group? How many are in her group?

IRIS: "Yes. There are 100's."

In terms of a core group?

"Fifty-two. It's quite large."

Does she recognize people in her group? Family members?

"Oh yeah."

In a previous session, Iris explained her core group was working with addiction – is that still accurate, or is that just part of one class?

"That is part of her "energy class;" "How to Heal Addiction." It is energetic.

Are all 52 of the class healers?

Yes, and peacekeepers. Peacekeepers are healers.

What activities do you participate in aside from teaching?

I study and play games. Mind games. An earth example would be playing chess by linking our lives with the board…"

A chess game played in multiple dimensions?

"Yes."

What other games besides chess?

"We don't have time for many games; we listen to a lot of music."

Where's it generated from?

"It's ethereal."

Are there musicians that help you create that music?

"Not really. But there is a group. I've never met them; but they are in charge of music."

Let's help Iris to meet these music creators. Are we inside or outside?

We are inside; there are hundreds here, it's (in) an auditorium.

Can someone come forward to help answer my questions?

It's a male. He looks like Bob Dylan in his 20's. He has a guitar, no hat. The guitar is slung behind his back.

If I may ask you some questions; are you someone appearing as Bob Dylan for Iris to be able to communicate with you, or are you actually Bob Dylan's higher self?

He says, "Higher self, yes."

If I can call you "Bob" - I've met your daughter and granddaughter in life, I've spoken to a number of musicians on the flipside who knew you. My question is, when people manifest music either here or on the flipside, is it math, are you generating it, or is it a combination of both?

He says, "Music is math but it's also emotion. It's emotion tied to math. And we all generate it, we send it down people to download it. But they download with their lives; anyone can ask us, if they are aware."

(Note: I think "download with their lives" means "by choosing their lifetime, they are equipped with a certain frequency that allows them to appreciate certain types of music.")

Do you create songs or just a method to create songs?

"We create the feeling of the song; they can hear it in their head, and they translate it."

Who do you hang out with over there? Anyone that we might know here?

"Well, John Lennon. Eric Clapton is here too."

Should we speak to John?

"Sure."

John, please put in Iris' mind what you've told me about your son Julian. Something you told Julian before you passed – if you were going to communicate with him...

"White."

Show Iris what that is.

"A white feather."

Thank you.

(Note: Some years after his father's death, while touring Australia, a local tribal chief asked for Julian's help in getting fresh water for his people. As a gift he brought him a large white feather and Julian named his foundation after the gift "The White Feather Foundation." This is one of those "proof of concept" moments. I don't know what to say other than it's a confirmation of who I'm speaking with.)

What do you want to say to Julian, in case I can pass it along?

"Tell him he gives me a lot of joy watching him."

He's become an incredible photographer; are you helping him?

"Um, no; that's all him."

About what age is John appearing in front of you?

He looks about forty with glasses.

John, you didn't like wearing glasses in life – yet you manifest with them; why is that?

He says, "I need them. It makes things clearer."

Your glasses function as a mechanism to help you focus?

He says, "It helps me to see things clearly – without them (over here) I was tortured by seeing things *too* clearly.

I'm curious your impression of my friend Luana, whom you've met via Jennifer Shaffer. What does Luana look like to you now?

"She's floating. It's not like she has wings, but she floats around almost as if she does; she moves and navigates as if she has wings... she has blue eyes, blonde hair, shoulder length."

(Note: I've had a lot of conversations with Luana since 1996, but this is the first time someone has described her in this manner. It's thrilling really.)

Let's ask Luana how she thinks I'm doing.

She says, "She's very proud of you, Rich."

Does Iris have question for John Lennon?

(Iris aside) I met him once. (To John) "Do you remember meeting me?" He says he does. I met Yoko at La Guardia airport; we were going to Camp Stanley; we were at the airport and first I noticed Yoko because she had like 8-inch platform shoes and hot pants cut down to her navel – and my mouth dropped because she was so hot. Next to her was John and then Eric Clapton.

(Note: Camp Stanley was a camp in the Catskills where Iris went during high school.)

How old were you?

I was 16. I was with my sisters; they sat at the table next to us and said "Hi." My sister said "Hi, we're big fans" and John gave us his signature with a little drawing... my sister has it.

John what a treat to see you here; you can always help Iris.

He says, "Her singing isn't that great."

Very funny! I want to thank everyone who has participated in our journey today.

And Rich... they all have really good feelings about you. You have a very good healing soul.

Let's thank everyone for the journey and for Iris allowing us to go deep to this place we've been.

*****

CHAPTER THREE: WHERE DOES MUSIC COME FROM?

"Mnemosyne" Mother of all Muses - Wikimedia

The Goddess of Memory was a very important goddess in the Greek world. She was the mother of the Nine Muses. A prayer was said to her before every performance of a play because the plays took days to perform, and the actors would beg for a good memory.

In terms of her myth, she met people after they died, and had them drink a cup of water from the river of memory, so that they could "remember all their past lives."

And then, just prior to people being born, she'd give them a drink from another river, which made them forget all of their previous lives – and just focus on one particular one.

When people do figure out where and what to call the filters that are on the brain, that prevent us from accessing this information easily, they should name those filters after her.

Mnemosyne.

The word *meme* comes from her, as does *mnemonic*. A music phrase that helps one's memory. "Every Good Boy Deserves Fun" in musical theory. "Good Boys Do Fine Always." "Red sky at night, shepherd's delight. Red sky in the morning, shepherd's warning." Thanks to our pal Mnemosyne.

Someone in our "Hacking the Afterlife" forum on Quora reminded me of a story I've told of how after speaking with Michael Newton on the flipside via Jennifer Shaffer (as seen in the film "Hacking the Afterlife") as I returned to my car I realized someone had typed the word "Mnemonic" into my cellphone.

I didn't know what the word meant and found it amazingly coincidental that my jeans pocket might have randomly typed the word for "memory." It's what got me to look up the word mnemonic in the first place.

Just a tad ironic that the Goddess of Memory has been completely forgotten by time. She's the actual "Mother of all the muses!" *How very amusing!*

Interview with Jennifer "Stone"

I got an email from someone about doing a "session" where we would take a shortcut to access her council. In most cases, I tell people about finding a hypnotherapist near them, or about doing the kind of mediumship that would put them directly in touch with a loved one. But in this case, this is someone who is working with clients as a medium and felt that she wanted to do a direct connection in the way that I have done in the past. (*Her name is Jennifer, although not the Jennifer Shaffer we find in other chapters.*)

There are many mind-bending events in this session, so I'll let the words speak for themselves.

Rich: Hello Ms. Stone. I just want to state upfront that I consider that we're scientists here.

"Jennifer Stone" - I've never considered myself that.

So, when you were at Harvard, where'd you live?

Cambridge and Somerville... in the Fenway for a while.

Let's talk about Jennifer's journey – who's Jennifer Stone?

(Note: These sessions on zoom or skype are informal. There's no hypnosis involved, often drinking coffee. It's filmed for reference, and with permission, excerpted later. I'd never met Jennifer before this session.)

Jennifer: When I was in the *woo woo* closet, I worked for the head of research at a hospital, doing psychic readings on the side, so I made up a fake name.

Did he ever find out?

Yes, and he found it fascinating – so I was worried for nothing.

(Note: We access a relative no longer on the planet.)

Rich: What do you look like to her?

Younger. She sees me in my 20's, even though I'm 53.

What are you wearing in this visual?

Shorts, navy blue surfer shorts. A bathing suit and sweatshirt over it.

Color of the bathing suit?

Mint green.

Do you own this bathing suit?

No.

Okay, so this is "new information." If you owned this suit, you could create it – but you don't. So, in this being able to communicate with people on the flipside, part of it is allowing them to show us what we look like to them.

Wow, this is crazy.

What's the sweatshirt say?

Nothing; it's plain – like I borrowed it from some guy, like I threw it on because I was cold.

When you're holding her hands, do you sense any emotion?

Peace.

What's that mean?

Like "finally." That's the vibe I get – like "Finally; I have some peace."

Is that for you or for her?

For her.

How do you think your sister Jennifer is doing?

She says, "FABULOUS!" That's how she used to say that word. That's hilarious.

Is that your point of view as a relative or from someone else?

Before you even had the question out of your mouth, she said "All of us."

Great. "When you hear the answer before you can ask the question you know you're connected." Can we talk to Jennifer's guide?

She's saying there's a lot of them. Not just one.

Let's invite one or two – your principal guide or person to come forward and have a chat with us. Is that a male, female, neither both, a light or nothing?

I get two – it's more like – I'm sensing one is a light. Like a pastel, pinkish lavender blueish color – and the other one is showing me someone I've talked to before. You probably know him, the big Hawaiian musician "Iz?" He came through to me on my mom's funeral day. I didn't believe it was him, so he went to a medium friend 3000 miles away and gave them the message for me; it was him! She's showing me him – so I guess he's more of a guide than I thought he was.

Israel Kamakawiwo'ole – YouTube screen grab.

Try not to judge it. I appreciate him showing up. But before we talk to him, I'd like to talk to this light.

(Note: I do this because there's context involved with speaking to a person who used to be on the planet. The mind may wonder how it could possibly be this famous musician responsible for the iconic version of "Over the Rainbow" could possibly be her "guide." Instead of addressing him first, I focus on someone she's never met but may be capable of communication.)

I'm getting "Yes," but I don't know who is saying it.

That's okay. "Yes," doesn't have to be spoken aloud. I'm going to address these to the light. How tall is this light?

Seven feet.

I'm going to ask this light if it can manifest as a human for the purpose of this conversation so we can address this person with more clarity; can you show her a being of some kind?

This happened while you were talking... and I'm kind of shocked, but it looks like a human woman, but she's not – she's not from Earth. She's like big, blonde... and kind of like... I can't describe it. She's not solid like you and I, kind of transparent but more solid than wispy.

Thank you for showing up today, can you give us a name or a letter to use to address you?

I got the name "Trixie" (Jennifer aside:) Which is crazy! Sounds like a hooker name.

Trixie! That's a great name, I love it. Can we call you Trixie?

She's laughing, "Yes."

Are you familiar with me, or what I'm doing?

"Absolutely."

(Note: I ask this question because sometimes they say "No." It helps me gauge what I can ask of them.)

Can you put in Jennifer's mind how you're familiar with me asking questions? Am I a punchline over there or what? Who told you?

This sounds crazy – she says she "knew you before you were born."

Doesn't sound crazy to me. Our friend Jennifer is seeing you as semi-translucent. Is that because you're incarnated somewhere else as we speak?

"No, it's just how I present myself."

Have you lived other lifetimes on other planets or ever a life on Earth?

"Never on Earth."

So, I assume lifetimes on other planets or other universes. Is that correct?

(Pause) I don't hear anything.

But let me ask, have you incarnated somewhere else before?

"Yes."

Has it been in our universe or some other universe?

This is the weirdest answer; she says, "You don't understand they're one and the same."

Okay, I think I do; kind of what we're doing – conversing outside of time, but you're saying it's irrelevant to think of it as another universe. Tell me what Trixie looks like to you.

She's Amazonian – like 7 feet tall, big, like a basketball player. Big bones, big hands, look like beautiful face – the hair is weird, bangs that are blunt cut, platinum almost white, it is white, longish, down to her back. I think she has this blue – royal blue headband, bangs are covering it, but it has a stone in the middle, stone is like a gold color; she's dressed in white.

Okay, take hold of her hand.

I'm trying, but I can't feel anything. It's like she doesn't have any matter; I can't feel anything.

Translucent? Is there any emotion associated with that action?

When I ... I guess I'm holding her hand, but I can't feel it... it's almost like touching her I realize she has eons and eons and eons of knowledge.

Like tapping into a library of sorts?

Right.

Trixie – is that a pun? Or a name you've had for a long time?

"Very much a pun."

Ok, "Tricksy." There are tricks here afoot. It's so cool to meet you. I'm going to ask you for a guided tour, but I want to speak to her guide Israel for a second. What's he wearing?

(Note: Israel Kamakawiwoʻole became world famous for his rendition of "Over the Rainbow/What a Wonderful World." I read that he had a dream about the song, and in the middle of the night, called his friend a recording engineer and got him to meet in the studio. The version we've all heard was "take one.")

The first thing I notice he's wiggling his bare feet and he's not overweight ... normal weight - same face he had in his last incarnation, he's just thin... *ner.*

What's it feel like when you take his hands?

Super warm. Like a lot of joy – like he's giggly, super happy all the time. Which is why he's wiggling his feet; this is very fun for him to do – he likes it. This interview thing.

How did it come about that you recorded that song everyone got to know you from? If you remember?

Let me see.

There was an incident as it was reported – I thought it would be fun to ask him to put it into your mind.

I feel like he's showing a party – for someone who passed... did he record this for someone else?

Let's ask him. Iz? Who inspired you to record that song?

He said, "For Gabby."

Do you know who Gabby is?

Another musician...? Named "Poo ha knee."

Are you getting that from Iz or your memory Jennifer?

From him.

(Note: Mind blown. On my first trip to Hawaii, I was given a tour by one of my brother's oldest friends. He took me to a Gabby Pahanui concert – who was considered a famous "slack guitar" player. I had all of his cassettes when I came back. It's a bit odd to know only one famous Hawaiian singer and to have Israel say that he performed that song for *him.*)

Gabby Pahanui (Wikipedia)

There was a famous Hawaiian guitarist named Gabby Pahanui. Wow, let me clarify this – Iz, you're saying that **"Somewhere over the Rainbow"** *was performed as an homage to Gabby Pahanui?*

He's laughing. He's saying – "She hu..." he laughed and said, "she hu!"

Is that Hawaiian?

Jennifer aside: I don't know. He's saying, "She hu, shee hu!"

(Note: Research tells us "Chi Hu" is Hawaiian for "Yippee!" "A phrase commonly shouted by residents born and raised in Hawaii during moments of joyful excitement. Also sometimes spelled as chi hoo, chee hu or chee hoo.

(UrbanDictionary.com) (Samoa: "siususu") From "Pidgin English" chee hu (chi who) "alright; woo hoo; yippee" In A Sentence: Chee hu, pau hana! (Alright! I'm finished with work!" (e-hawaii.com) I know Jennifer Stone doesn't speak Hawaiian slang, but Iz does.)

Who was there to greet you when you crossed?

"My mother ..." He's showing me her in a uh, in a muumuu – old school muumuu – I don't think people wear these anymore.

Was it a kahuna or your mom?

It wasn't a kahuna... he's saying "Auntie... auntie."

(Note: I wasn't aware of this, but Hawaiians refer to caregivers as "Auntie." "In Hawaiian culture, to call an elder auntie or uncle is to communicate endearment and respect, along with an implied familial bond." *Quora.com*)

Was that a welcome surprise to see her?

He says "He was very happy. He says he was ready to go." (Jennifer aside:) How did he die? I don't even know.

(Note: Israel K suffered from obesity throughout his life, at one point weighing 757 pounds... He endured several hospitalizations because of health problems. Beset with respiratory, heart, and other medical problems, he died at the age of 38, survived by his wife, Marlene and their daughter. *Wikipedia*)

I don't know, but I know he was overweight. Anything you want to tell your family or fans who every time they play that song, cry?

He says, "It brings me a lot of joy – it's like..." (Jennifer aside: He showed me a ball bouncing... It bounces back up to him – "Like the love (comes to him) and then he bounces it back down to us – like a ball bouncing back and forth – his music gives us joy and our joy gives him joy; it goes back and forth like a wave. He shows me a kid's bouncing ball."

(Note: I've spoken to a lot of guides, and many council members. This is the first guide I've met that lived on the planet recently. The idea that he is a "second guide," came forward at the same time as her main guide, Trixie, would likely mean that they knew each other in a previous lifetime, which I eventually ask.)

Are you hanging out with Gabby since returning there?

"All the time," he says.

Are you playing ukuleles or other instruments?

He says, "They play the ukes, but other stuff too – they can play whatever they want, but they're good at everything."

Are you playing with any other musicians?

He showed me this older African American guy who used to sing with Billy Holiday... It's Louis Armstrong. (Jennifer aside:) Holy crap!

That's wonderful; the singer of "What a Wonderful World."

(Note: Can't put a finer note on this portion of her interview. She saw a musician she didn't know, never met as being associated with her on the flipside, and when asking him a direct question about his life and journey, he reported performing his iconic song as an homage to a musician she had never heard of. And then when I correctly guessed the name of the musician, he spoke to her in Hawaiian slang, a Samoan phrase she had never heard of, nor had I, that I had to research to learn it's meaning.)

Later in this same interview, her guide "Trixie" (an Amazon of a woman) suggests we have more to look at:

Richard: Let's put that memory back into the time frame – anything else she needs to see in this library?

"Jennifer Stone" She wants to... she wants us to go over and meet this little, little old man who kind of runs the place. She wants us to say hello and to give him a little thanks for taking care of all the ... she calls them books. He's so cute – he's probably just under 5 feet. I don't know his age; his face is timeless. He looks human, really old but really young at the same time – I can't describe it; a million years old.

What's his name?

He says "Huey." (Jennifer laughs.) That is so not what I was expecting.

(Note: At a later date, years later, Jennifer Shaffer and I interview him, and he refers to himself as "Five." Maybe he was referring to "five feet tall.")

Nice to meet you Huey – can I ask you some questions?

He says, "I'd be delighted."

Are you aware of what I'm doing? I know it sounds like I don't believe it.

He says, "In general, yes, but he's too busy to pay much attention to the specifics."

That would make sense. Have we spoken before?

He says, "Yes – but not in this manner." I don't know what he means.

Like I was filming someone asking you questions, and I happened to be in the room at the same time?

"Yes."

(Note: I just had a flash of a session from my book "It's a Wonderful Afterlife" who was talking to this librarian (him! who else?) who was sarcastic and funny. He's the fellow who was asked; "what is the meaning of a shift in consciousness?" "What or who is God?" He replied "You humans think it's important to name things to get a handle on them. But in terms of a shift, imagine yourself a crab on the ocean floor and you open your eyes and realize you're in an ocean. That's a shift in consciousness.

To the question "What or who is God?" he said "God is beyond the capacity of the human brain to comprehend, it's not physically possible. However, you can experience God by opening your heart to everyone and all things." A sentence I've thought a lot about since he said it – and here I am transcribing this session and he popped into my head.

In a subsequent session with medium Jennifer Shaffer, he confirmed to me that indeed, he is "all librarians" and appears to each one in his own fashion, dependent upon their syntax and experience. Wow.)

I'm curious what your opinion is about people talking about a shift in consciousness – what would that mean to you?

The first thing he says, "It's been a long time coming; we've been waiting and waiting and waiting."

You mean "we" in terms of humans?

"No, the flipside people." He's saying that he "gets more visits now than he used to and he's excited because he didn't have enough company until recently. He likes it; his thing is "the more the merrier."

(Note: He's saying because consciousness is shifting, he's getting more visitors in the "Akashic records" from average people. That people on the flipside have been "waiting a long time for this to occur" and now it is.)

Did you choose this job? Or was it given to you?

He says, "Both."

I was writing about this today – "What or who is God? I'm curious what your answer would be?

He's pointing to all the little balls (of light) and saying, "This is God." (Jennifer aside:) Probably because he's a librarian. He probably has a lot of time to read.

Has your name always been Huey?

He laughs, says, "My name is whatever you want it to be."

What do your friends call you?

He's chuckling; "They call me Maestro."

(Note: Maestro is defined as a "conductor of music" or "a great or distinguished figure in any sphere." As noted, later he refers to himself as "five.")

I understand it's a ridiculous question – speaking to a million-year-old person – what does it matter what his name is?

Jennifer laughs.

Why does everyone see the library differently?

He says, "It exists, but not on any kind of plane we can visualize or understand."

You mean it exists etherically, like seeing a rainbow they see it from their rainbow?

He says, "Yes and no." You and I, Rich, we're physically unable to conjure what it is so we have to put these constructs around it – we see a tv screen or a scroll or a glowing little ball.

I was curious, since everyone sees it differently; that would mean it isn't a place – but in terms of relative experience to that person experiencing it.

He says, "No." He's scratching his head like "How do I explain this to you people?" He says, "It's almost like um... oh f*%k." He says he can't explain it to me... He's saying, "There are so many dimensions and (they're) so weird in other dimensions, there are no words (invented yet) to explain to you how it exists...– the best I can tell you

is that what you perceive it to be is as good as what it makes on our side."

Same goes with us having this conversation. But let's say Jennifer and I are on another planet and we're able to access this – it would be different if we are using words or syntax... he's saying, "This is beyond words?"

He says, "Yeah: you can't conceptualize it."

Same goes for "God" I suppose. What is it that you want to tell people?

He's saying, "Spread the word about my library because you don't remember anything down there." He's referring to us on Earth. He says, "Reading doesn't make you smarter, reading makes you braver." He's using light balls as an analogy, if we discover what's happened to us (via the library), we'll (come to) understand we have crazy phobias from stuff that happened in the past; we can learn why we're afraid of spiders or windows and it will make us braver.

A version of "The truth sets us free?"

He says, "Yeah; yeah."

What's the best way to access you?

He's saying, "You're doing a great job Rich... of learning – he says, "Dream time is particularly easy, but you have to set the intention before you go to sleep." He says, "That's the easiest way, set the intention you want to come visit and find these books and with practice you can get here very easily." He's saying, "For most people," and

he's got this cute little old man look – he's making a sad face – he's saying, "They'll never find their way here."

In their lifetime?

"Right" he says.

In the future another lifetime?

He says, "Possibly."

Were you ever surprised to see someone who stopped by to visit? Someone surprise you?

Okay, this is crazy but he's showing me James Dean with a cigarette hanging out of his mouth.

James Dean: Wikipedia

Let's focus on this for a second – you're talking about the actor?

"Correct."

You had met him before; you knew who he was before?

"Correct."

Okay, I had a conversation with him not to long ago (via medium Jennifer Shaffer). Are you aware of who he has reincarnated as on the planet?

He says, "Yes." He's not telling me who it is. It's like he's smiling, it's a secret perhaps. He doesn't want me to know.

I'm not supposed to tell her?

He says, "She really doesn't need to know that."

You mean it's not up to me to turn on the lights in the theater and say, "It's only a play?"

"That's right."

It was surprising having a conversation with James Dean. I was asking him my usual questions ("Who was there to greet you, etc) and I asked, "Are you getting ready to reincarnate?" and he said he already had." Odd thing was I know this actor he was referring to... and he said "Yeah, I'm that guy."

(Jennifer aside:) Wow; talk about six degrees of separation.

I texted a friend who is best friends with this actor and asked, "Has your friend ever had someone tell him he was the reincarnation of someone?" And he texted back JAMES DEAN. Later, he told me since knowing this actor, that his whole life random people would tell him that.

That must be kind of weird.

Well, he's got his own life and journey. He's a happy guy, has a family and is a successful actor with a great career.

Wow that's such a cool confirmation.

Is this accurate Maestro?

He said, "Oh, indeed your friend is him. It's true..." and um.. he's saying, "I need to get back to work."

(Note: Mind blown yet again. I'm speaking to a person on the flipside through a woman I've never met. This fellow on the flipside is reminding me that we've met before, that the actor that I know that I suspect is the "Reincarnation of James Dean" is actually the reincarnation of James Dean. I could not write this scenario if I tried.)

Okay. We'll let you go. But what kind of work do you do? Cleaning, categorizing, fixing up energy?

He says, "The books/energy balls are my children and I take care of them like I ..."

Like a mother?

"Like I... would if I had my own child." I get the feeling he doesn't have or never had kids – this was his full-time life.

Have you ever incarnated on Earth?

"Never."

That must be disconcerting for you to deal with so many Earthlings.

He's laughing, as if we are the children. He's saying, "this isn't just all Earthlings, this is everyone."

Okay, you've got a lot of work then. Thank you.

(Jennifer aside:) That was amazing. I don't know how it all works; I don't know how I got this gift of "talking to dead people..."

Let's ask Trixie that question. What does she say?

"Because you asked for it."

Now you know.

This was awesome, thank you.

Thank you. Wow.

*****

In this interview, we not only learn that her guide is someone (the higher self) who was famous for singing one of the most famous renditions of a classic melody in history, but that her guide wanted us to meet the "librarian."

Also, as noted, I reached out to the best friend of the actor who was noted as the reincarnation of James Dean. I asked simply "Has anyone every told your pal he was the reincarnation of someone?" And without missing a beat he texted back "James Dean."

Later he told me that their whole lives people had wandered up to him out of nowhere and said "Hey, I'm sorry to bug you, but you are the reincarnation of James Dean." So many times that he'd given up thinking about it. And apparently, he's had a number of "unusual events" around that memory of that lifetime.

A CONTINUATION OF THIS CONVERSATION WITH THE LIBRARIAN VIA MEDIUM JENNIFER SHAFFER.

As I often do, when I hear something mind bending during a session with someone not under hypnosis speaking about someone on the flipside, I often ask Jennifer and Luana

Anders to take up this conversation where it left off to see what else I can learn.

My comments are in italics, Jennifer Shaffer's replies (*How many Jennifers are in this book by the way?*) are in bold.

Jennifer Shaffer with the author

Rich: Okay, let me ask about a session I did the other day with a woman over skype. In her Akashic library, instead of seeing "books" she saw them as tennis balls sized light; energetic swirling lights.

Jennifer Shaffer: That's how lights attract lights – our whole existence is light.

Her guide was showing her this library, we met the librarian; a million years old with an eternally young face.

I got an image of Yoda.

When we asked for his name, he told us "Huey."

They're saying, "like the essence of Yoda." (Jennifer aside) I asked is that how he looked? And they said, "No."

Let's ask Luana to bring him forward.

He's here. They have him blocked in (scheduled). She put him in my head...

Let me ask you a question.

(Jennifer aside) Is this someone you knew?

No.

He's morphing into various different – he morphs into different looks from what I'm getting. Whatever it is... whoever it is... (He's changing into the perception of him.)

My first question; "What's up dude?"

He showed me stacks of infinite records a mile high... "that's what's up."

Are you the only Akashic librarian or one of many?

Library

He says, "Source." He showed me being him and shooting out thousands of pictures of his image in different lights. If I'm getting this right – he said "Source." He says, "Our soul is like the ocean... each wave is a different person."

So, you are the source librarian – people see different variations of you in their Akashic libraries?

He's saying it again; "Source." I think he's saying he's "God."

Let's clarify that.

He says, "You see what you want to see."

Well, we've heard God is not a person, per se, but more like a medium or a nexus...

That's what he showed me; like everyone is a light and everyone is connected. Everything that's on earth, all the different layers of the planet.

Have you always been The Librarian, or did you become the librarian?

Jennifer smiles. He showed me coming from other galaxies, being a part of someone else's world - he became his own librarian... (Jennifer aside) It's funny, you ... it's like he became his own god – the way they talk about it in the Mormon church where they talk about becoming your own God in the afterlife.

Instead of God or deity, let's use the word Librarian - it's easier to conceptualize... you came from another realm originally?

He says, "Yes."

How many years ago?

He says, "Tens of millions of years, "square root of pi" kind of answer."

Was that a realm anyone is aware of on our planet?

"Yes" he said.

Not in our universe, but another realm?

He says, (Another realm) "That's connected. It's like we (in our Universe) are the power source for the other galaxies."

Okay... your universe is the source of other universes?

"It's complicated," he says.

Just trying to clarify. We've spoken to people from higher realms, give us a level...

He said, "Eleven."

Are you in touch with people from there?

He says, "Yes." He says, "He needs a lot of people; he needs an army. He's the source for them – (Jennifer aside) I'm asking, "Are we the power source for him and his universes?" and I'm getting "Yes."

(Note: This seems to refer to a previous conversation where we learned that dark matter or dark energy is the source of matter in other universes; discussed in a chapter with scientists.)

But you're the librarian for all Akashic libraries?

"No." He says, "There are a lot of libraries."

So, the other libraries that you're not in charge of, others are in charge of?

"Yes."

How many libraries are you in charge of?

"It's like you take the population of Tokyo and you multiply that by a billion."

So, everyone in our realm?

"No."

Are you the librarian for everyone on Earth?

"Yes."

And some other places too...

He says, "We're connected to all of that – he's in charge of all of that."

In my interview with you, you said the books of our past lives are not about history but were about fear; the times we conquered fear in our past lives.

He said, "Yes. The opposite of fear."

Like "How I overcame fear in a previous lifetime?"

"Yes, that's why past life regressions help."

So, what is love if not the opposite of fear?

"Love is the heart center." He showed me it's connected to everything, oceans, seas, the earth.

We're connected heart wise to all people and all things? The ocean, an object, a table?

He says, "Yes."

On a quantum level – things don't come into existence until we choose to observe them according to quantum mechanics. Does that apply to everything?

"Yes" he said.

What do you want to tell us Maestro?

He says, "To stop fearing the unknown. The more that you love, the more that opens you up, heart wise, the more knowledge comes to you."

So why did you choose to show up to this guide during this session. She wanted me to meet you – why?

He said, "It should be in your books, the discussions we've had."

It will be.

(Jennifer aside) He's smoking a cigar. A Cuban cigar.

How long have you been smoking Cubans?

He says, "100,000 years." (Jennifer aside;) I know they weren't invented yet.

Did they exist prior to being on the planet?

"Everything did."

How is that?

He says, "When we open ourselves up, we reveal things that have always existed, we get things. Somebody was really lucky getting the first cigar, someone lucky getting Microsoft."

You're saying those things existed, but our conscious awareness of them does not – until it does? Is there something you want to show us so we can become billionaires?

(Note: My questions may sound flippant, but when I meet someone like this, an intellect that is hard for me to keep up with, I try to throw a few curve balls if I can.)

He showed me your heart center.

So, tell me how can people access Akashic libraries?

He showed me lying down – he showed me meditation. He says, "If you don't judge anything you can get anything. If you're not fearful of things coming in – it's very challenging to not judge what you see or hear."

Should people focus on you in their meditation to go to the Akashic records of their many lifetimes?

"No," he says. "They should focus on their hearts."

What's a question for their heart? To say, "I'd like to visit my library?"

He said, "Another way to say it is "I'd like to visit who I am elsewhere."' Using the word library helps everyone get there."

How about using "heart library" instead of Akashic?

He said, "That's what it is but – if you want people to get there, you can't use that word – they might think it's something else." He says, "You should use "Akashic" because it's taken thousands of years to get people to hear the word – even if they're not religious. Akashic means "heart."

I think in Sanskrit it means etheric or "invisible."

He said, "But it also means "heart.""

I asked you before if the geometric shapes people have seen were books – of those fractals are books; is that correct?

He says, "Yes."

You said calling them "Akashic books" is the right term –

He showed me something being pressurized... "Since there's no time in space, it's a record of time where you are."

Okay; like a packet in time? Who creates them?

"Our higher self does – that's how we get out of this lifetime – we have several outs."

We create the packets.

He said, "Yes."

How many does a person have?

He says, "Thousands. They are not all just one lifetime. Everything makes up one big shape – love, hatred, all these things, loss, that all becomes fractals - eventually they become cohesive and turn into "your books."

Can I access someone else's Akashic records? Are we allowed to do that?

He said, "Yes; everything is connected; you can see whoever you want – everything that's affected them."

So, what's in the books, functions like a URL or a link?

"Yes."

I'm aware the brain may not actually store memories in engrams – but function as a "link" to the off-site memory. That theory is that we don't store info in the brain but offsite?

He says, "Yes." He showed me that.

So, we have our own personal cloud, and the cloud is our fractals filled with memories from all of our lifetimes?

He said, "Yes."

Wow. Do the engrams in our brains serve as a link or a URL?

He says, "Yes. It also comes back though – as well - both ways. If we're feeling something on the planet, we get information coming from there, maybe not our past lives but something else."

Is it possible to access other people's past lives?

He says, "We're in the bandwidth." (Jennifer aside) It's like me (Jennifer the medium) thinking someone is going to die – it's a frequency I'm translating. I pick up that frequency."

Okay, thank you Mr. Librarian.

(Listens) It's one of his people (is speaking with him) – he says, "He's able to talk through people."

What does that mean?

He has a medium up there – he or she or whatever - is talking through someone there right now... He's showing me you. He says, "Because your research is helping people and there's a buzz up there about it."

I asked if you ever met anyone from the planet who impressed you over there, someone in the library, and it was someone from our class.

He's showing me James Dean.

Yes. Anyways, thanks for answering our questions; I'm sure everyone has a lot of questions, and we're like kindergartners.

He says, "Well, sometimes you learn from kindergartners."

****

As I say, mind officially blown.

Basically, the Librarian is saying the same thing that Prince was saying – that everything is frequency. That everything we experience, see, hear, enjoy, taste, feel while on the planet is frequency, and everything we experience, see, observe, mentally construct while off the planet is also frequency.

To quote the physicist Mino who appeared in a dream to someone and said "We are both particle and wave, like light. When we are on the planet, we experience more particle than wave, but off planet we experience more wave than particle."

If one thinks of experience as quantum physics – they can see how we are both particle and wave. Light is both particle and wave, and in the experiments done with light, they've demonstrated this fact. That light functions as both a wave and as particle – and that carries over to our experience of consciousness as well.

Both particle and wave. When we're on the planet our experience is more particle than wave, and off planet it's more wave than particle.

Apparently, everything in between is frequency or music.

Anthy conducting a minor symphony. Note the hand clutch.

CHAPTER FOUR: SOUL MUSIC

Robin caught flagrante delicto with unnamed pal.

Robin Williams began showing up in our book "Hacking the Afterlife."

At some point, it felt as if the book was too long, and the chapter about Robin was more about me dining with him and my observations of his effect on others than anything related to his actual journey. So, I took the chapter out.

Then the next session, *apropos of nothing,* Jennifer said **"Robin is here, and he wants you to put his chapter back in the book."** My mind swam a bit (was she in my computer too?) and then I said "Ok. Will do."

He shows up often in our sessions (as does Prince) and always has prescient things to say about mental health or about his path and journey or sometimes just silly, hilarious advice.

My questions are *in italics*, Jennifer's answers are **in bold.**

Richard: First let's say hi class; how are you doing?

Jennifer: Luana showed up and then Robin Williams.

So, Robin; tell us - what's up?

He says, "He's in New York." Some kind of an award or tribute is going on for him.

(There *was* a tribute for Robin in NYC on Sept. 19th, 2018, when this was recorded. *https://donyc.com/events/2018/9/14/robin-the-ultimate-robin-williams-tribute-experience*)

What's the formula for you to talk to us?

He just showed me like Hiroshima blowing up. Like this big cloud going up.

Like a nuclear reaction? I mean, is there a formula?

He says, "Yeah, there is."

Just for you and us or for everyone?

There is not really... he showed me a 3D image of a body, then he showed me all the different planes (lines) coming in... kind of like Vitruvian man?

Vitruvian Man by Leonardo Da Vinci? Robin used this image with you before you're probably not aware of it.

(Jennifer aside) Not at all.

Robin, how much do you slow yourself down to talk to us? If that's the right term.

He showed me everything pointing in, to the heart; he says, "He has to slow his heart down to match the heart he wants to talk to."

But what's the formula to do so - half speed? One tenth?

"One third."

In order for you to slow your frequency down to speak with us, you slow it down about a third?

He says, "It makes sense because it's one third of the body." He just showed me that.

How about in terms of Jennifer elevating her frequency or energy? Does she have to move it up two thirds?

He said, "In my case, I just have to be."

Okay. That makes sense. She doesn't have to change her frequency because she's already tuned this way?

"Yes." (Jennifer aside) You must know I've never thought of this.

Is Jennifer more tuned than the rest of us – what percentage?

He says "75% more tuned."

Comparatively between me and her?

He says "50% for you... you're getting there... you go up to 80 sometimes he says..."

I guess it depends if I'm paying attention. Correct me if I'm wrong here.

He says, "Caffeine affects it too... it helps you ask questions."

It allows you to bounce around or focus?

He just showed me marijuana...

Okay, and I'm sure Luana is helping as well (with this communication.)

Jennifer taps her finger on her nose. (Meaning "correct.")

So, it's this idea of opening up channels to communicate with them, but also slowing down the frequency or the wave over there ... so it's not like we could create an app where everyone could tune in because each person is different?

He showed me a thumbprint.

Which makes sense. Everyone is unique – so the thumbprint is unique to each person. In order to communicate would it be like a ham radio operator who keeps dialing until they get a response?

Hey, says, "It's like something that... it's like being and nothingness going back to meditation. Opening your mind to slow your heart rate down."

I know it's not like folks could just dial that frequency in...

He said "Someday." (They'll figure out how to adjust the frequency.) Jennifer aside: Wouldn't that be cool? We just figured it out.

I know some scientists who are trying to do that – design a device to communicate, but if each person is unique...

He just showed me evolution, like the monkey, how much they can hear...

Based on all their lifetimes?

He says, "Yes." (Jennifer aside) Even people like me though, with all the fears I had before (with this work, speaking to spirit); once I got over it, it was like I was just ready to go. Once you get over it (the fear of being able to communicate) you're ready to go. He just showed *me* being a violin.

One that is out of tune, out of whack?

He says, "Not very much."

So, all of your Jennifer lifetimes – from various forms of talking to spirit - you've been honing your ability to be able to do so in this manner in this lifetime. Now it's easier for you to play that violin of who you are?

Yes.

You're a Stradivarius.

I was shown that... in the form of a piano, like a Steinway... However, there's no hierarchy; it's just a tuned instrument.

Like I asked my concert pianist mom who is on the flipside about what kind of piano she is playing over there, and she responded, "All of them she ever played," then Jennifer, you saw her as a young girl in front of the piano.

......

Well, let's unpack this if we can. Sometimes I'm in the heat of the moment, or in this case the heart of the moment, and I'm asking questions as fast as Jennifer can answer them. I know her well enough (and she clearly says so in this interview) that these are not topics she's invented, thought about or made up before.

It's what makes us a unique team to converse like this. She's open to whatever pops into her mind, I'm open to asking any form of follow up question. We hear in the previous book, from Luana, that if one thinks of "11:11" as a formula – we meet "at the decimals."

As explained, each 11 represents a hallway. One is ours; one is theirs. They need to "slow down" their "frequency" in order to be able to communicate with us, either through dreams, sounds, lights going on and off, or some other method of communication.

We've been told in our hallways, meditation, sleep can help increase our vibration (or block out the cacophony of the day) so that we can "meet at the decimals."

Robin is saying the same thing here. That he slows down his frequency about a third to communicate with us. In Jennifer's case, she doesn't need to "speed up" or increase her frequency to communicate, as she's already "built that way." (Meaning whatever filters, she should have - are not there, or were not in place like many others have.)

For a scientific discussion of "Filters on the brain" I recommend watching Dr. Greyson's "Is Consciousness Produced by the Brain?" on YouTube or his recent book "After" for a discussion of filters. There's a discussion of the medical cases that point to how frequencies appear to be blocked by our conscious mind while we are awake, perhaps to allow us to experience things fully.

However, some people don't have those frequency blockers or have had them altered by a consciousness altering event – a near death experience, head trauma, or while under deep hypnosis, they are able to bypass those filters that prevent us from "hearing" or "accessing" this information.

Interesting to note that his reply to "So how can we build an app to help people do that?" he showed her a fingerprint. Each person has their own unique print (or frequency) and so that form of communication would have to be on a person-by-person basis – so that they could "tune themselves" to the frequency of their loved one on the flipside.

Also, worth nothing, this description of how Jennifer's "many lifetimes" as a medium or someone similar have each contributed to her abilities now. That's a topic touched upon before – musicians, artists, doctors, etc, appear to choose lifetimes that will result in the qualities they seek further down the road. It might be on their tenth lifetime that they get to a point where they can use them the way they've wanted to.

I know this seems esoteric, and further if we consider the source; Robin is someone who is known for comedy, known for his lightning quick mind. However, Robin on the flipside is just another lightning quick mind who is observing the nature of reality from his new perspective, and whether he's "Robin Williams" of *Robin Williams fame*, or Robin Williams, the fellow who's had 22 different lifetimes prior to this (I'm making up a number) and in this one, he got a chance to experience using his wit at lightning speed in front of an audience – either way, I can't *not* quote him because "it's not something that sounds like he would say" – but rather, I've come to realize that we need to adjust our hearing.

We don't know much about what our loved one's sound like on the flipside, based on all their journeys, and our reactions to what they're saying are based on our own prejudices and limitations on this side.

*****

(Another session. My questions in italics, Jennifer's replies in bold.)

Richard: Okay, I'm curious; Robin anyone who wants to come forward, Luana anyone we haven't spoken to?

Jennifer: Bill Paxton is here.

Hi Billy; you want to say hello?

There was a person you talked to yesterday, he is giving me images of Ojai as you were talking... was this guy a biker?

I think he is.

(Donal Logue the actor, author, friend of Bill's. I had him craft three questions for Bill on the flipside, and Bill answered all three correctly – to the point of Donal saying, "That is uncanny.")

Bill wants you to talk to his friend, the bike rider. He needs your help.

Okay, Billy, but I think I scare people when I say Bill wants to say hello. So, anything else you want to say?

He said, "Thank you." He's saying "It's rough getting to the front of this class... then they make fun of you (when you're up here) "just because..."

Burt Reynolds showed up six weeks ago but didn't say anything. Does he have something he wanted to say? If he doesn't want to talk it's okay.

Robin says, "He doesn't yet know how to communicate."

Well, you're welcome to chat with us – Burt, I think you met the film producer Jonathan Krane in our class. He can help you.

(Jennifer aside) Did Jonathan have a heart attack?

(Note: Jonathan D. Krane was John Travolta's manager, produced a number of feature films and three of mine.)

Yes.

I didn't know this... but he's showing it to me – he showed me the arm hurting, fell over.

It was about a year ago that Jonathan checked out... I was thinking as weird as it is, out of all the people I've worked with, he was the only film producer who took me seriously as a filmmaker. It's disconcerting to realize there was one guy and he's no longer on the planet.

But he can help you now... it's funny – he can help you now, and all of them went like this – (Jennifer shrugs.)

What does that mean?

Like they're embarrassed they didn't help you before.

Sydney Pollack is part of our group, I met him through Jonathan. Sydney, I was talking to your daughter the other day. You know Phillip Noyce, the filmmaker...

(Note: In our conversation with Sydney, he mentioned sending a note to Phillip Noyce. Phillip corroborated that he did get the note from Sydney just prior to his passing, and the content of the private message.)

Phillip confirmed the note you said you sent him was the actual note you wrote. Phillip said "Yes, that was the note."

Who is the guy with big hair? He showed me Tina Turner.

Luana was friends with Tina, they joined Buddhism together.

The guy who sings "I feel good."

James Brown? Is he there?

Yeah. Looks like it.

Slide on in James.

They're all laughing now. Prince did a lot of James Brown's dancing moves. Prince just bowed and did the "I'm not worthy" bow to him.

He was the original. Everyone learned from him. Who was there to greet you when you crossed over James?

He says, "His whole family." (Jennifer aside:) Did he know Luana? She was showing me Tina Turner... that was the connection – she's showing me that connection.

(Note: Six degrees of Luana. She knew Tina Turner, both joined Buddhism together (SGI) and Jennifer is saying that James is showing her Tina, that's his connection to Luana.)

James, you led an unusual life, it was a bit all over the map. So why did you choose this lifetime?

He says, "It was the simplest way to feed his family."

You were such a great dancer and great singer.

(Jennifer aside) Elvis just stopped by.

That's nice, we can get to him at some point...

(*Continuing*) James (Brown) wants to speak. He says, "He chose this life to be an influencer, he influenced everyone to "knock it out of the park." He gave them that "by being African American, by breaking the boundaries to do whatever they wanted to do. By giving everyone else an easier path to do whatever they wanted to do."

That makes sense. Thank you. Does Elvis want to talk to us?

He does. He showed me Priscilla.

What about his daughter? Is he in touch with her?

He says, "She's hard to reach because of her beliefs."

That's okay, it's allowed. Who was there to greet you when you crossed over?

His manager? (Jennifer aside) I don't know anything about him.

I know who he is. Did he appear young or old when he saw him?

Middle aged.

(Note: Colonel Tom Parker died January 21, 1997. Elvis died August 16, 1977; 20 years earlier, but as noted "two thirds" of our conscious energy is always "back home.")

That must have been pretty unusual for you – you couldn't get away from the guy in life and there he was to greet you on the flipside.

"That's how he knew he was no longer here, because he was greeted by him."

Who else came to greet you?

He showed me five individuals.

Was you mother one of them? I know you were close; when did she come forward?

(Note: We'll hear more about who greeted him later in the book.)

"She was right there with him." Was he tormented by the manager? I don't know anything about him.

In life, yeah.

He's showing me the man was like an equal with his mother...

Colonel Parker controlled his life...

I asked him if the manager apologized for his behavior and he said "No, but Elvis just understood why."

Does Elvis have any regrets about checking out early? Or was this an exit point as in "time to go home?"

88

(Note: We hear about "exit points" often – where people have a choice to "take the off ramp" but either don't or stay around for some other reason.)

He said, "He had two exit points before, but he didn't take them."

Do you have any regrets?

(Jennifer listens) Aw… he loved Priscilla. Says "His heart broken over losing Priscilla… he was so heartbroken over her."

(Note: When Jennifer says she doesn't know anything about Elvis, I know that to be accurate. Elvis and Priscilla separated on February 23, 1972, and filed for legal separation on July 26.)

So, when you first met Priscilla did you recognize her?

"Yes. Instantly."

From a previous lifetime?

"Yes, but he didn't know it then."

Did you have a relationship with her in a previous life?

"Many." He's showing me… It's like they had opposite roles.

You mean like she a princess and you were a slave?

"Something like that."

What about your musical ability? Where did that come from? Did you have that before?

He's saying "Yes, a couple of times before. He wanted to understand what it was like to feel like everything was out of his control when he did music."

Okay. Who was the most surprising person for you to run into on the flipside? Who impressed you over there?

He's trying to show me ... someone in a surf movie... He's trying to show me a surf movie.

Someone you worked with in a surf movie? Someone who did a movie with you, and you got to the flipside and you met this person and that impressed you? Okay, I'll look that one up.

(Note: I figured he'd done many, but I think he's referring to "Blue Hawaii" made in 1961. His close friend on that movie was Robert West an "American actor, film stuntman and songwriter... known for being a close confidant (of) Elvis Presley. (Wikipedia) West died in 2017, but according to these reports roughly two thirds of our conscious energy is always "back home" on the flipside. Sometimes people have a near death experience and see people who are still on the planet. So, if Elvis ran into this friend, he would be surprised to see him as he was still alive when he crossed over.)

He says, "This is a great class."

Thank you. Any last words for us Elvis? Anyone in our class want to speak? Lu, anything you want to say?

Luana's voice is so calming and soothing, I love her voice... she's saying "Everyone just has to be more open, and interpretations come in so many ways...

Well, the fact that Colonel Parker controlled his life, wouldn't let him travel, go anywhere, for Elvis to meet him on the other side... is kind of funny.

He's saying, "But he understood it."

Interesting that he said, "He wanted a life where he was completely out of control." So that was perfect because the person who helped him get out of control was the guy who managed him – meaning he did a good job. Never thought I'd be rehabilitating Colonel Parker's image in a flipside session.

"Right," he's saying, "That was the role he played."

....

Luana didn't know Elvis but knows others who knew him that have shown up in our class. James Brown showed up because knows members of our class and Elvis swung by because all of these people "vibrate" or "exist" in a similar frequency.

Elvis showed up in a recent podcast.

Tricky Dick and Elvis. (National archives)

OUR PODCAST WITH ELVIS

This is an edited transcript of the conversation between Jennifer Shaffer (in **bold**) and yours truly (*italics*).

Rich: Jennifer, it's close to your birthday of 7-1. What were you doing on your birthday 7-7-77? You were a wee toddler.

Jennifer: I think it was around when Elvis died. (He died in August of 1977). I just remember I was being placed in a living room, my dad came back from a run, and we were watching the news. Why did you ask me that question?

Just thinking about my friend Dave whose birthday is next week on 7.7. Luana is there anybody that needs to come forward that wants to talk to us?

(Jennifer makes a face.) It's Elvis.

Well, well for people who are not familiar with our book Backstage Pass we have spoken with Elvis before. I know I asked him some of the some of the same questions, about his experience crossing over.

He just said "Blue Suede Shoes" ... I'm actually hearing the song which is kind of nutty. I'm not thinking it. (A pause) I think he's making fun of me.

Well for the folks who haven't read "Backstage Pass to the Flipside," Elvis, who was there to greet you when you crossed over?

He said, "He recognized a child," so I don't know if he had a child... or Priscilla had a pregnancy that didn't go right... um... but it felt like a child. I know that wasn't the answer the last time.

(Note: In the previous interview he mentioned his mother as one of the first to greet him; I was aware of their close relationship.)

It's okay because the more we speak to people about the experience, the more people add to their story. He knows we've asked the question before.

Right, but I am still seeing somebody a child and that's what he wants to mention.

I see, so he's here today to talk about this?

He says, "Yes, he's trying to bring this point forward… which (he says) is especially for people that have lost a child before it came to term - for whatever reason."

We've heard that often, people being greeted by a child and the experience of seeing that child.

(In terms of people who've reported seeing a baby in our interviews; Harry Dean Stanton, who said aloud to eyewitnesses at his deathbed, "Hand me the baby" and in our interview with him, told us he was greeted by a baby that didn't come to term in 1962, (when he was 26) told us this a week before the memorial. Jimi Hendrix mentioned a child he was supposed to have but did not, and others have done the same, whether or not historians are aware of those miscarriages.)

(Jennifer aside) I believe in the thousands of readings I've given that before the spirit enters the body, they know what's going to happen whether or not it's going to be terminated, whether or not it's going to be come to fruition or whether or not it's there's something wrong and they have a miscarriage.

Countless times those children report even though they're not born here, they're born "over there." They get to help you with the other kids that are born later, they help facilitate that, so I believe he's bringing that up... like 'you still get to greet the loved ones that didn't necessarily make it.'

A very interesting topic. And the reason you want to talk about it, sir, is because you want people to know the process?

He says, "Yes."

In terms of this child that greeted you, was it a boy or girl?

He says, "It was a girl."

Was this somebody you knew from a previous lifetime or is this somebody you knew from this one?

(Jennifer aside) I'm getting that it wasn't with his wife Priscilla...

But was she somebody that was supposed to come to you in this lifetime or perhaps later on?

No, it wasn't something that's supposed to come to me this lifetime, but I knew that this person or found out after the fact that this person didn't have the baby...

So - it was somebody you might have had a baby with but didn't arrive for whatever reason and so then when you recognize this being, are you seeing them as a small toddler, or are you seeing them just as light or as energy... or how do you see them?

(Jennifer aside) That's a great question because he showed me the process. He was showing me as he was coming to

the other side… and Elvis said, "You can only imagine how disgruntled I was at first (crossing over)."

He says, "But then all of a sudden my heart was just completely full of joy and (saw) that there were no mistakes that were made. That every one that was made… was supposed to be made…

It was all part of the journey you had planned in advance?

He says, "I didn't feel bad about anything… I was told everything was exactly the way it was supposed to be."

That's beautifully put. Now just to point out that some people have a hard time with this because of course first their brain freezes when we say your name Elvis, because they can't get past the fact that we didn't know you.

And he just set Prince in front of him… (as an example of someone we've chatted with, but don't know.)

Put him in front so we'd realize we could talk to you even though we don't know you or didn't invite you today to chat with us? Okay. So, Elvis Aaron Presley, I have been to your birthplace in Tupelo Mississippi, as I just happened to get lost there, and stopped in front of your home while looking at the map.

Is that what you want to come and talk about? The process of incarnation or do you want to talk about music a little bit?

He said, "Thank you," and he says, "No. He wants to speak about the process." He said, "I know that would have helped me if I was to hear (about) that before I left the planet."

The information we're discussing resonates with people on some level?

He says, "Whether you believe it or not, it will resonate with some part of your being."

There's also this idea that we have a higher self that is aware of what we're doing or watching us on stage and watching our podcast in in the midst of their disbelief allows their higher self to hear an alternate reality. They things that happen on stage are not set in stone, but often improvised, is that correct?

He says, "Yes." He's showing me like, "Let's say 10 things were planned in your life; like having a child, getting married, your work being a singer," he said. And he says "And then from that... he's showing me a grid - so if you have 10 things or 10 points on the grid happening..." He says, "Then you have 100 points behind and underneath that, which we believe are coincidences." He's saying, "and then a thousand beneath that."

He says, "There's so much work that we're not consciously aware of, to have those things happen, and there's different ways to get to that point there's different ways to get to wherever you're supposed to go. To connect those dots."

We sort of have a grid that we've laid out for ourselves but correct me if I'm wrong, sometimes you don't connect the dots for whatever reason?

He says, "Correct. And that's what you have to make up in your next life (if you miss the connection.)"

Let me ask about your life review... I'm sure it was with lots of friends, family, teachers... What was that like for you or what was your review like?

He says, "It was long, long, like a huge download with tons of information."

Does everybody simultaneously get that information?

He says, "Yes."

For the most part you felt...

"Joy," he says. (Jennifer aside) I'm wondering if there is a better word other than joy...he said, "Love."

He says "It's like, I felt love in my life, but I didn't feel unconditional love." Like, he was loved by people, but he says, he "Didn't know the feeling of that unconditional love that you can have for someone else."

He says, "Everything was filled to the brim." He's just showing me his heart completely filled, filled up with love, like there was not one space missing.

He says, "And (the life review) it's like revisiting all the most amazing things from your life that fill up your heart." He just showed me it was like examining all the major moments from his lifetime, whether they're big, small or indifferent - he says, "Those accumulatively fill up your heart because everything else just kind of goes away."

If I could just talk to you about process for a moment, the idea you're onstage during a life review, and everyone in the auditorium experiences the ups and downs of your life. Is there an MC or someone who plays the role of the announce on "This is your life?" Is it your guide or a teacher?

(Jennifer makes a face.) **He says it was Jimi Hendrix!**

Really? Wow. Jimi has shown up so much when interviewing musicians on the flipside; it's the weirdest, oddest thing. Are you joking because you're aware of this class?

He says, "No!" He's saying, "God is that big ball of energy of life that we make that we're all a part of." He says, "It is in everyone so it could be anyone that's interviewing me it could be anyone doing this interview."

But I'm asking, literally was it Jimi? Or a metaphorical Jimi?

He said, "It was (actually) Jimi, and that was part of his softer landing coming over to the afterlife."

We can't judge it as we've heard it so many times has to be as to not be fantastical for us.

(Note: For those keeping score, Harry Dean Stanton met Jimi at Monterey Pop during his journey to the flipside, Jimi was there to greet John Lennon on stage when he crossed over, both played "Blue Suede Shoes" (the first mention of the tune in this research. When I asked, "What was he playing?" Jennifer said, "I'm seeing some blue shoes." He clarified what kind of shoes, and how it was a song "everyone knew.")

Jimi was guest hosting the Tonight Show when Charles Grodin arrived on the flipside. We've asked Jimi about his journey, who greeted him on the flipside, and he's said that he "likes to help other people transition so they can have a soft landing." It's like he's saying, "Put me in coach, I can play that part and help them make the transition.")

Elvis, if I can turn to Jimi for a second? We've interviewed you before ("Backstage Pass to the Flipside") we talked about his journey...

(Jennifer puts up her hand) Hold on. (Jennifer asks Elvis) "Why are you showing me her?" (to me) I just saw someone who's still on the planet, but they must not be doing well or something is going on with them.

Well let's ask, Elvis, why did you put that image in Jennifer's mind? Who is it?

It was Barbra Streisand.

I was writing about her yesterday (for this book)

Shut up.

I'm not shutting up. I was writing about her yesterday because my friend Kutenla had me give her a copy of a CD I made in Dharamsala with the Nechung Monks. But I gave it to James Brolin and said, "I directed you in a movie, but we've never met." Film was "Cannes Man." I took it over after shooting began... But the CD is the meditation that the Nechung Monks do to put the Oracle of Tibet into a trance.

If it's a CD of prayers and chants, they're saying "We need to pray…" or they're saying something and they're showing me… hold on a second.

Let's ask Luana if they want to discuss chanting. She was a lifelong chanter, Buddhist SGI; does someone want to discuss the process of what that does for your frequencies?

He says "Yes! And about the frequency of getting more connected or feeling you are already connected but feeling more connected…"

We've had a number of people in our class mention this before, Anthony Bourdain.

They're showing me chanting as well as church music. He says, "That's important to help connect the two sides of the veil."

Elvis you were from the gospel music, church singing world, what would be an avenue to connect?

As soon as you said gospel, he said "method." Or "Methodist." He says, "Put on some music as the method, if Gospel is in your background, then Gospel music (is too) If it's what puts you into a trance, whatever music lifts your heart."

(Note: Elvis was baptized Pentecostal. While some argue Pentecostals and Methodists are the same, one is older than the other; both considered Protestant religions).

I was curious about how certainly frequencies are involved – like when we hear Elvis voice, or our favorite music, the sound is so distinct get hat frequency of who or what Elvis was or what he represented to us or the time in our life.

He says, "The same goes for other music, religious music, Christmas music - any kind of religious music where you're in that space of family, of being loved. If it moves your heart whatever it is… (i.e.) it could be punk rock…" Tom Petty just showed me "Alice in Wonderland" so whatever that song was.

Alice in Wonderland? Movie or book?

(Note: Tom appears to be referring to his song "Don't Come Round Here No More" where the video was shot as if it was part of the Alice in Wonderland story – something I wasn't aware of until I just searched "Tom Petty" and "Alice in Wonderland." The song is about something completely different, but the video uses "Alice" as the backdrop.)

"Not the movie but the song," Tom is saying.

I don't know the song, but in the book, Alice takes a pill, she gets small, it's an altered perspective. Are you saying that music changes your perspective, puts you into a holistic health trance?

He says, "Yes." He's saying "It can help heal you. Music helps to heal. It heals the soul; that in turn fills your body. It heals the soul... and that in turn heals your body."

I just want to clarify something, Elvis. I'm trying to get to the heart of this. It sounds spiritual, but you're talking about something science based?

He says, "Correct."

The point being it's it doesn't matter what your belief system is, put on, crank up the tune if that elevates your heart. Crank it up? I read years ago about people treating all kinds of illness with sound therapy. It makes sense, since we are all vibrating atoms, if one can find the right frequency perhaps, they can restructure problem areas over time or with intensity. Correct me if I'm wrong Elvis, but you're talking about the idea of the music elevating people – not only because it's connecting to a happier time, but it's also connecting you to your higher self?

He says, "Your future memories as well. Because if you play it live now but you could be helping yourself in the future when you hear it again."

So, let's say in a previous lifetime you were someone who liked Beethoven's music? Maybe you heard him live, and then in another lifetime, you hear it again, and you connect to who you were when you heard it the first time? Tapping into who you were before?

"Yeah." He says, "Yes." He showed me an example. There's a song that Coldplay sings, "Viva La Vida." He showed me that song... the song has church bells ringing, Roman Catholic choirs sing "Nobody wants to hear me" – (Jennifer aside) I mean I'm hearing that song now, that song came into my head from somewhere, I wasn't thinking about it, but Elvis says "A lot of musicians do that – they are remembering events from a previous lifetime. That Chris took the past of something that he was..." (Jennifer aside) I'm seeing it now, and connected to that past, and Elvis says "A lot of musicians do that... they don't know consciously that they're doing it (writing songs with impressions from a previous lifetime). Some do know consciously, and Chris Martin actually might but because they know when it's just... kind of when it floats in your head... how to grab it."

(Note: A word about Viva La Vida. Lyrics are:

"I used to rule the world, Seas would rise when I gave the word, Now in the morning, I sleep alone, Sweep the streets I used to own, I used to roll the dice, Feel the fear in my enemy's eyes, Listen as the crowd would sing, Now the old king is dead! Long live the king! One minute I held the key,

Next the walls were closed on me And I discovered that my castles stand, Upon pillars of salt and pillars of sand..."
For some reason I can't explain, I know Saint Peter won't call my name, Never rule this world, But that was when I ruled the world." (*Viva La Vida." Words and Lyrics by Chris Martin.)*

(Note: It brings to mind George Patton's poem "Through a Glass Darkly" where Patton recalls all of his previous lifetimes as a warrior.)

In this case, Elvis is referring to this particular song because Chris Martin may have had a memory from a previous lifetime. Perhaps as King, or someone who knew the King well enough to write about him. (And of course Elvis is often referred to as "King.") What Elvis is saying is that musicians frequently write about previous lifetimes without knowing about it.)

Well, in your case Elvis, you didn't write songs, but you lived inside of them in a way that made people feel as if you were singing to them.

When you said that, he said "I would sleep with them."

Do you mean emotionally? Literally?

He was just talking about the music, like holding on to the piece of paper (with the song written on it) and he would connect to it, yeah.

Let's talk about "Blue Suede Shoes" you popped that song into Jennifer's mind. I know she's not aware of who wrote that song but we've had a number of people reference that tune on the flipside.

(Jennifer aside) My dad loved that song and I forgot about that too! He's saying, "Take all of the nuances of this podcast, the underlying threads dealing with my dad, it's completely packed full of signs."

So, (Jennifer's dad, Jim) what is it about this Carl Perkin's tune that connects so many people?

My dad just said, "It's so much fun! It reminds him of his 57 convertible when he used to race cars." (Jennifer aside) I just want to clarify that I, Jennifer haven't seen a blue suede shoe in my life.

Well, when we first talked to Jimi, when Jimi crossed over at some point, he was on stage playing that tune. Later we talked to John Lennon and when he crossed over, he found himself on stage with Jimi playing that song. Later I discovered they'd both recorded the song a year apart, separately.

(Jennifer aside) That's crazy and now here is Elvis talking about blue suede shoes!

It was one of Elvis signature tunes, breakout hit.

(Jennifer aside) Yeah, but I've never heard him sing in spirit! That was really cool to literally hear him.

So, Mr. Presley, what's up with the song?

He says, "It's a song that connects generations."

Elvis, have you talked to Carl Perkins? I assume he's on the flipside (Note: Carl passed in 1988).

He says, "He's still writing away. He's still writing away."

Have you performed any of new songs on the flipside? How does that work? We had Carl Laemmle tell us a few weeks ago that people can create all kinds of vistas, including auditoriums or shows. Is it like that?

He's showing me it's like somebody coming up and saying, "Hey I want you to check out my arena that I built (with my mind). Will you come play in my arena?" That's what he's saying.

Somebody has mentally constructed an arena which means all the seats, all the acoustics - everything that you could possibly imagine?

I asked, "Do they try to recreate your experiences that you've already had?" He said, "Both. They try to recreate both; the experience of being on stage and the roar of the crowd, plus the backstage, minus the drugs and alcohol."

Yes, we've heard that – no brains to get addled by drugs and alcohol. But then when you walk on stage?

He said "Being on stage, it's like being on acid or LSD, but it's not because you're more euphoric. Because there's such great pleasure associated with it, right?

And you don't take for granted anything. Elvis says, "I would walk in, and before, I might have taken for granted the stage, the floor." He says, "When you walk into something that was built or reconstructed," he says, "You pay attention to every detail because you don't want to miss anything!"

(Jennifer aside) "Wow. I don't have the words. He just showed me when he was drinking and was on pain pills... He said "I didn't have the wherewithal to appreciate the

depth of what it took for that moment in time, because of course you're trying to remember the lyrics, you're trying to remember the cues, trying to remember the rehearsal… almost sleepwalking – which is not cool…"

So those frequencies … the frequency of your memory of you performing the song, the frequency of the person who wrote the song, perhaps the frequency of all the musicians who played with you, your sidemen and everyone that's ever loved that song filling up the experience…

I'm sure the downbeat reverberates out across the universe and gets a lot of people to show up in the auditorium once they hear "Elvis is going to sing!" That must be thrilling for a lot of people.

He says, "Yeah because you can attract a crowd of people from different countries at the same time. All can come see him all at once."

So, let's pretend I'm in your audience… my higher self is watching you and my stage self is on stage… that guy's not aware of the concert unless I'm asleep and then the filters are down. When I wake up, I might have a memory, "I dreamed I saw Elvis last night." Is that how it goes?

He says, "Yeah. But he says it's like being able to watch it on TV and then jumping into the television set."

Cool! That's a beautiful example; jumping into the television.

He says, "And you're playing along with you don't have to wait. No one is there to tell you not to jump in, but there's a reverence for it and nobody will go that doesn't have that frequency."

You can't force people into the audience right to join you onstage?

"Right," he says.

So Luana, how did Elvis elbow his way onto your VIP list today? Does everybody just back up when he shows up?

She says, "It started yesterday with you writing about Barbra Streisand."

Okay, I was connecting the dots to seeing her a few times, at the Clinton Inaugural, in a diner in Beverly Hills, then with Kutenla, the Oracle of Tibet.

(Jennifer aside) And I didn't know anything, like I was fighting saying her name, but they were like saying "No, no, no it's important. Tell him." It shows how interpretation can be wrong – I immediately thought they were showing Barbra as some kind of health warning, but it turns out it was so you could connect those dots. And then the idea of "Route 66" came to mind, just seeing that number, my dad's favorite tune. Nine times out of ten they're putting the thought in your head.

Thank you, Elvis, for the illuminating conversation. We'll catch you out on Route 66!

*****

I've played the tune "Route 66" quite a bit. In honky-tonks and dives, restaurants and mansions – I was the Shanghai film festival in 1996 with my film "Point of Betrayal." I ran into some French filmmakers I knew from Cannes, who invited me along.

We got to the French Ambassador's reception, one of the snootier filmmakers said, "Monsieur Martini? The reception is for invited guests only." He might have been looking at my tennies as he said it. I saw a piano. I asked the Ambassador's wife if I could play it. She said "*Mais non*, it is badly of tune." I said, "Let me be the judge of that." Couple of errant keys, but I avoided them and dove into "Route 66."

A few seconds later, looked over my shoulder and saw the Ambassador and all the guests were dancing. Rocking out. All of them, even the snooty fella, kicking up their heels. Music does soothe savage beasts everywhere. ***Mais weee!***

Anthy Martini and her protégé circa 1959

"THE QUEEN OF SOUL"

This interview is worthy of repeating because I never met Aretha, nor did Jennifer Shaffer. I had seen her in concert, and know people that she knew (Sydney Pollack, Ray Charles) who show up in this interview to corroborate what she says.

Because of those connections, I consider her *showing up* not out of the realm of possibility. However, I was aware of some details – like she didn't "leave a will." I thought it would be a fun exercise. *"Did you or did you not leave a will?"*

This interview appears in the first book "Backstage Pass to the Flipside." In terms of frequencies – here's someone who tapped into many of them. In terms of who "brings her in" Prince is someone I reviewed for Variety, met him and his entourage backstage at one of his shows, have friends who knew him well, and he started showing up in the research just after he crossed over.

Numerous times he's confirmed details about his life – and given us some controversial tidbits to consider.

To be clear, in this interview Aretha reveals the existence of a handwritten will, instructs me to reach out to her niece to discuss it – both accurate. I was startled to find her niece was her executor (nor did Jennifer know) and she replied to my email "While I converse with my mother in heaven often, I do not believe that your medium is conversing with my aunt."

Which is fine, I am not trying to convince anyone of anything. The point is to understand how frequencies work and report whatever it is they say verbatim.

My questions are *in italics*, **Jennifer's replies in bold.**

Rich: Okay Luana, does anyone need to talk to us?

Jennifer: Prince is coming in...

Rich: Mr. Rogers Nelson, they just released the catalog with 10,000 new songs of yours, unreleased tunes. How do you feel about that?

He says, "Amazing. It makes him feel good; it outweighs the sadness."

Prince, is Aretha over there with you?

(Nods) She says, "She's having a blast! She's having so much fun... like *aiii!*" (Jennifer listens) What? Ok. I feel like she's still "learning how to heal herself... I felt her (illness)"

(Jennifer aside) Does she have a sister? She's up there with her... wait... no, two are up there with her... one is... down here?

(Note: After the session was over, I looked it up. Three of Aretha's sisters are with her, none are still "down here.")

I'm aware that she didn't leave a will.

She says "She does have a will, but they don't know where it is. It's not with an attorney."

Okay, please be more specific?

It's very old. Did she have a lot of husbands? How many relationships did she have? I'm seeing five.

(Note: Wikipedia tells me she was married twice, but indeed, had five long relationships.)

I don't know, but whatever...

She's laughing... she's trying to give me a timeline.

The person you were married to will know where it was or his heirs?

"No, they won't know where it is. (It's) One of her sisters feels like..."

(Her sister) knows where it is?

"She won't know but she will know..." She's explaining that "She won't know but *should* know."

What's your sister's name?

(I'm getting) something with an S.

(Note: I didn't know it at the time, but her niece Sabrina is the executor of her estate.)

Then we don't have to worry about (helping them find) it?

She says, "So, *you'll know* that when they find it, *you already knew* they'd find it."

Okay then, who's going to find it?

"Her sister, or someone related to her sister. She wants you to write about it..." (Jennifer listens, looks confused) I'm not saying she'd make it up, I'm saying it's hard to... – (Jennifer aside, eyes wide) I can't believe I'm talking to Aretha right now! I just have to go with it.

She might want to talk about the song "Nessun Dorma." She sang it at the Grammys.

(Jennifer continuing) I've never heard her voice up close. She's putting me in a sweat... she wants to go back to the first thing (she said). Her sister (or someone related to her sister) has the will... feels like it's in a house in the 1980's...

In Aretha's house?

She says, "Not in *her* house."

(Note: Sabrina found the handwritten will in her home. *AP News "Three Handwritten Wills Found in Aretha's Home" May 20, 2019,* Nine months after this interview.)

They're all laughing.

Miss Franklin, look around who's here in (Luana's) class. Ray Charles is here – we've spoken to him. (Ray starred in my second feature film "Limit Up" playing God.)

She says, "She loved him." Luana's telling me she cut up that velvet rope and (Aretha) walked in.

Ray and Danitra Vance in the film Luana and I wrote; "Limit Up"

Aretha who was there to greet you when you crossed over?

Prince says, "He was there and Ray Charles (as well.)"

Miss Franklin: anything you want me to tell your family?

"That I'm fine. I have no pain."

What was your favorite song?

She loved (the song) you said earlier – she's holding a flower... that thing you said before.

"Nessun dorma?" Okay, she substituted for Pavarotti at the Grammys, did an amazing version of this Italian aria.

She's saying "The lyrics are so amazing. They're super important."

They are? Well, it means "no one's asleep." I guess that's a metaphor that no one dies. "Nessuno dorma."

She said, "She had a premonition before that... just the music."

(Note: I don't know if she meant a premonition about passing away, or about doing the song.)

Well, she stepped in for Luciano Pavarotti at the Grammy's. Can we ask; how's Luciano doing?

"He's here – he's mad about his death."

Luciano, you went up and down with your weight... so it wasn't unexpected.

So much anger. Um; he says, "He was overweight but happy – but he was up and down up and down."

Well, welcome to our group, Luciano – and say hello to your friend Aretha.

He says, "Six degrees of Aretha Franklin."

Luana, is this exciting for you to meet Aretha? The Queen of Soul?

She says, "There's no hierarchy (here), but she adds spice to the class."

Anything else?

They say, "come on back."

Okay, we soon will.

*****

Nessun dorma indeed.

PART TWO

The following session was filmed on Sept. 7TH, 2018 after Aretha's televised funeral. My questions in italics, Jennifer's responses in bold.

Richard: Hi class. I'll leap right in. Aretha, we're back, we met last week, can we talk to you?

Prince has her on his arm and he's walking her up the aisle.

Anything you want to say about your funeral Miss Franklin?

"Extravagant" she says.

When you crossed over, who was there to greet you?

She showed me dancing with this guy – he brought her into a memory.

(Note: As we'll learn later, the person she was dancing with had an important role in her life John Hammond, iconic music man who had a hand in everyone's career from Robert Johnson to Bob Dylan.)

Someone we know?

Someone associated with her...

I read that Stevie Wonder came to see you (before she crossed).

"Two days before," she said.

(Note: I don't know if this is accurate. But when discussing time and dates, I'll defer to the person I'm speaking with.)

What did he say (to you)?

He said, "It's okay (to pass); I've got a lot of friends up there."

Who have you been visiting with, Aretha?

"Everyone." She just showed me Marilyn as well – (Jennifer listens:) Let me try to say this as she said it; "I was the African-American Marilyn." The class is laughing along with her.

Aretha, there's a video of you playing "Nessun Dorma" for your granddaughter (on YouTube) – It popped into my head; were you an opera singer in a previous life?

"Yes."

In what era?

"16th century... Paris; somewhere in Paris. And she married somebody Italian."

Let me ask you a musical question, was the coloratura which you had in your voice, that you carried throughout this life – was that unique sound related to your previous lifetime?

"Yes, yep." (Jennifer aside:) She's showing me my brain (Jennifer's brain) and what I'm doing here (as a medium), and how my ability to use this (to speak to the afterlife) – is more accepted now. It wasn't accepted in all my lifetimes, but I can use it now because it's carried through all of those lifetimes. I would have struggled with this ability if I hadn't figured it out.

So then do most musicians carry their frequency of music from life to life?

"Yes."

What singer did you admire (during your life)?

She says, "Sammy Davis Junior." (Jennifer aside:) I saw Sammy show up earlier... He was hanging out with Prince.

Silly question, but were you friends with Michael Jackson?

"Sure." She's like "Of course I was! That's such a *stupid question*. She loved him."

Aretha, what do you want us to pass along to your friends and family?

She said, "Tell them to breathe." She says, "They're still looking for the will."

You said it was on a computer your sister had – (but I learned) all your sisters are gone.

There's someone like a sister to her (still here).

Okay, well, you did say it was going to be found in October. That's when I said, "Then I guess I don't need to worry about it."

"They're still not looking in the right place."

Things could change... it may be that they're going to find something.

If they do then I think it's going to be contested...

(Note: Ding! It is being contested.)

So why were you born into Reverend Franklin's family?

"He wanted to change the world like Martin Luther King."

In terms of choosing the neighborhood to be born in?

"That's what she charted," she says. **"That was her math."**

(Note: The "math" referred to, is the path she "charted" like a musical score.)

Who was your biggest influence?

"God."

(Note: Not something we've heard before. People say it *here* often, but rarely during one of these sessions.)

I mean on the planet – who was it that you want to give a shout out to?

(Jennifer observing). He was white – trying to figure out who it is...

A singer?

"No."

A record producer?

"Yes." From New York. Feels like.

I can look it up.

"He believed in her and also he kind of saved her from her own family." (Jennifer looks at me) I don't know anything about her family. (It's).. her friend from New York. She met him when she was like 14."

(Note: John Hammond signed Aretha when she was a teen and took over her career. As noted, he was responsible for everyone from Robert Johnson to Bruce Springsteen becoming part of our musical songbook. This would make sense, even though I had to research this to see who it could have been.)

So, what was your favorite song?

"Somewhere over the rainbow."

A fitting title for our discussion. Thank you, Miss Franklin.

PART THREE

This ensuing session was recorded on March 26th, 2019.

Richard: Hi class. Hi Jennifer. The other day, I had an entertaining class without you because I got to go see a movie and our class went to see it with me.

(Note: I went to a screening of *"Amazing Grace."* As I sat in the theater, I had an odd feeling our entire class was there.)

Aretha what did you think of the movie that I saw about you this weekend?

She's saying "I was surprised. The lengths of it... – the lengths it took to get it out there."

Let me ask you Aretha, why did you not like this film so much that you didn't want it out there?

(Listens. Makes a face) "Body image issues." She just... I'm asking her, "It was really about body image?" And she replied, "You're one to talk."

Correct me if I'm wrong, but watching the film, I got the impression that you were ill during production.

"Absolutely." She says, she "had issues from diabetes" – that "her blood sugars were off."

(Note: It is not public knowledge Aretha had diabetes or symptoms of diabetes; she died from pancreatic cancer, but I found an article where she revealed she suffered from those same symptoms. "...one thing that isn't widely known about this artist (AF) is that she is diabetic." https://www.diabetes.co.uk › celebrities › aretha-franklin)

I noticed you were coughing off camera; you looked like you were in pain.

"I was." She says, "Her whole body was in pain." She said, "She was suffering from a number of things."

Let me ask our pal Sydney Pollack, (who directed "Amazing Grace.") What did you think of the film?

(Note: There's an interview with Sydney in "Backstage Pass to the Flipside." I sent the private details he mentioned to one of his daughters, she reported the interview was "absolutely accurate.")

"There was something wrong with his hair," he said.

Ha, okay, your hair was bushy. I hate to be the critic Sydney, but part of the film was out of focus. While watching it I thought I "heard" Ray Charles say: "I could have filmed this better!"

"Ray is funny."

Another still from the film Limit Up

In the film, Reverend Franklin said Aretha had only called him the night before and said, "C'mon down." Why didn't she ask her father to participate earlier?

She tells me that her father "took Aretha away from her mother," it felt like.

(Note: According to her bio, her mother died when she was younger.)

Aretha, we asked you earlier whom you met when you crossed over, and you told Jennifer that you were dancing with a man, who felt like a manager when you crossed over. Was it John Hammond, the famous record producer who signed you when you were 16 or 17 years old?

She's telling me "He took over for her father." (With her career).

He signed her to a record deal at Columbia. Sydney, what did you think of your movie?

"Love." He loved it. He just showed me hearts going up into the sky... like there's love there.

As a director, what would you have done differently?

He said, "He would have put Aretha more on a pedestal."

For better angles I imagine. The film was as much sacred as it was revelatory.

"That's right," he says, "but that didn't make her look good." He says, "There wasn't the money at the time."

Just to clarify, the main reasons you didn't want the movie to be released, Aretha, was how you looked?

"All of it." She felt "it wasn't optimal."

What did our class think of it?

They said "It was amazing. Even though she felt she could have done better as a performer."

There's a moment in the film that is otherworldly – it's during a call and response portion, where Reverend James Cleveland is calling out, Aretha has her eyes closed and is singing her responses, but the microphone isn't on her, and she isn't aware of it. It's an extreme close up, but you can see that she's in another place, transcendent.

"She was."

(Note: A reminder that Jennifer has not seen the film, and at this point, I didn't mention the name of the film either. So, she's not giving me her opinion, but the opinion from those who've seen it.)

Then Reverend Cleveland moved the mic over to her so we could hear her.

Hold on. She keeps showing me Whitney Houston. (Listens) She says she had a great love for Whitney, felt like she felt a great responsibility for Whitney – I don't know why.

Okay, I'll look that up.

(Note: I did. Aretha was very close with Cissy Houston, Whitney's mom, and took care of Whitney often. They were very close, and her bio says they spent a lot of time together. Not something I knew, or that Jennifer could have known.)

But before we get off the film, I wanted to say the film shows what a profound instrument you have as a singer; it's on full display in that film.

She says, "She realizes that now." (About the film)

It will be revelatory to those who see it...it comes out next month. It's called "Amazing Grace."

(Startled. Jennifer asks) It's called "Amazing Grace?" That's the song that Dave Chappelle told me she sang to him. I didn't know that! That's so cool.

May I ask what Martin Luther King thought of the film?

"Powerful."

I learned that Dr. King knew Aretha's father. Aretha, in a previous discussion you said a girl with the name S has your will. Who is that?

Did she have a daughter?

I don't know – I don't think so.

It feels like (the name is) a Shannon… or Shawna? (The name turns out to be Sabrina.)

I'm sorry, I didn't mean to interrupt Reverend King. I felt your presence in the theater, for whatever that's worth.

He said, "Thanks for inviting me."

After the film, I asked everyone to give me a one-word review. I wish I'd written them down, as each reflected their persona.

(Jennifer aside) I asked the class, "If we should ask you guys to come to the movies with us?" and I heard an overwhelming "Yes." I asked, "Do you put that idea in our minds to go to the movies as well?" and I also heard a "Yes."

Like sneaking friends into the drive-in in the trunk of your car? Next time I'm in the theater I'll think of all the folks that may have suggested we attend this film.

Luana just said "Thank you."

For what?

"For filming this, for putting this out there."

*****

The Queen of Soul remains the *Queen of Soul*.

CHAPTER FIVE: A FIFTH OF BEETHOVEN

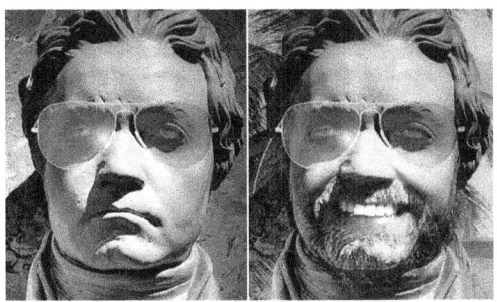

Beethoven sculpture made in his lifetime. *Rock Icon (photoshopped by author)*

In the book "The First Four Notes: Beethoven's Fifth and the Human Imagination" (by Matthew Guerrieri, Knopf 2012) the author suggests that the most famous of the first four notes of any symphony (Beethoven's Fifth) is a metaphor for *"Fate."*

Like "the French Army is knocking at the door." (As it was in Vienna when he wrote those notes.) According to a biography of Beethoven, by Anton Schindler in 1855, someone claimed that Beethoven was asked about the "meaning of the first four notes of the symphony and he reportedly replies" **"You are too dumb."**

Guerrieri notes that the French composer Hector Berlioz attended a concert with his teacher of the Fifth, the teacher said, "It so moved me and disturbed me... that when I went to put on my hat, I didn't know where my head was." The next day, Berlioz reported the teacher told him "That sort of music should not be written."

Berlioz is famous for Symphony Fantastique among other pieces, that audibly depicts a war zone, complete with the rolling drum and finality of the guillotine. ("March to the Scaffold" reported by NPR: https://www.npr.org/sections/deceptivecadence/2013/03/06/173633385/marches-madness-off-with-his-head)

In college I studied the piece for my Humanities major, ("The Impact of the 20th Century on the Humanities" which I graduated Magna Cum Laude at Boston University in 1978) learned about the leit-motif concept of repeated passages, the "idee' fixe" of his composition, and was startled that the music created strong images, the same way that "Afternoon of a Faun" by Debussy, evokes images of his pastoral trips to America when he wrote it.

As an aside, but not quite an aside, when I was in Paris visiting the Pere Le Chaise cemetery, I stopped by to see some of the famous graves, Jim Morrison, Edith Piaf, Oscar Wilde (with the multiple lipstick imprints on it), I suddenly heard someone say "Hello!"

The tomb of Edith Piaf with author John Connell

It was clear as a bell. I swung around in the cemetery, looked to see who was greeting me, and in front of me was the tomb of George Bizet (composer of Carmen who passed at the age of 36).

I looked over my shoulder, looked around to empty space and replied, "Bonjour to you sir." Unfortunately, thieves stole his bust in 2006, but who knows if it wasn't George behind the theft? Overlooking a favorite pub perhaps?

Back to Beethoven's *"You are too dumb."*

While the book about the beginning of the Fifth goes into fanciful detail of what he might have meant – he literally said what it meant. It's the interpretation that trips people up.

"Du bist zu dumm."

From An Etymological Dictionary of the German Language"
"Dumm, adjective, 'stupid, silly,' from Middle High German tum, tump), 'stupid, foolish, weak in understanding, dumb…'
'Dull in sense and intellect' may be the primary sense of the adjective… Words expressing the perceptions of one sense are

often transferred to those of another. Hence Gothic dumbs, 'dumb,' Old High German, "deaf, dumb."

(https://en.wikisource.org/wiki/An_Etymological_Dictionary_of_the_German_Language/Annotated/dumm)

"You are too deaf to hear the meaning."

Beethoven often spoke of dreaming about music that came from the great beyond, or as he called it "the ethers." There was no common reference in religion or language aside from "heaven" to talk about "beyond the spheres" – but he didn't use the word heaven to describe where music came from.

Beethoven first noticed difficulties with his hearing decades earlier, sometime in 1798, when he was about 28. By the time he was 44 or 45, he was totally deaf and unable to converse unless he passed written notes back and forth to his colleagues, visitors and friends.

(https://www.pbs.org/newshour/health/what-caused-beethovens-deafness - 12-19 by Dr. Markel on PBS)

So, when he answered the question; "what do the first four notes mean?" he was acutely aware of what going dumb meant. He was ten years into his journey into profound loss of hearing and was aware that sound was something that was no longer part of his repertoire.

"You are too deaf to hear what it means."

But even **"*Du Bist Zu Dumm*"** is literally what it sounds like when it's played. *"You are too dumb."*

Beethoven was also going deaf at the time, so it literally is a metaphor inside the metaphor. Like his music. Like all music. I think it's a brilliant answer and not a sarcastic reply at all.

If one hasn't a clue where music comes from, telling them where it comes from is pointless. They won't be able to hear it. Might as well continue writing.

From an interview with Beethoven via Jennifer Shaffer on our podcast "Hacking the Afterlife."

At some point during the interview, the musician Prince appears in Jennifer's mind's eye, and she notes it.

Rich: Prince, please come forward tell us what do you want to tell us the man who owns his own color?

Jennifer: He's saying "He likes red too. He's putting you (me, Richard) in my mind's eye. He's saying again, "You need to have music accompanying the books of yours, have music on in the background while you read them."

Let me clarify. Prince what you're saying is not that I should play music, but that perhaps music that will assist this kind of research will help? This research that we're doing talking to the flipside. That music helps you to focus.

He's saying, "The frequency of music is like a bandwidth that you can connect with, yes."

Should I suggest when people listen or want to talk to someone on the flipside, they put on a particular piece of music that connects them emotionally? Like if you want to talk to your grandmother and you knew she loved Bing Crosby. Would you put on some Bing Crosby songs and think about them?

He's sharing with me a figure skater no idea why.

Please correct me if I'm wrong but did you the figure skater in her mind as metaphor? Something, who used to figure skate mentioned - she said there used to be stunts like triple jumps and no one could do them, but when someone finally did do one, it was like everyone suddenly could do them; is that what he's talking about? Watching someone like us communicate and talk to people on the flipside helps people to learn?

He says, "Yes."

I was reading about how music not only helps people with Alzheimer's because the part of the brain with music is still functioning but also an article about how sound and the human voice can help rewire the brain or actually affect certain illnesses like cancer. Like the musical tone or the focus of that tone helps cure the illness. Is that accurate?

He says, "Not completely." So, what my interpretation from what I'm getting is that it's not necessarily music that heals you but brings you back to where you were before you got the illness; that's one method.

Let's use something more common, like dementia. People have said that plaque is involved with blocking, but we have heard that where music is stored is a place that isn't affected.

They showed me a violin has a very high frequency - like I don't know the terminology...

Yes, it would be considered higher frequencies...

I'm getting like a guitar has a frequency, and frequency relates to health... drums would also generate a frequency... I'm just seeing a certain physicality of it all.

I've read about physical therapy where they put giant speakers in a room and the thump of the percussiveness physically affects the body. Prince, allow me to ask for names of musicians that you think could help people if they used their music as a healing technique.

I keep coming back to Beethoven.

Which symphony or tune?

I'm hearing "The Fifth."

Luana, can you bring Beethoven in? Prince is talking about you; what do you think about that? Is he accurate?

Hold on. They had a debate up there about it... they had a debate on what rings in the all-encompassing... like is it piano? Violin? It's everything at different... like it's everything with different frequencies and different tones.

But Ludwig we've talked to you before, I wanted to ask you about the healing nature of music. Prince is saying one of your symphonies is the most effective.

He's saying, "The Fifth; that healed him."

I think I know what you're referring to. It was a dark period of depression over going deaf. Was that it?

He says, "Yes."

So, the Fifth healed Ludwig?

That's what he's saying. "It helped him."

I'm partial to your Ninth symphony sir.

Well, he said. "So, if you have to have music to get you out of something, start off with his first symphony, start at the beginning and go through all nine. He's saying "Why not? And when you get to the fifth symphony, crank it up because "I'm really gonna wake up the neighbors."

He's also showing me the root chakra – the pelvis where the root energy center exists. Like listening to it there, "It has… it makes that effect on you. Has a healing effect if you listen to it with your root chakra."

So, you crank up the Fifth symphony and you will feel it in your biscuits? The "Biscuit Rattling Fifth?"

He's laughing.

Beethoven likes that. Okay let's return to Prince, please.

Prince is saying "The point of me breaking the velvet rope and coming in…" and he actually physically showed me him breaking the rope… is that "You, Richard, have something connected with the music you're playing and channeling and the whole class is up there wanting to help."

I was participating in a zoom group the other day and filmmakers were talking about the late great composer Bernard Hermann. I told the story of how in college a friend asked me to escort her on a date with this older fellow. He had this amazing penthouse over Manhattan and he brought out some killer pot. I got stoned, wandered around his place and saw these gold records. I realized "Bernie" the guy with killer pot, was the composer Bernard Hermann.

I've composed the music for two of my films and I had no clue who he was until years later. Can Bernard come forward?

He's here.

Do you remember this event?

He says, "Yes, but vaguely."

Is it okay if we talk to you?

He says "Yeah, I'm the one who put the thought in your head." (To do so)

If I may, you worked with Hitchcock quite a bit, have you been hanging out with him on the flipside?

He says, "No. He's moved on."

Who was there to greet you when you crossed over?

Who's the guitar player that's famous? I'm sorry.

I don't know. Jimi?

"Yes." He says, "He's hanging out with Jimi."

(Note: Revisiting this passage, it appears that Jimi has greeted quite a few people on the flipside.)

Have you been hanging out with Igor Stravinsky?

(Jennifer aside) I don't know who that is, but he says "Yeah." But he's planning his next return. He says, "He's planning his next return like a ski trip."

How about David Raksin? (Composer of "Laura" and an old friend of mine.) David are you around can you come forward?

He's showing me a record – so I don't know if he produced records or... wait, he was a composer.

(Ding!) That's correct. Just like Bernard and in fact they were friends I knew David briefly - okay David do you want to show Jennifer where we met?

Did you meet in a park?

We drove around a park in Spain in a Jeep together. A music fest in Biarritz, then to the Basque country. He told me some great Bernard Herrmann's stories. But Bernard back to you...

I tell you what I'm feeling – that "somebody stole from each other."

Yes, that's why I brought up Stravinsky's name. Having listened carefully to the Firebird Suite, I found elements of it in some of your scores. Did you lift music from Stravinsky?

He says, "Sure did." There's like, there's something with three - like "three pieces."

Bernard, correct me if I'm wrong but composers have been borrowing from others for centuries. It's attributed to Stravinsky actually; "A good composer does not imitate; he steals," right?

He says "Yes!" (Jennifer taps her nose.)

I think it's hilarious Stravinsky wanted to point that out.

He kept putting it in my head; he was moving away from Bernard in my eye, and I'm like "What is it? You're not talking to each other?" And they started laughing and I'm like he's hiding something he doesn't want me to know about" And it was because he didn't want Bernard to steal his ideas for his next lifetime.

I can tell you that people will say "Bernard Hermann never lifted music from Stravinsky" but I just got it from you and not from me. That's pretty hilarious that he was the one who mentioned "stealing." We just heard it from Igor himself. So, Igor, you're planning on returning soon, is that right?

She laughs. "Yes." He was just trying to show me how he wasn't letting Bernard know - like he might steal it.

How about you Bernie are you planning on coming back soon? Funny, I looked up the date when we met and it was literally a few months prior to you passing. Did you have a heart attack related to smoking pot? He was only 60.

He's laughing and says, "Karma's a bitch." He's showing me it happened in the street. He was just walking along and then he died. It might have happened in his home – but that's what he's showing me – out in the street and keeling over. He says, "It was a heart condition that was undiagnosed."

He's saying, "He felt like he was out on the street looking not so good… he says he had a precognition coming into this world to leave it early."

(Note: Mr. Herrmann was in L.A. to work on the score for "Taxi Driver," directed by Martin Scorsese. His wife, Norma found him dead, apparently of a heart attack, Dec 25th, 1977.)

Sorry to hear it.

He says, "No excuses; he's not giving excuses."

Well, thank you for all the great music which includes not only Psycho, but the Twilight Zone theme which scared the hell out of me as a kid.

He says, "Then you're welcome."

*****

I know this all sounds fanciful, problematic.

But it's pointing in a direction. I'm asking specific questions to people on the flipside. If someone else asked these questions, they might get different answers – but then again, they might not. There's only one way to find out.

And if someone does ask them the same questions and gets the same answers, what are we to make of that?

There are people convinced "tricksters" are out there, manipulating information for some nefarious reason. There are people who look carefully at these reports and when they see an error – are adamant that it's false.

A friend, Mitch Katlin sent me a quote from William Blake the other day. It was from the book "The War of Art" by Steven Pressman (2011) and it's a chapter that begins with the Blake quote:

"Eternity is in love with the creations of time."

He breaks down what that might have meant and suggests "that would imply that the Fifth Symphony of Beethoven was waiting to be written."

"By Blake's model, as I understand it, it's as though the Fifth Symphony existed already in that higher sphere, before Beethoven sat down and played dah-dah-dah-DUM (*Note: "You are so Dumb"*) The catch was this: The work existed only as potential – without a body, so to speak. It wasn't music yet. You couldn't play it. You couldn't hear it. It needed someone. It needed a human… to bring it into being… so the Muse whispered in Beethoven's ear." He brought it forth. He made the Fifth Symphony a "creation of time," which "eternity" could be "in love with." *(Pg 116. "The War of Art." Black Irish Entertainment LLC (November 11, 2011)*

Could be.

But the fun concept behind this book, behind the research into this field, is to offer that we can ask Blake what he meant, we can ask Beethoven what he meant. We can have different mediums ask Beethoven the same question multiple times and see if he changes his tune.

So to speak.

"Ludwig after the check cleared."

CHAPTER SIX: THE FREQUENCY OF LIFE

Sherry Talbot Martini in her music class

The more I reflect on music in my life, the more I realized it's a running theme. An idee fixe.

Music is how we find love. Make love. Give love. It literally is what love is, or in Michio Kaku's book, the "string theory" of quantum mechanics. But as the flipside research has shown, it also appears to be the medium, the vehicle, the fabric of consciousness. To reiterate string theory:

> *"If we had a microscope powerful enough, we could see electrons, quarks, neutrinos, etc are nothing but vibrations on miniscule loops resembling rubber bands. If we pluck the rubber band enough times and different ways, we eventually create all the known subatomic particles in the universe. This means that all the laws of physics can be reduced to the harmonies of these string. Chemistry is the melodies*

one can play on them. The universe is a symphony. And the mind of God, which Einstein eloquently wrote about, is cosmic music resonating through spacetime." (The God Equation: The Quest for a Theory of Everything by Michio Kaku. Doubleday 2021.)

Can you see the musical theme in your lifetime?

I was pulled on stage by Chaka Khan when she was singing with "Ask Rufus" in our local high school. Beautiful woman, a year older than me, singled me out of the crowd and pulled me on stage. Perhaps only so that 30 years later, when sitting at her table with Edna Gunderson of USA Today, at the birthday party that Whitney Houston sang for her manager, Clive Davis, I could lean over to her and say to Chaka; "Hi. You pulled me onstage in high school. Thanks."

Music functions as a time machine. *It's why I'm writing this book.*

It's not about my journey through music. It's to point out that we all have a journey through music.

That we hear songs that move us, remind us, make us remember – but I'm saying something a bit different. The music itself is outside of time, it carries the energy or frequency of that moment in time – so I can listen to Abbie sing, or Bruce sing, or myself play a song I wrote when I was 18, and I'm right there – outside of time – back in time, reliving that moment.

Music is the fabric of the universe. Music is the fabric of life. Music is a key to recalling life. Music is the last thing that goes in the Alzheimer's brain, music is the medium that keeps us alive, music is the thing that makes us happy, music is the thing that makes us weep, music is the essence of who we are.

Yes, we are strings, all reality is strings and notes and keys and frequencies – all vibrating, but not in cacophony. In harmony. And when you meet the person you've known for many lifetimes, they resonant the way two guitars on stands resonate with the right note is struck – the way glass can break when one sings the right note that makes them explode.

But let's chat with some folks no longer on the planet who remain on the planet through their music, shall we?

This is an excerpt from the documentary on YouTube: "Talking to the Flipside with Paul Allen, Junior Seau and Dave Duerson." Jennifer Shaffer and I are interviewing Paul Allen a day after his passing. Paul, aside from creating Microsoft with his pal Bill Gates, created the Jimi Hendrix Museum in Seattle, and started a brain institute to study the brain.

My questions are *in italics,* Jennifer's replies **in bold.**

Rich: So, Paul, look around the class, can you see all the musicians that are here? Who's the person you most want to talk to or play with?

Jennifer: He says, "Prince." Jimi Hendrix showed up before, all the guitar players showed up before, I wasn't sure if it was because of when you said he played guitar (instead of piano). They were here to greet him.

So, Jimi what's your opinion of Paul, what have you guys talked about on the flipside so far?

That he had a connection to Jimi while he was here, but he didn't trust it either.

Paul did something that's related to Jimi – both were from Seattle.

He showed me a huge building. He showed me like this huge foundation in front of different artwork and stuff... He showed me the Cleveland Hall of Fame thing.

Correct; it's like that. (Ding!) It used to be called the Jimi Hendrix Museum; he created the West Coast version of the Rock and Roll Hall of fame.

He's showing me all (Jimi's) his guitars, his shirts, the tie-dyed stuff. I love that.

Correct; (ding!) I've been there (Jennifer has not). They also feature things from Kurt Cobain. Paul have you run into Kurt?

Yeah. He's saying he's worried about Courtney. What I'm seeing is that (Kurt) is planning for a return – I'm asking could you change the outcomes from there? He's showing us here – how (this research into the flipside) we are changing their outcomes.

Okay. So, when we examine this stuff, we change our future because we become more aware of it?

We affect our future now by the work we're doing here (in this class). Whatever's happening elsewhere affects what's going to happen in the future. Kurt Cobain said that he saved Courtney by leaving... and that it also helped his daughter.

Kurt, anything you want to tell us or your friends and family?

He said, "He's happy to have Paul Allen there."

Who greeted you on the Flipside, Kurt?

Kurt says, "He was greeted by his dog."

What kind of dog?

"A little dog."

(Note: It's a common thing to meet a beloved pet on the flipside.)

Kurt's plaque in his hometown of Aberdeen.

Okay Paul, how do we get people in your brain science foundation to consider what Jennifer and I are doing, so we can help them speak to you with this ongoing conversation?

He says, "It will not take much – you need to write them."

What would you like to tell them in terms of opening up their research?

"Stop making everything "science based." Open up… to be open to (alternative) reasons... Tell them to be open to the way he left and why things happen."

Who is they? You mean the way people leave, the way they die?

"Yes, and (to) pay attention to that."

But can we put them in the right direction for that?

He says, "You can't, not right away."

(Note: Is he really saying, "Drop science?" The quote is "Be open to the way he left and why things happen." He's suggesting in order to "understand science" one has to be open to "non-science answers.")

(Later in the interview) So, Paul, look around anyone you want to talk to?

He says, "Prince."

Talk to or play with?

He said he wants to play (with him).

What would you want to ask Prince?

"How he wore those high heels."

Prince told us dancing in high heels "killed him."

(Note: When asked about why he was addicted to opioids and how that killed him, he said "No, dancing killed me." He said he was addicted to jumping off pianos in high heels which led to ankle injuries which led to hip injuries which led to pain pills.)

What kind of guitar do you have over there, Paul?

He showed me a Ukulele.

I see. Because that's as far as you've gotten (in terms of mentally creating it)?

He says "It's got a higher vibration. There's no hierarchy (including guitars). It's softer (in tone)."

And easier to play. George Harrison has spoken with our group, he's a huge fan of ukuleles.

Paul says, "They're playing together."

George with Rainbow; photo Olivia Harrison (All Rights Reserved)

If you had one song to play... what would it be?

Something... sunshine?

You mean "Here Comes the Sun" or "Good Day Sunshine?"

"Good Day Sunshine." (Jennifer aside: I don't know it.) They're showing me them tap dancing over there.

I think you had a recording studio on your yacht, you put out an album with your buddies. Anything you want to tell your friends or Julian Lennon?

Jennifer nods. "Yeah, he does have a lot of love for him."

A specific sentence for him?

He says, "He loved him more than he knows." He's showing me two different kinds of feathers. (Jennifer aside:) I remember the story of how his father sent him the white feather, but also there's a black feather that got introduced. He says, "Tell him to look for the darker feather; tell him to look for the darker feather, it's all one, it's the same."

A white feather with black feather? What's the metaphor; look for balance?

"Yes."

Like yin yang – balance. Does he need balance in his life?

"Yes, but who doesn't?"

(Note: I sent Julian this message from Paul Allen about looking for darker feathers. He said that indeed, he has started to notice them. His reply was; "Yin yang.")

Dennis Hopper just showed up. Were they friends?

Well Dennis and Luana were... did a couple of movies together. What does Dennis want to say?

He says, "It's a long line to get to talk to you."

I'm sorry. It's Luana's fault.

"Tell Rich...." hold on. He says, "Tell you, don't be fearful about giving his family information."

Okay. I don't really know them well; I knew your ex-wife.

He showed me all the connections.

Don't be afraid of mentioning it in public and having someone else pass it along?

"Yes."

So Dennis, what are you doing over there? Creating any kind of artistic endeavor?

He says "He's creating sounds. That's why he's part of that group."

We had people creating their environments; where do you hang out, or what kind of sounds do you create?

He says "He's recreating the sounds from earth.... exploring sound barriers."

For whom? You or pals?

Jennifer laughs. It's like "For our podcast up here."

(Note: I think he's joking that he's creating a background music track for our class.)

What kinds of sounds?

He showed me the movie with ... what's his name, the movie with the bear?

"The Revenant" with Leonardo Di Caprio. You mentioned it last time...

Something connected to you about that, I don't know what it is.

Do you mean with the director or Leo?

Maybe Leo with this environmental work. The afterlife research - it's green because you're not wasting energy.

My question would be "Is anyone in this class aware of what Jennifer is talking about?" Or should we just keep doing what we're doing, and they'll eventually figure out where we are?

You just have to put it out there, they'll find us.

Are you doing any playing of music?

"That too; at night."

What kind of stuff you play? Blues, rock and roll?

"Everything. But right now, he's focusing on the ukulele."

I would guess it's because it's hard to construct a Stratocaster or an amp – like what Prince can do – a ukulele is easier, has only four strings, there are only about ten chords...

I'm asking him "Is it a better frequency?" And he's like "No." It's like you said, "It's easier to construct."

Maybe one day we can tap into music on the flipside. That would be a great way to prove the flipside exists.

Does Paul know the guy who did the Titanic film?

Jim Cameron? Could be. Paul made a few films; most were money losers.

He says, "It's just money."

I heard the other night, Questlove, the drummer for the Tonight show, was bereft about Paul's passing. He wrote that he's going to miss your encyclopedic mind of music – and Questlove his own encyclopedic memory.

Paul says, "He knows everything by its time period."

Well, take a look around; we have all these musical people in our group.

He says, "He loves Aretha... and Whitney."

Thank you, Paul Allen. Catch you on the flipside class!

****

Later on, we did a session with Junior Seau's widow, and she was able to connect directly to her husband Junior. During that interview, I asked him to show Jennifer "where she met him before" and she was startled to recall the above conversation.

Junior came through a few times, along with football player and fellow CTE sufferer to report that "Joe Namath has cured his own CTE with hyperbaric oxygen therapy." The main reason I've posted these interviews on YouTube (MartiniZone.com) is to help people access this concept.

It's not mine. It's not Jennifer's.

It comes from the flipside.

FRANKLY SPEAKING

Chairman of the Sidewalk

Typical afternoon, I turn on the camera and say:

Rich: Hi class, who's here today?

Jennifer: Jimi Hendrix and David Bowie just showed up.

Is that related to someone I asked to come today? Could you put in Jennifer's mind why that might be?

Okay, now John Belushi showed up.

On the drive over, he popped into my head, and I asked aloud why we hadn't seen him in a while.

(Jennifer aside) Shut the front door!

No, really.

I believe you. I'm seeing George Michael as well.

He's associated with one of the folks I asked to join us today. But let me ask George Michael. Do you still sing over there on the flipside?

He says he does. But now he's writing more.

How does that work? Are you singing old songs or writing new ones?

He showed me that Elton is channeling him – "he's putting tunes in his mind." (Jennifer aside) I'm not judging it; he just showed me projecting thoughts into his mind. (Pause) Frank Sinatra!

Correct. (Ding!)

It was who was in my head; I just couldn't think of his name.

Does he want to talk to us?

(Listens) He was just talking to Marlon Brando and then Anthony Bourdain.

Anthony's a great interviewer – Anthony, you want to help us with this one?

Anthony says, (he asked Frank) "He wanted to know how Frank made it through unscathed." "The mind," he said. Sinatra says, "He had many people around him where Anthony felt more alone, Frank had a crowd, where Anthony had millions of people who watched him... but not a group to support him."

Frank, you gave something to Quincy Jones.

He comes through smoking a cigar. Was it a cigar cutter? He showed me something small... almost like a picture of a... (Jennifer flexes her hand.) He gave him a ring.

That's right. (Ding!) Quincy said he'll never take it off.

He says, "He gave it to him from the heart."

Quincy was his arranger.

He says "That's what Anthony did not have. He had people to micromanage him." Frank says, "I loved Quincy."

Frank, who was there to greet you when you crossed?

Did his wife die of chest cancer? Or maybe a girlfriend, one of his first loves who died of cancer or something along those lines... She's beautiful... a brunette that was like Marilyn Monroe. *(Ava Gardner?)*

Were you surprised when you saw her?

He says, "She was there before he crossed over, so he wasn't surprised."

You saw her in your hospital before you left Frank?

He says, "In his home." (Jennifer aside) I don't know how he died, feels like he was battling cancer.

(Note: He died of bladder cancer and some other afflictions in 1998. The brunette Jennifer is seeing is likely his second wife Ava Gardner who died 8 years before him.)

So, who did you seek out when you got to the flipside?

He says, "Rock Hudson." That's what he showed me first.

Did you work together in a movie or just friends?

I asked, "Do you mean that kind of friend?" and he said "No, just friends. They "got" each other. They had walls up for different reasons."

Are you aware of any other lifetime you had on the planet?

"Yes." It was in Europe is what it felt like.

Someone poor or successful?

He says, "Successful."

So, when you decided to come back were you aware you were going to pick a golden voice?

He says, "Not when he landed, but yes."

What do you regret?

He says, "He really doesn't have any regrets, but he does regret some heartbreaks with siblings or children. It feels like... someone committed suicide over him... he says, "He could have been a better friend to Elvis."" (Jennifer listens;) Oh. He's such a mobster.

You want to go down that path with Frank?

He says, "Yeah."

So Frank, a lot of your friends were criminals.

He says, "It was different back then," he says. "They killed people for fun – he put a guy on a wheel and people shot at him..."

Who did that?

I don't know... He's telling me "Joe Pesci played that person in a movie."

(Note: I remember my father weeping as he read the biography of Frank. Such an icon for people of his generation, so sad to hear about his journey outside music. The idea that Joe Pesci played a real character in "Good Fellas" (based on

Nichola Pileggi's "Wise Guys") is disconcerting for those who know the violence of that kind of character.)

We're not judging ... what do you want to tell people who loved you?

He said "Breathe." (Jennifer aside) That was interesting.

It helps you sing too. (Frank was famous for modulating his breath like a trumpet player to elongate notes.)

He says, "To not do drugs. He's saying drugs can be brought down in a metaphoric or etheric way and it's why people connect or try to ..." He's saying "It's like I want them to love. If you love, you'll be more afraid to hurt. You'll be more afraid to kill someone if you love someone. If you just connect you have to compartmentalize the hurt."

Do you feel you imparted that with your songs?

He says, "Yes. I made them think of other things, I got them out of their heads, yes."

There are people in our class whom you helped.

He's showing me Aretha, and Whitney Houston when she was a little girl. That's what he's showing me.

Whitney, can you come forward?

He says, "He's helping her daughter... from the flipside."

(Note: This was before Whitney's daughter passed.)

Okay. If I can ask you Whitney, who was there to greet you?

She says, "Elizabeth Taylor." (Jennifer aside: I'm sorry to ask; Is Elizabeth still here?)

No, she's now part of the rat pack. Liz, you want to talk to us? Who was there to greet you?

She says, "Her first of 5 husbands..." I have no idea about her life; she says, "She was there to greet Michael Jackson."

And you greeted Whitney; why did you greet Whitney?

She says, "To let her know it was ok."

Do you have any regrets?

She says "Many. She's working with her daughter up there."

(Note: Liz has three, two with Richard Burton, one adopted, and another with Mike Todd)

Whitney, what do you miss about being on the planet?

"I miss the lights." She showed me like the lights onstage. Performing lights.

What was your favorite performance?

She's showing me the Olympics... didn't she sing there?

(Note: She did. It was for the 1988 Seoul Olympics. "One Moment in Time" which she performed live. I could ask Jennifer if she watched those Olympics, I know I did not, was not aware of this event, nor that she sang there.)

What was your happiest moment singing?

(For the film) "The Bodyguard."

What about you Frank? Your happiest moments?

He says, "When somebody recognized him..."

What do you mean?

He says, "As a good singer."

How old was he when he was first recognized as a good singer?

He's saying "9 or 19..."

Who was this person who recognized him?

He's showing me he had a suitcase... I don't know. Showing me a suitcase, traveling somewhere... dark suit; it was probably someone in the mafia.

I think his first contract was with the mafia.

I didn't know that – he's showing me...

Mafia means "my family" in Italian. Frank, what's your favorite song out of all your tunes?

He says something with sunshine.

You are the Sunshine of My Life?

He's showing me Elton John – something that they... they've been showing me Elton a couple of times... and George Michael.

Let's talk to this other singer I invited today, a friend of George Michael's.

Freddie Mercury!

Yes, who I asked to come by today. How does he appear to you?

A little big, bigger than he was then. Short hair, with an earring, short, short hair...

What do you think about this movie "Bohemian Rhapsody?"

He says, "They got the ending wrong." He's telling me over and over again – "It just came from one person." (Meaning only one person helped create the scenes.)

How did you like Rami's performance?

"A plus" he says.

The film on a scale of one to ten?

He says, "It was a five." Jennifer laughs.

Freddie was from Zanzibar. And Freddie's real name was...

Faruk?

That is, it.

(Jennifer aside) Shut the front door!

No that's it. I think the film honored your journey – gay people have given it a thumbs up, you did fall in love (Jim), and they got that right.

He says, "They shortened it, the (actual) timeline... they were together a much longer time."

Did you know him before this life?

He says, "Many lives. He showed me he was a female... before."

Was Freddie or Jim the female?

He says, "Jim."

Who greeted you when you crossed over?

He started singing "Mama."

Any regrets about your life and this journey?

He says, "None."

Do you miss anything?

He says, "Feeling, smelling. Tightness of the outfits, the tactile of the piano, the guitar, the kiss, the lips..."

Are you playing instruments now?

He says, "Yes." He's showing me something like an organ, but it takes up the whole universe...

What was the genesis of the song Bohemian Rhapsody?

He's showing it was him as a kid... he was young...

But the lyric; "Mamma, I killed a man?"

He says, "Metaphor; a broken heart."

Okay. When you wrote that song it was about someone breaking a heart? When did you realize you were gay?

He showed me as a baby. "When he was born."

What do you want to share with us about your journey or path?

He says, "Not to worry; I'm doing fine, I'm doing amazing, there are not words to describe it."

Did you know David Bowie?

Through the song "Under pressure." He says "It was an honor to sing it with him. Then he showed me the rocket.

Major Tom? David's last record, Dark Planet. David Bowie's journey into the flipside. So, Freddie what should we tell your fans and friends?

Jennifer makes a peace sign... "Peace and love. To live your best in it, authentically don't let anybody tell you differently."

Thank you, sir!

Luana just went whew! This is exhausting. She's showing me that they give you questions to ask... it's a flow, it something that is orchestrated, but it's improvised.

*****

It's unusual to hear all these folks come forward. We've interviewed them at other times in other sessions, recently a long conversation with Elizabeth Taylor about her journey, her love for James Dean, and her love for the actor who James has returned as. Literally recorded him (the reincarnated portion) talking directly to Elizabeth, learning new information from her, and recounting old details. It's something I've filmed, but has been kept private at this person's request. But in the interview he accessed Elizabeth on the flipside through Jennifer and had a long chat with Elizabeth about their journeys together and love for each other. It's mind bending, but why I do this research.

CHAPTER SEVEN: IT'S ALL FREQUENCY

Jim Morrison standing off stage in Per La Chaise Cemetery, Paris. Photo courtesy of Elizabeth Stanley. All Rights Reserved. (Look at the ghostly figure behind her pal)

THE MUSIC OF CEMETERIES

Some years ago, as I was winding down my writing music reviews for Variety, I got an unusual proposition. Was I interested in covering a music festival in France for the magazine?

The editor Bruce Haring had been invited, but couldn't go, so I went in his stead. France has this very wise program that takes tax money and puts it to the arts. In fact, half of every ticket sold in France to films, goes into this art fund so that French citizens can make films, create music about anything.

So, I went off to Biarritz to cover this festival for Variety. It was financed by the French government, and they put me up in a nice hotel on the beach and made sure that I went to all of the musical offerings. I met the composer Alexandre Desplat there – at the time, he was unknown, and gave me some of his CDs to see if I could show them around Hollywood.

But here I was at a composer's festival, and it was before I wound up composing music for my films. This trip also got me an invite to visit the producer of Elton John's records, and I got to sit behind his piano, in his studio where he recorded all of his hit tunes.

One wonders if the instrument itself remembers those who've played it. Those hours behind the ivories, moving the keys – the way some mediums can sense a presence with the object that someone has left behind – could instruments carry the same frequency? The same vibe?

Another session with Jennifer Shaffer in Manhattan Beach.

Jennifer: Billy is here.

Rich: Hello Mr. Paxton. What do you want to say bud?

Is there something like "100 with Prince?"

This guy I'm talking to on Tuesday, feels as if somehow Prince has been visiting him.

"Yes, he is."

So he asked.

"The frequency."

Correct. (Ding!) He asked Prince to show him a sign, if it was the case, and his girlfriend turned to him while watching a rock concert and said, "Did you hear that riff that guy played was a total Prince riff?" He said he was in tears. So, how'd you do that?

"Frequency. He put her awareness towards the guitar player." Prince says, "I have a crew that makes things happen."

Who helped you?

He said, "Luana."

So Luana has been helping you to communicate. Okay. Well, what do you want me to tell this fellow Coby?

He said, "Just be open."

Open to the idea that you're guiding him?

Prince says "Hey, people follow Jesus!" He's laughing. That's just him being funny.

Would it be useful to tell this guy you are his guide?

He said, "You have to explain about the frequencies. He's tapping into Prince's frequency – it might not be so much that Prince is a guide, per se, but he shares a frequency that Prince has with his own past lives..."

This guy is a musician.

I feel like Prince was a teacher in the spirit world with him before he came here.

Prince, is that accurate?

He says "Yes."

In between lives, Prince has met this guy.

Like a 100 years ago, that's where the 100 came from; He says, "That's why it's still so fresh."

I need to put it in a way so that I can parse it... and next thing he'll be jumping off pianos.

"Yeah."

Rich: Okay, back to you Luana.

Jennifer: She's like "It's busy here!"

I have a question about a tweet from your old friend about David Crosby – you introduced me to him one day at Hugo's restaurant.

(Jennifer aside) Don't tell me. (Listens) She said, "He's cuckoo crazy... he was like that back then too." (Back in the day with Crosby, Stills, Nash and Young). She said, "She feels like he's missing the point to whatever he's tweeting."

Well, in his tweet, he said he thought Jim Morrison wasn't a great poet or a great singer; we talked to Jim briefly in "Backstage Pass." I was curious what he might think about that.

He says, "He totally misses the point."

Mr. Morrison, do you want to say something about this comment?

He says "Obviously, I don't say anything well." (Jennifer aside) He's being sarcastic.

Oddly enough, someone sends Jim's attorney a card every year on the anniversary of his passing and signs it "Jim."

How about this, anything you want me to tweet to David Crosby in response from the Flipside?

He says, "Tell David he should have said that when he was around."

Well, is there something more poetic to say to him?

He says "David wasn't any good either, singing (his) lullaby's..." He says "Let him stew in it. He obviously craves attention and that's how he's getting it." Jim Morrison is telling me "He loved to write, he loved poetry, he loved writing... and that's the irony. Like he didn't want to be a singer, just wanted to write."

So, people should do what you love.

He says, "He's writing now, making poetry in his mind." He's also saying, "Don't criticize people who can't defend themselves."

Well, you can defend yourself now, Jim.

"Right." Then they showed me Michael Newton. "We can give a response as long as it heals people, and a response to David's comment doesn't heal. If the response is a way to open horizons, we can get a response, but he's saying that

he doesn't care. Jim just brought in Will Shakespeare. I think it's his birthday.

Will, is it your birthday?

He says "Yeah."

Are you pals with Jim Morrison?

He showed me the both of them. He says, "Their energies are similar, their mannerisms are similar."

Jim, what do you want to say to your fans or friends or family?

He says "Live life. Hold on to nothing. Give yourself an opening even if it's only to be confused with what has been given, what has been told to you. Find your own path. March at the beat of your own drum. Even if you've stolen the drums. Be different! And make a different path. Don't follow everyone else or the same path. The same is so ordinary.

Is that it?

He says "Oui."

That's funny – well you are living in France as we speak. That gorgeous Pere La Chaise cemetery. You're so French mon ami. Let's break this down – you and fellow poets, like Will Shakespeare are in the same relative frequency?

He says "Always."

And you share frequencies?

He says, "They all do!" Then Prince showed up, David Bowie showed up (to demonstrate.) He said, "We all use the same frequencies."

For music and writing?

I'm hearing "Your solar plexus is the same color as gold – there are different energy centers." (Jennifer aside) He's showing me chakras...

I think it was the great sage Sponge Bob who said, "My spirituality is so hard I broke my chakra."

They are saying, "Everyone can get information, there are melting pots in all kinds of different areas, it's whoever is open to allow that information to come through. If you allow that space to show up it's much easier..."

What are some of the ways for people to connect to their higher self?

They're saying "Through mediation or music... writing... painting. Channeling music, allowing it to flow through you. Channeling writing.

How can we pass that along to people?

They say, "tell them to meditate and visualize where their happiness lies. Meditate on 'where is your happiness,' what is your purpose, what you are passionate about, dive in deeper and you'll discover what is it that you want that to do.

So, when complications arise to your dream, if you've already seen the end result, then conflicts become a speed bump?

They're saying "It's a hiccup. Just a hiccup. If you are in your truth, there are no roadblocks, just different ways to go around."

If I may paraphrase, they're saying "Meditation is a key?"

"Some people call it prayer."

True. So, Jim, what's an effective prayer or meditation to help people?

(Jennifer aside) I just got this overwhelming sense of love... He says "putting love into everything that you do. Visualize what love looks like to you and then get that feeling of love within you."

Do you mean related to another person?

He says "No, could also be a project – if you want to do the thing you love – you can send love to your friends, family before you see them."

How do you picture love?

He says, "You don't picture it, you feel it."

So, can I love the lottery numbers into existence for example?

(Jennifer aside) They're laughing.

He says "Just know that everyone can have money – if you love what money can do or the purpose of what it can do that can help others, and change your relationship to it, it will get you more money – things will show up."

Wealth of love?

"Yes."

What more can you want?

*****

CHAPTER EIGHT: "WE'LL BE RIGHT BACK"

The Author on Merv Griffin with Charles Grodin.

It's another Thursday in Manhattan Beach. I've driven to Jennifer's office; on the way I've thought of a couple of people who might want to come forward in our class. But I wanted to leave space for someone on the flipside who wanted to speak with us – someone I may not know. I start the conversation, the same way.

Richard: Hello Class!

Jennifer: Hello.

Richard: I was thinking how when we work together, we create something else when together, because I know my questions aren't the same as you normally get in your day-to-day practice – people come in to see you with their grief... the loss of a loved one, and I'm here saying things like "Hey, let's talk to Picasso."

I've only had two out of thousands of my sessions ask me questions like that… and it's only because they've read your books.

Luana anyone want to speak to us first?

Did you mention Dick Clark to anyone? Is he still here (alive)?

No. What does he want to say?

I just got shown a photograph of Dick Clark.

Who showed that to you?

Luana.

Okay Luana, bring him on in, we're open to you.

I know it's not the person you asked or requested to speak with (and I have not told her that yet either.)

Well, Dick Clark is somewhat related to the person I want to talk to… You see a pic of Dick Clark? What's it look like?

It's a photo in black and white of him.

In his era, doing American bandstand?

"Yes."

Luana, are you giving Jennifer a genre?

"Yes." (She taps her nose, Luana's way of saying "correct you are sir.")

That you have a music person for us to speak with?

Like Elvis...

Does having Dick Clark's photo in her mind's eye help you or Jennifer to focus?

"It helps all of us."

What does that mean?

"It's supposed to help you and all of us to focus on him."

Okay, this person passed away a number of years ago, so people are talking about him, and we've talked to this person before...

Are you talking about David Bowie?

(Note: I leave in most of the times we get the "wrong" name, so that people who are focused on that sort of thing, can get off the "afterlife bus" return the book for a refund, etc. In most cases she gets the name in between one and six tries.)

No, but he's welcome to join us. Someone said to me "You're out of time" last night. I thought to myself is that a warning? Or a pun? Because "You're out of time when you're outside of time."

Whenever you're in that matrix, you're outside of time.

It's a way of singing or writing a song I think – allowing yourself to be outside of time... I don't know who was singing to me. It seemed like a male voice. We're talking about someone from our class... somebody who was of Tom Petty's era, who performed with Tom who is no longer on the planet.

I'm drawing a blank.

Luana, let's look around the room, who needs to speak up.

George Martin...

Okay, he's related to this fellow.

George Harrison.

Correcto-mundo. (Ding!) Today's the day he died 17 years ago. He didn't want to show up to you?

He says, "He's busy."

That's fine. What's he busy doing?

"He's talking to other people in the class."

Two Georges. From the archive at Beatles.com

So, George people are talking about you cause it's the anniversary of the day you checked off the planet. The new white album came out. You said George Martin... can we talk to George Martin?

(Jennifer aside) Sure, I don't know who he is.

Luana, do you know who that is? Can you bring him forward?

"Yes. Yeah."

Mr. Martin, can I ask you some questions, do you mind?

He says, "He got them this morning."

Okay, because I was talking to George Harrison this morning to prepare for our questions... So, Mr. Martin...

Did he die two years before George?

I don't know... I think after... I know one of your sons.

He says, "It was five years after."

(Note: That's correct. Ding! George Harrison died in 2001, George in 2006)

I met one of your sons in Cannes.

"Was he a little bit of an asshole."

He was funny... he's odd, a bit unusual. But you have two sons.

Do they have a big age range? And personality range?

I think so – yes. But the second son, show Jennifer what he's doing.

"Producing." I saw records flying.

Yes, correct, mixing records that George worked on. Show Jennifer who you worked with?

Freddie Mercury came through.

That is correct. (Ding!) He produced one of their records. But...

Did he produce "The Beatles?"

Yes, correct. (Ding!) He did.

He showed me that right away, but I got confused.

Yes, but when Freddie Mercury jumps in what can you do? But tell her about your background George.

Does this go back to Dick Clark?

Let's see...

I just saw Johnny Carson as well.

George, you used to produce some comedy records with comedians, one of them I'm going to ask to come forward. Can you put him in Jennifer's mind? She'll know him as a movie star.

David Bowie came through again.

Sorry David, I don't mean to put you on a waiting list... I'm the encyclopedia of useless info. Some of the people you worked with included Peter Sellers.

I loved the Pink Panther.

The Beatles liked those early comedy records, George Harrison was a fan of those records that George Martin produced. Have you talked to Peter since you've been on the flipside?

Yes. He's hanging out with Robin Williams.

Okay, can we talk to Peter?

Yeah.

Who greeted you when you crossed over?

He says, "His animals." Um... then it felt like a sister... but he's laughing. "It was his wife!" Jennifer laughs.

So, your first wife?

Something like a second wife.

Was it her physically or higher self-greeting you?

"It was not her higher self," he says. (Jennifer aside) I know nothing about his personal life.

(Note: Peter had four wives, the first three are alive, the fourth has died and is interred with him (he died in 1980.)

Peter, you were friends with our friend Hal Ashby who is also in class. Movie called "Being There." One of the best performances ever given in a film. What do you miss about being on the planet?

He misses the ocean... I asked, "Can't you just go to the ocean?" He like "It's not the same. The salt."

The water on your feet or the salt air in your lungs?

He says, "The feel of freedom." He's just breathing in.

What do you regret if anything?

He's so funny... he showed me like these big clown shoes that he couldn't fill... He says, "It was not taking enough risks."

Before we let George Martin go, I forgot to ask, who was there to greet you when you crossed over?

He says, "It was his mum."

What do you miss about being on the planet?

He says, "I miss the parties, the laughter, the perfume."

Do you regret anything?

I can almost smell a woman walking by with Chanel. It's interesting... um. He says, "Not really; but if I did have one regret; he wishes he spent more time with his kids."

You have two sons, Gregory and Giles – I met Gregory, and Giles is the one doing all the Beatle records ... a message for Gregory?

He's laughing. He says, "He needs to bring down his heart rate."

How does George appear to you? Hip, well dressed?

Old school.

What about your son Giles, what would you like me to tell Giles?

"Something about the third song."

You mean The White Album?

"Something about the 4th album," then he said, "White Album."

He's saying there was a 4th cd? Is he talking about that?

"Yeah, it was a 3-cd set, he says, but there was a longer version on the 4th cd. It needs some undoing."

You mean it needs some work? I don't think they'll work on it.

He says, "I know that I totally know that. You asked for specifics. It's the 4th album the 3rd song..." He says, "His son already knows what he's talking about as he considered it."

He considered it but he didn't do it.

"He cut it too short."

The third song on the 4th CD, you think he should revisit that.

"Yes."

Giles did the "Love" CD for the Vegas show and put that together.

(Jennifer aside) Wow.

A monumental piece of work... Giles is talking about doing another one.

Are they thinking of doing something like what "Mama Mia" did? A movie with all the songs?

Could be. There was a movie that did that "Across the Universe" - it had all the Beatles songs...

(Jennifer) I never saw it.

They did a re-release recently... a Broadway musical director directed it.

He said, "I think she needed to be kicked out."

You didn't care for that?

He says, "Not at all. It was a piece of *crap*."

(Note: Nothing quite like a review from the Flipside – No offense to Julie Taymor. It's just one man's opinion, and for what it's worth, I enjoyed the film. Jennifer has never seen it.)

What do you think Giles should work on?

He said "He just wanted to focus on this album…"

But any advice for him?

"He needs to be outside and focus on getting outside. Traveling."

John Lennon anything you want us to tell Yoko as we didn't ask before?

(Pause.) "She talks to him every day."

Okay, let's go back to George Harrison again – who was there to greet you when you crossed over? I know what you said before, but now I'm asking again just to see if it's the same answer. Who was there to greet you when you crossed over?

I see a horse. I see a woman on a horse.

That is exactly what you said before. Thanks. So, what do you miss about being on the planet?

(Jennifer aside) That (horse image) makes sense to you?

Totally. What do you miss?

"Richard Branson."

You liked him?

(Note: I had no idea George Harrison and Richard Branson knew each other. Apparently, they were good pals. https://www.virgin.com/richard-branson/my-memories-sir-george-martin)

"Not really" he said.

Ever the comic. Then why do you miss him?

He says, "He misses having fun with him."

Goofing around. Getting your weird sense of humor.

"Very weird," he said.

Do you think it's odd that I ask you questions like this?

He said, "No, I'm kind of used to it." (Jennifer aside:) You talked to him at night, he showed you laying down and talking to him.

Was that you singing to me last night? (I heard someone sing the words "Out of time.")

"Yeah. He's showing me your face while you're talking, I always think that's weird…" hold on.

I'm out of time?

"Yes, because you're able to talk to them."

Or do you think I should write a song called "out of time?"

"Yes."

Did you like my new stab at a tune I put on YouTube "To be or not to be?"

"Yeah, it was kinda groovy," says John. Will (Shakespeare) just said "The title was fantastic." I forgot that it was already written.

"The title is fantastic?" (Obviously mocking me from the flipside. It's allowed) Well, your name is on it Will. (When I

posted the song, I put Will's name for the lyrics). Sorry, Will there are no residuals.

He said "I'm going to sue you and show up at your door. Or in your dreams."

"Knock knock." "Who is it?" "It's some dude dressed in 16th century duds saying "What dreams may come? They've arrived."

He said (the song) "It's brilliant."

(Note: Okay, I'm flattered. I just got a flipside compliment from John and George and Will Shakespeare, or at least in my egocentric mind, I'm allowing that to be the case. They could have been totally mocking me, I have no clue. I know Jennifer has not heard the song – but I took "To be or not to be" and set it to music and put it online. Why not? Either way, NO ONE WILL EVER BELIEVE that these fellows are complimenting me, nor would I deign to claim so (or put them on the album cover.)

What do you want us to tell your pal Russ Titelman, George?

He just got a chair and sat down.... "Way back in the day." (Like I'm droning on.)

It was after your Beatle years that you knew our mutual friend.

Jennifer: Did he (Russ) do something with writing, editing of his music? A Producer?

That's correct. (Ding!) Russ produced a number of Grammy winning records, including one of yours. He also is an excellent photographer and let me use one of you he took in our last book.

"He's one hell of a producer, one hell of a chap." (Jennifer said this in an English accent. Jennifer listens:) "Thank you," he said, "You have a nice accent."

Okay. So, what about Russ Titelman, what do you want to tell him?

He showed me taking a volume knob and turning it up.

What does that mean?

(To George) Really? (To me) That's what he's doing.

His hearing isn't so good so maybe that's related to it?

Yes. (Taps her nose) Tell him to "Turn up the volume..."

It's a pun, "turn up the volume Russ, it's also a way to hear George." What's a good way for Russ to reach out to you George, or for you to reach out to Russ?

"Through his guitar." I'm seeing him playing a guitar...

So, while he plays guitar think of George?

I hate to ask this, did George play guitar?

Yes, it's funny because it shows how much you don't know about the folks we're talking to.

"He (Russ) should channel him (George.)"

Russ took some great pix you... one is in our book.

"That was really cool."

I know we asked your permission to use that pic...

"There are better ones he said, someone's arm is over somebody and looking off in the distance, 70's..."

There's one in the street.

Is there another one when they first met up in LA or saw the beach together?

A photo of you that Russ took at the beach?

He's just showing me the beach again.

(Note: I asked Russ about this, and he can't remember taking any pictures of George by the beach, but confirmed he has some things of George's.)

(To me) Did you know the woman on the horse?

No, I didn't. I knew your wife's sister - your sister-in-law, George.

When you pushed her away (meaning "ignored her") she said, "Tell him to knock it off."

I think you said that it was your wife's higher self who greeted him on the horse.

Which wife died from cancer?

One of his earlier wives, it's possible... his current wife, her sister went out with my brother. I didn't know George's wife Olivia, but I knew her sister –

"She's still here on the planet."

Yes, correct. I'm sorry they didn't marry (as we've discussed before, when George said he remembered my brother hitting a home run during a softball game at his house.) I'm just trying to give Russ a message from you George. Anything other than "turn up the volume?"

Hang on. "He needs a haircut." Is he losing his hair? He's joking, showing me like trying to do the combover. Wow, he's a ballbuster George is.

So, he's busting Russ' chops about his hair and his hearing? Russ has a fine assortment of cool hats. Maybe he's just being silly.

Hold on, "Something to do with a pick." It feels like there's a pick he has that could have been George's.

George may know this story – as I've mentioned it before, but I was there when Eric played that song for his son; "Tears in Heaven." I had the guitar pick from that session.

"And you lost the pick."

That's correct. (Ding!) Russ sent me another one with Eric's name on it... are you referring to that pick?

"No."

So, Russ has a George Harrison guitar pick?

Might be on the wall. "Framed."

You're saying use that pick to talk to George?

"No." Who has the artwork? You know about George's artwork?

I don't know – Russ has artwork of George's? He may have at one point. I know he had one of his statues of Buddha.

"Russ needs to listen and not to doubt, he's been trying to show him signs all the time... 11:11 is appearing, like he's trying to contact him."

(Note: There's a chapter on the recurrence of "11:11" in a previous book where we talk about each 11 representing a hallway, and they have to slow down their frequency, we have to "speed up" ours so we can "meet at the decimals.")

Does Russ have a guitar or instrument of yours?

He says, "He had or has 3 instruments of his." I'm seeing a harmonica.

I don't know – at one point he may have had his piano... are you saying that if he takes the pick out, that he can communicate with you?

"He's just giving you brash."

A brash?

"Yes, he's teasing you."

So, I'm saying he should use the pick, open his mind and heart and play the guitar and he'll hear from you George is that right?

"Yes."

Thank you, George, Mr. While-My-Guitar-Gently-Weeps. Perhaps George does listen in as well, I guess. Kind of like "Alexa" always listening. What did I hear this morning? Oh yeah, your song "All Things Must Pass..."

"Gas." (Jennifer makes a face, as if saying something to George.) Seriously?

All things must pass gas. Okay, that's a little sophomoric.

(Jennifer aside) It's not coming from me.

I heard that song this morning...

(Jennifer aside) That's a song?

Yes, "All Things Must Pass" - a beautiful song by George. Let me ask how you see him; is his hair long or short?

Shorter.

Can you see his face?

Yeah. Smiling.

So, can we talk to Peter Sellers? He's a friend of George Harrison's.

It's a Brit invasion! (laughs)

I know!

"Yes." He's here.

Hello Peter. Mike Myers is a huge fan of yours. Peter what do you want to tell Mike or your fans?

Laughs. He showed me "The Pink Panther" ... (listens, seriously, then laughs.) Just now, I thought he was asking me something serious, and he said very seriously "Please watch the Pink Panther movies, so you'll prefer to go outside."

What do you miss about being on the planet?

"A lot of things, not just one thing." He says he misses the sense of smell.

Who do you hang out with on the flipside? Stanley Kubrick came by our class.

I keep getting Robin Williams.

Perfect, well, that's a logical person for you to hang out with. You guys make each other laugh?

"All the time – they try not to think (when together), because if they think they will make each other laugh."

There's a fellow that I met years ago, the man who directed The Pink Panther, he was a client of my pal and producer Jonathan Krane, who we've spoken with before, Luana knows him from "Group" (we spoke earlier to Sydney Pollack who reminded us that he was in group with Luana). I've met his daughter Jennifer a few times... whose mother is the first wife of this fellow. Luana, can you put this fellow's name in Jennifer's mind?

Blake? I saw my son, Blake.

Correct. (Ding!) Blake Edwards. Directed Peter in The Pink Panther. Can we bring Blake Edwards in?

Sure... he's a tall guy. Was he a tall guy?

He can be tall over there. It's allowed. (People appear on the flipside, as they prefer to appear. Even though he might not have been tall here, that's how he's appearing to Jennifer) How does he look to you?

I see him with brown hair, looks like he's from the 70's; he has on wide collars, and he looks really thin.

Hello Blake. Do you recognize the people in our class?

"All of them. It's a special club" he says.

I don't think you worked with Luana...

He says, "Not then, but since. Twice through you."

How did you cross over, who greeted you when you got there?

Felt like his heart gave out – from whatever complications he was having. Sometimes I'm shown that for other reason. I'm seeing that it was like was in his lungs, and he's correcting me; "No it was my heart." (For the record, he died from pneumonia according to wikipedia)

Who was there to greet you when you crossed over?

Why is Tom Petty coming in? (Listens) Okay. Got it. He says, "A guy named Tom was there to greet him."

That's why you saw Tom? Close friend or a soul group member? (Often the case)

From his soul group. (Everyone has them, they're the people you normally incarnate with).

Did you know Tom in this lifetime?

He says, "Yes, in this lifetime," he did.

Were you surprised to see Tom waiting for you?

"Yeah." He was really happy.

What's Tom's last name?

Something like Tom's son... not Tomason ... I don't know.

Sounds like Tom's son?

Look for the Tom part...

(Note: Blake Edward's daughter told me it was likely Tom Waldman, who wrote a number of the Pink Panther scripts, an American who was a close friend who died 25 years before Blake. https://en.wikipedia.org/wiki/Tom_Waldman)

Was this someone you served in the military with?

Was he a pilot? He's showing me someone in a plane... a WWII plane.

What was Tom's occupation in this life? You guys worked together in England or Hollywood?

He says, "Everywhere."

Primarily – where was Tom living?

"England."

Did he work with you on your films?

He says, "You can say that."

(Note: If it was Tom Waldman, that is accurate.)

Blake, what do you miss about being on the planet?

He says, "The water and the breeze and the cold air." He doesn't miss the rain.

What do you regret if anything about your life here?

"More outings," he says. It was towards the end it felt he was like heartbroken.

Over not getting out.

"Over someone."

I'm sure Jennifer does not know who your second wife was, Blake, but if you could put her in Jennifer's mind so she does?

I'm seeing a singer... what was her name... I know that's not his wife... but she showed up. Liza Minelli.

Well, his wife was a singer, correct, also an actress but is mostly famous for appearing in other people's movies. Put a song in Jennifer's mind.

Jennifer smiles. (It's raining as we film this, she looks outside at the dark clouds over the ocean.) He says, "The sun will come out tomorrow."

Okay, but what are songs where people sing them that are bigger than life?

Oh! (Seeing it) "The hills are alive!" He was trying to help me to get there. Julie Andrews. I know every song from that film.

She's still on the planet, she's still rocking, but is there anything you want me to tell your daughter Jennifer?

(Jennifer smiles) Did she have blue eyes? He said, "Tell her I loved her from the moment I saw her blue eyes."

(Note: Jennifer, Blake's daughter, says her eyes were blue as a baby.)

So, why'd you let her appear in Heidi?

Jennifer makes a face.

Don't judge it.

He's throwing it back at you. That's funny. He says he thought "She was mature enough." I don't know what he means.

Do you Jennifer know what I'm talking about?

(Jennifer aside) No!

So, Blake, you let her appear in that movie that interrupted the Super Bowl... and she was chastised for decades, except now it's something people ask her to sign autographs about.

Was that in 67?

Could be... Anything you want us to pass along?

(Ding! Correct. Film was made in 1967, interrupted the Super Bowl in Nov. 1968)

He says, "Tell her she doesn't have to worry about cancer;" she's worried about cancer.

Stop worrying about cancer? Why?

He says, "She worries too much."

Does she, have it?

He says, "No." She had a scare, I think.

(Note: This is accurate)

She's got kids as well, anything you wanna tell your grandchildren, Gramps?

Jennifer makes a face.

If I can't poke fun at Blake, I don't know who I can.

He says, "Tell them to stop asking their mom for money." Laughs. He's kidding about that. That's a joke.

(Note: Blake Edwards was responsible for many laughs in his film career; all the Pink Panther films, Breakfast at Tiffany's and others.)

Who are you hanging out with on the flipside, Blake?

He showed me the brat pack... he showed me Frank Sinatra.

You're hanging out with Frank? Do you hear him sing, or just watch him beat up mafia guys?

(Note: We interviewed Frank in another session, he was funny and sarcastic. I tend to be flippant when someone else mentions someone we spoke to in the past, just to see if that alters their answer.)

He says, "They play guitar together."

Did they play in life?

Blake played piano I think... Frank is learning (to play).

(Note: This is a common refrain so to speak. People can create "mental constructs" of instruments and then play them.)

So, you're constructing the guitar to play it with each other? Is it 6 string guitar?

He says, "It's four."

That's a ukulele...

What's up with the ukuleles over there? (We've heard this before, Paul Allen said he's learning to play a ukulele.)

It's easier to play, three or four chords and you can sing almost any song. George Harrison used to hand them out like candy. Has Frank learned how to play the uke?

He says, "Yeah."

If I asked for a song to sing, what's the first thing that comes to mind?

Hold on. I can't understand this song.

Give me the lyrics. Frank, if you're going to sing a song with Blake what would you sing?

(Laughs. It's raining as we film this interview.) "The sun will come out tomorrow." At first it felt like "November Rain," but it was our peanut gallery throwing stuff out there.

Rich: Okay, so back to Dick Clark. So why did he show up?

Jennifer: "To say hi."

What do you want to say, Dick?

I asked him – he said "He got a lot of bands out there..."

He made many musical acts... later in life he told a couple of off-color jokes and people filmed him doing that and people were like "oh my god! Dick Clark went blue!"

He's saying, "I can't believe you're bringing this up."

I'm sorry, it was just in the zeitgeist.

(Note: It was a clip in Michael Moore's first film "Looking for Roger")

"I was better than soul train," he says.

I beg to disagree. Tell us who was there to greet you on the flipside?"

He says, "His cat. He had a little pushed up nose... an orange tabby."

Your cat?

He says, "Yes, it died 3 years before he did."

Was that surprising?

"Yeah."

Did you believe in an afterlife?

(Wags her hand) He says, "He wanted to."

Once your cat was there you realized you were somewhere else?

He says, "It was a soft transition – like with Harry Dean." (Stanton – as reported in "Backstage Pass to the Flipside.")

I'm going on the radio Sunday night, what do you want me to tell people about you showing up in our class??

He says, "Tell them I didn't mean those off colored jokes and I'm sorry."

What else?

He says, "To keep making music, even though you might not think you're good at it, someone else might think you're great at... it... (Jennifer aside: he just showed me Kanye... "Another man's trash is another man's treasure.") "Don't give up based on what anybody thinks or tells you."

Does that apply to life or music?

He says, "Everything."

What do you miss about being on the planet?

He says, "He misses the interactions with people."

People you worked with or people in general?

He says, "Where you get to be surprised about answers... he misses... this is interesting – he's showing me how you don't really get to keep your thoughts on the other side. When thoughts come out, people see them. You can't hide your thoughts over there. Like he misses having a normal conversation, listening to someone else and being surprised what they're saying."

Like what we're doing. You were one of the consummate interviewers.

"Thank you."

And you integrated music on your show and rock and roll and the New Year's Eve shows... you were like the workingest man in show biz; what was that about?

"Not as many as Merv."

Why did you say that?

He showed me Merv Griffin. I did know Merv – he discovered my mentor, Lisa, and she showed me where Merv is buried.

Where is he buried?

In Westwood. Near Marilyn Monroe.

How far are you from Hefner, Merv?

"I was there before Hugh Hefner was there."

Okay, but how far are you from his tomb now?

He's showing me they're near each other.

Anyone else need to come forward? Luana is that why you showed us Dick Clark?

"Yeah, to bring Merv in."

Dick did you know about our class? Have you heard about this class, or have you been observing all along?

She says, "You're able to go in and download everything that's there (in previous sessions of our "class.")" So funny, it takes ten seconds over there to download everything all the classes.

Luana, this seemed like a convenient way – for you to show us who wanted to speak to us...

They had to show up (and a photo appeared of them) otherwise I wouldn't have known.

Luana holding up a photo is an effective way to bring that person forward? Was this helpful for Dick Clark?

"Yes, it helps them go to their people."

Just to clarify – someone joining our class – Dick Clark for example, he has his loved ones, family friends, and this kind of class exercise helps him to reach out to them?

"Yes."

Okay Dick, this will be a chapter in a book sometime in the future, what was your favorite band you introduced to America on "American bandstand?" Who were your favorite artists?

He showed me... Stevie Nicks, Fleetwood Mac, The Pointer Sisters, The Beatles, Elvis... (listens) "That shook up everybody," he said. He showed me something in black and white and then... he "likes Ryan Seacrest." He showed me Ryan looking up and said "Somehow he handles it all. He just deals with whatever, he has no life because of it."

Any tip you want to give him?

He says, "Don't make off color jokes." He laughed. "No. Ryan should give us tips."

Any last words?

I'm seeing Marie Osmond singing... "May tomorrow be a perfect day, may we find love and laughter along the way, may god keep you... until we meet again..."

(Note: One of the Osmond's signature tunes.)

Who put that in Jennifer's mind?

My dad. He showed me the time when he danced with Marie. She picked him out of a crowd – my dad carried that photo next to my mom's picture for the rest of his life. Let's ask my dad about the healing thing… when I asked him to give me a blessing.

*****

"All things must pass… gas." I could never have conceived of that comment, nor could Jennifer. It is bizarre as well as comic at the same time – and ladies and gentlemen, I submit that as cornball a comedy comment is it is - it could only have come from the flipside.

Dick Clark American Bandstand - Wikimedia

CHAPTER NINE: MUSIC THAT HEALS

Clarence Clemons Photo Wikipedia

Another day in Manhattan Beach, talking to the flipside.

Rich: Luana, who else did I invite today?

Jennifer: Is the other person you want to talk to in music?

Correct. Luana put in Jennifer's mind who the lead singer of the band was that we're asking to come...

I'm seeing an African American... played in a rock band that is famous... I don't think I know his name... (Ding!)

But you might recognize the instrument he played or the lead singer of his band. Let's focus on something else. I met this guy, can you put the place in Jennifer's mind?

Felt like a party or a bar. (Ding!)

Yes. It was a party in the Hamptons. I was at some event, saw him by himself and I spoke to him.

I'm getting a saxophone. (Ding!)

That's correct. He played with...

Springsteen. That guy! I don't know his name. (Ding!)

Clarence.

He was trying to tell me "Terrence."

Clarence and I have someone in common, someone he used to date, lived with her years ago, a close friend of mine.

I'm getting Shaka... Shaka Khan?

Yes and no. Her name is Chacon. (Ding!) Lilia Chacon. That's correct. Clarence who was there to greet you when you crossed over?

He said, "His grandmother."

Your nephew is touring, how's he doing?

He said, "Way better."

(Note: Clarence Clemmons nephew is playing saxophone with the E Street Band these days.)

Clarence anything you want to say to Bruce?

He says, "Tell him to slow down."

All right.

He says, "There's something going on with Bruce's ear... left ear... maybe he's losing hearing in it." (Sometimes she sees an ear because they're saying "I'm talking but he's not listening). He says, "He needs to write more."

Okay. Clarence, can you bring your friend Danny Federici forward?

(Note: Danny Federici sat in with my band in LA one night, he was pals with our guitarist Bob Bernstein. I could not believe how he made my keyboard sound – he was amazing. He died after Clarence, was also a member of the E Street Band.)

Danny Federici, who sat in with my band. YouTube

Danny, who was there to greet you?

He said, "Clarence."

How'd that happen?

He said, "He saw him before he left."

(Note: This often means, "in the hospital." Like the way dementia patients begin to see their family or loved ones who've crossed over, it's because the filters on their brain have shut down.)

When you got over to the other side... what happened?

He says, "I saw Clarence as younger... and Clarence said "We have to get going because we have to play." We went on stage, and we played but I didn't have my instrument!

He was missing a keyboard?

It was from a memory that they both had.

Where was the show the memory came from?

He says "Chicago."

You're on stage, and are you standing in the place you normally stood?

He said, "No; there wasn't room for me."

Did you see the rest of the guys?

"Yes."

Did anyone recognize you?

"No."

What song were you singing?

(Jennifer aside) That one where the girl was pulled onto the stage.

"Dancing in the Dark?"

He said "Yes."

At what point did you realize you were in the afterlife?

He said when "He was put in the audience, was looking up and there was no one at the keyboards..." something weird like that...

Bruce mentions it in his show where he had a dream his dad was in the audience, and he saw himself standing next to his dad and looking at himself singing on stage.

That's what he was showing me ... I know it wasn't him...

So, Danny, you see the band playing without you... then what?

They all laugh, then Clarence and the rest of they all come to him and laugh and say "Dude, we're never going to let anyone else play your keyboards!"

Do you remember playing my keyboard?

He said, "Yes, twice."

(Note: My band "Imminent Disaster" played the House of Blues twice, and our guitar player Boo Bernstein has played with many session players. One day he asked if Danny could "sit in" and I was in awe of his playing. I forgot that he did two sets with us until he mentioned it.)

Wow. That's correct.

He says he "changed everything... (all the controls)."

*****

That's another time that a musician has told us that when they crossed over, it was like walking onto a stage. In John Lennon's case, I asked him when he knew he was on the flipside, and he reported "walking onto stage and playing "Blue Suede Shoes" with Jimi Hendrix. I didn't know that both he and Jimi recorded that song a year apart, separately, and have no idea if they played on stage together, but I do know that when "Sgt. Pepper's" came out the Beatles went to see Jimi, and he did a version of the title track in his show just for their benefit.

And recently, when interviewing my friend Charles Grodin who had crossed over to the flipside, he said that he saw himself on the set of the Carson show, something he did often in life, but instead of Johnny in his chair, Jimi Hendrix was conducting the interview.

When asked about that, we were told that Jimi likes to participate in these "constructs" – to help people have a soft landing. Because they all know him, remember him, and are often thrilled to see him.

Charles was great friends with Paul Simon. During the interview with Jennifer Shaffer, I asked him *"Do you have any message for Paul Simon?"*

Charles and Paul were great friends, Chuck got an Emmy for directing their antiwar special, they remained lifelong friends. At one point Chuck made me the imaginary manager of a pretend musician named "Hutch Saxony" and told me to negotiate a music session with Paul.

What Chuck wasn't saying was that *he was* Hutch Saxony. He had this unique skill where one could play any melody to him, and he could improvise what sounded like a "believable tune" on any topic.

We went into a sound stage with Grammy winning producer Russ Titelman who had an engineer set up a track and Chuck sang three poignant songs. One was about a man walking along on the beach with his dog. "My dog." Sounded like a touching song someone wrote somewhere. Completely improvised. Completely from somewhere outside his mind.

Paul and Charles would play elaborate games with each other – like sending over lawsuits over something trivial. "You ate the last pickle in my fridge when you were over last weekend, so I'm suing you for damages." And then Paul would countersue Chuck about some imaginary slight. It would go on and on, with legal paperwork and long involved faux lawsuits. "No! You at the last pickle!" "No, you did!"

But when Chuck passed, I asked if he had any message for his pal, Paul. He said, ***"Tell Paul to not worry about his last song."*** I asked "Why?" He said, (through Jennifer) "Because his last song **is not** his last song." I sent that to Paul in an email and heard back.

"Richard: Chuck's words have an absolute connection to what I am doing. Rather astounding if true! Thank you. Paul."

I find it both mind bending, but at the same time quite logical that Jimi Hendrix is still an icon – that people report seeing him, meeting him, talking to him – and when we asked him why he was showing up so often in these reports, he said it was "something he enjoyed doing."

I'm enjoying reporting it.

Three amigos; Gene Wilder, Joe Bologna and Charles Grodin are all backstage now.

MUSIC HEALS

Nancy, Michael, Ron – Photo Courtesy of the Reagan Presidential Museum; Pete Sousa

In the research, it's always problematic when people are faced with accusations of misbehaving during their lifetime. No one exemplifies that conundrum more than the Michael Jackson, one of the greatest artists of the modern era, and who was accused of abusing his power and position with children.

In a general discussion of abuse – which has been doing in the other books "It's a Wonderful Afterlife" – we find people who do hypnotherapy can access their "life planning" session where they discussed in advance things that would occur in their lifetime, including abuse.

It's a profound thing to realize that what happens onstage stays onstage, that our reasons for choosing our lifetimes, for choosing the events that occur to us, or that we cause may have been planned in advance.

With that being said, I must warn readers, listeners, that we're about to dive into the topic.

My questions are *in italics*, Jennifer Shaffer replies **in bold**. This was filmed on March 12th, 2019, after the screening of

"Finding Neverland" on HBO (which Jennifer and I had yet to view).

Rich: Last week we interrupted Prince who had shown up with Michael Jackson. Sorry about that. Is Michael here?

Jennifer: "Yes."

So, Michael, you've been in the news lately.

He says, "He's happy that it's out. It's healing and it's helping others."

Anything you want to say about it?

He says, "He didn't know how harmful it was. He really loved those boys, like he was ... (trying to find the words) there was a love he didn't know... he was so separated from…"

His emotions?

He says "I meant what I said, I know they're healing, they're healing now, I know Oprah interviewed the boys and (know) how it's helping to break the cycle for everyone..." – Not only was he iconic, you know as a pop star, but he's... he didn't... I don't know how you could say this but he's saying, "This was part of his life's path."

I was going to ask him that.

He said, "Yeah."

Prince, please help him with this if you can. Michael, are you saying that you chose this life to not only hit the heights musically but also to hit the depths?

He says, "Absolutely."

We've learned this in the research, not from this case or these boys... but from other people - they signed up for a lifetime and agreed to experience trauma to teach others.

(Jennifer aside:) I asked him, "Is that (also) what you want to be remembered by?" and he said "Yes."

So, it's to help teach a lesson in overcoming negativity, overcoming trauma?

He said, "Yes." He showed me all the layers of it.

Who's idea was this? (To have this multilayered lifetime). Your guides? Your teachers? Who came up with the idea of teaching negativity in a healing way?

"It was the environment," (or "construct") he says.

Let's go back to your life planning session if we can... Prince can we help him go back to his life planning session?

He says, "He has it – he says that all of it... it was everything."

So, was it your teachers who suggested this? My question is, did you suggest it or your teachers, that you would teach that lesson?

He says, "It was all of us, everybody agreed upon it." He showed me something interesting. He says, "You don't have a body (back) there – when you agree upon something like this, you don't feel it, you aren't connected to it at all..." (Jennifer aside) That was interesting. I went to a spirit space, where you are looking at people who don't have bodies, you're looking at how things can work - it's like looking at a blueprint... sort of thing.

From an engineering perspective? It's an abstract thing?

He said, "It took him becoming famous so that it would get to a point where this (revelation) would be so big that they (abuse victims) could heal from it."

How do they heal from it? Specifically thinking of people who were traumatized by some physical act in their own life. By exposing something on a global scale - it helps people to heal.

He says, "Correct."

What's a message that might help heal people?

He says, "Just love. Have self-love. Know that it or what happened to you wasn't ... know that you didn't cause it."

You mean specifically those boys? Or everyone?

"Everyone who has been in it," he says. (Experienced trauma or abuse.)

So what caused it?

He says, "His surroundings did." (Meaning "all the factors combine.")

Let's say we're looking at it like a play and we're outside the theater, and we say "We're going to examine these things in this play, but it's going to be difficult to examine these things, but the purpose is to heal people by exposing it?

When he left the planet, he said "He was taken directly back to his (life) planning session."

May I ask, why were you taking that drug that knocked you out, Rohypnol?

He said, "To help him leave."

You were in a hurry to get home?

He had his bags packed, waiting.

But you wouldn't deliberate try to end it all?

He said, "No."

May I ask, was your consciousness still working while you were in that stupor state, what was your consciousness doing?

He said, "He was getting ready to go. Bags packed." He showed me like a Mayflower moving truck. I just saw the fire.... you know when he caught on fire?

During the Pepsi commercial... Some did say you never quite recovered from that. If I may ask – did someone abuse you emotionally or physically? If so, who abused you?

He says, "His father abused him emotionally, and allowed that (other abuse) to happen by being in that industry. But as to who molested him; it felt like an uncle."

You were molested by someone close?

He says, "Yes. It was someone in the music industry – just feels like an uncle."

How old were you?

"Five" he said.

Someone in the music industry?

He said, "Yes."

But I'll guess that this "Uncle" was abused as well... the cycle has gone on for everyone. I'm not trying to mitigate it or point a finger.

He said, "He knows that."

You said you were... glad... that this documentary came out?

He says, "Yes, that was the point. He had to leave in order for it to come out – because it was so big, many people are able to heal in this way. It took someone as big as him in order to help people heal."

Okay, I think I understand. Michael thank you – I felt bad because you showed up two weeks ago and we tabled our discussion because we were talking to (a famous scientist).

He says, "It was to get in your head for our discussion now."

I haven't seen the film yet and am not looking forward to it. But I understand why it needed to be made now. Thank you for explaining that.

*****

Again, I know this is traumatic for victims to hear. But it is in the research; the abuse we experience in life might have another intended lesson or profound level of teaching. It's not opinion, theory or belief; it's in the data and footage.

CHAPTER TEN: "FEELS LIKE A THOUSAND YEARS"

The Master of Time at Oxford

Some of this interview was in the book "Architecture of the Afterlife." However, as happens often, people do show up and reference previous interviews they've done with us.

In this case, there was an interview with scientists that considered themselves skeptics. Physicists who are on the flipside. Later in our podcast, we interviewed David Bohm and Krishnamurti, but in this Stephen Hawking gives some insight into how it can be that people can "access a time frame" that might include music or musicians from previous eras. (Physicists interpreting string theory or the music that is coming from the spheres.)

At this point Jennifer is recalling an event from when she was a toddler, where she was left in a car and overheated – then years later recalled the event in detail as the source of her "gifts."

Rich: So, this is your first experience with spirit?

Jennifer: Yes. They're showing me they did something to my heart to make me cry aloud. My folks told me the only reason I was alive is because I cried (and they heard her.)

Let me clarify this; you are showing Jennifer this first incident, and she'd later get stronger and better at it?

They tap their nose – "That's correct."

This relates to a conversation we had a couple of weeks ago, talking to our "science all stars" and asking about dark matter and energy – and someone said it was related to the medulla... back of the head, said it was the access point – and I looked it up – it's the brain stem – you pointed to where it comes up through the neck. It's the gateway. Jim step in... and any of our scientists – how do we access source while in our body? Is it related to the medulla? The brain stem? Or the pineal gland?

I feel it's the pineal gland... feels like a combustion – both have to work together. He says, "It's like they have to not work and work together, rewired almost."

Is the pineal gland a filter? Or a limiter?

He says, "It's an un-limiter."

So, it functions like a stereo receiver?

"Correct," he says. "The frequency that gets tuned in... um... the pineal gland is like... the receiver, the filter is the medulla."

Whose idea was it to make the pineal gland a receiver? A group idea?

They're all talking at the same time. It's kind of funny – it made sense as you would want it to be through your feet and showed me a person with their feet in the air... and your body doesn't need to be working in order to access it.

Okay, is the pineal gland in every human being?

They're saying "Everybody's pineal gland is open but it's like having..." I hope I'm seeing this right. "It's like when you have a flat tire on your car doesn't work – if you have too many disbeliefs, it just doesn't work."

But let's talk about the physiology – if the pineal gland works with medulla.

He says, "Its yin and yang."

Some kids are able to communicate freely...

He says, "All children are."

So, when they can't around the age of 8 is that because their skulls harden and their reception goes down?

He says, "Both. The skull hardens and um... it's the disbelief and the parents, etc."

If you're asleep, does it work easier? Does that somehow affect the pineal gland?

He says, "100 thousand percent."

During sleep the medulla is quiet, but is the pineal gland like a homing beacon?

He says, "Yes."

Okay, very good – do our science all-stars want to do a follow up on this dark matter issue? One gave us a formula, one gave us images, one gave us a forest and absence of a forest...

"The shadow. Right."

Note: Speaking recently with a Harvard neuroscientist about this, he mentioned the work of Dr. Viola Pettit-Neal which points to a structure in the brain that functions as an "antenna" for information (the caudate nucleus).

Anything you want to tell Jennifer to continue this conversation?

They just showed me a balloon flying up.

Who's here?

Stephen Hawking is here.

Does he mean "a higher message?"

I'm seeing the thoughts that go up (to them on the flipside) the difference is that I have a receiver to get the thoughts to come back... (Jennifer aside:) Say it again? In the information superhighway, you're allowed (to have) messages to flow simultaneously. Like a car.

You're talking about the vehicle of dark matter? Is it dark matter you're referring to?

He said, "Yes." Thoughts go up. That alerts the people you're calling or would like to speak to, to be around.

You're answering a question I was about to ask – "How does this work so Jennifer can speak to spirit?" The answer is "the questions go up, and the answer comes down?"

He says, "It's like being on a racetrack but much faster, I have few roadblocks and no flat tires."

Let's break it down – is Stephen standing or sitting?

Standing. He has these little glasses on.

Wire rim glasses?

Yes. He's wearing a suit, and a red bowtie, a blue shirt – darker colored. Feels like a blue suit with a lighter blue... it's something like he wore when he was 19... dusted off an old college suit.

Question at hand is "How Jennifer able to communicate with you? Or how are we able to communicate with people on the other side, it's like an information highway?

He stays "She stays in her lane."

That you should or shouldn't stay in your lane, or that's just her lane?

He says, "It's like I have my own lane but there are 100,000 cars swirling around everywhere." (Jennifer aside) I can see the road, but I can see it's a metaphor for being able to speak to spirit.

I see; she's in the midst of all those other cars, but she has her own unique frequency that helps her?

They're showing me how much this work strengthens the pineal gland because of it.

In terms of people who don't have her gift... who don't have the ability to speak to spirit?

It's funny, he says, "It's like owning a car, think of a Fiat or something, something old or beat up in the beginning, then by learning this and doing this more and more, your energy becomes more efficient, and you become more like a Ferrari." (Jennifer listens:) I asked, "Is it like a car getting less efficient as time goes on? And they said, "It's the opposite. The more you do it, the more green-lights you're going to have."

I keep hearing in this research, a shift in consciousness is happening; why we're on the planet at this point in time.

They say, "It's still only the top 1% that are aware of it."

Correct me if I'm wrong, how can Jennifer and I help facilitate this shift? Or can we?

"Film." Film... that's what he's saying.

What would you like to tell people on the planet that would convince them on some level that this actually is you talking?

He says, "That it's backed up by science."

I heard a funny story about you the other day that Jennifer could not know. You were on your way to a reading of a Simpson's episode – Hank Azaria was telling this on the Late Show. You were running late, and one of the actors at the table read, Harry Shearer said something funny about you being late.

He's saying, "It had to do with the concept of time."

That's correct. He said, "<u>The man has no concept of time.</u>"

(Note: This is about as mind bending a detail as I can imagine. Jennifer did not watch the Colbert show, and then neither did

Hawking. Hank Azaria telling a story on the show where he said, "The funniest adlib I've heard was from Harry Shearer" and he told that story. Stephen Hawking was not in the room when it was said – he was running late.)

How could you be aware of that?

Jennifer: Me or him?

I know you're getting it from him. That's exactly what the actor Harry Shearer said.

He's saying that he said, "The man has no concept of time."

How do you know he said that?

He showed me how illusionary time is.

Tell us how Stephen put that sentence into your mind.

He showed me the word "time" and then showed me it is dissipating out into the future... that's how he showed it to me. Disappearing into the future... He's in my lane.

Geeze Louise, you're riding in her car and in her lane. You're in her frickin' Ferrari!

He said "She's a Lamborghini!" He showed me the music outside as an example.

A: I asked Jennifer a question she could not know the answer to; B: you could not know the answer to because you were not there when the joke was said Stephen. So how are you able to access what was said? Did someone tell that to you Stephen, later on? Or are you able to access that time frame of that moment in time when it happened?

"Instantly," he says.

Help me with this concept... Are we speaking about the holographic universe?

(Jennifer aside) I'll share with you the image he showed me. He showed me a disk being pulled out.

Like a DVD or CD? And each disc...

"Each disc is the Akashic record of that moment in time." That's what I (would) refer to it as.

Like slices of time? It's part of the Akashic record, but you are accessing slices of time?

"Yes" he says.

These slices of time exist unto themselves, so when I ask about a particular slice of time, we can access that time together, is that correct?

He says, "Absolutely."

You access it simultaneously... and people like Jennifer are able to as well?

I asked him while you were talking "Are you getting it (the information) out of Richard's head?" I'm the skeptic here and he says, "No," He showed me pulling out an old floppy disk. He's showing me tons and tons and tons of numbers and just homing into whatever is in our lane.

So, the numbers, is how the event, or how the information is stored in its frame of time?

He says, "Like Pi, down to the (specific) numbers."

(Note: Just to emphasize this point, Stephen is saying that time is holographic and if you can "access the floppy disk" – his analogy, not Jennifer's or mine – but that giant floppy disk of information, people can learn more about any event.)

In speaking of dark energy, we got a formula from someone – "Negative pi times infinity." And Pi was included. Is that what dark energy is?

"Yes" he says.

And you guys said the other day that dark energy is source? Are you saying that dark energy is consciousness?

"You have to" he says.

But if source is dark energy... that means if we're going to access slices of holographic time...

(Jennifer aside) I'm seeing everything in holograms.

So even us, here in this room – we are slices of time, but let me ask you, is this idea of accessing slices of time is that the "second coming?" Is that related to understanding this kind of information as some form of epiphany that might include the concept of "a second coming?" Not from a religious perspective, but because once we realize there is not time, we can see that Jesus never left.

(Jennifer laughs) Stephen just went and got my dad. (Jim was a Mormon bishop).

That's hilarious.

My dad says, "Yes."

One more time please. Past, present, future...

Oh, they're showing me the outline of a human being, when we pass away, it's like with people who have lost a limb...

Phantom limbs?

He says, "That's dark energy, what dark energy is – phantom energy of something that once existed in that space. So, when people pass away it (that space) still has that energy" – that's what I see when people come in and out (of their bodies in spirit form)

You did say that the energy field is like dark energy.

(Jennifer aside) I'm so glad you're filming this! I would never remember any of this. Hold on. I asked "How come I don't remember what is given to me (during a session) and what I heard is "It negates being attached to it."

So psychologically it's a good thing to be detached - otherwise you'd be associated with every murder you've solved. Let's talk about "The Second Coming."

My dad is laughing right now about that.

Here's my point – this idea of a "second coming" – or that "Jesus is returning" is related to our work. In a number of interviews, we've "brought Jesus back" because we demonstrated Jesus never left.

"Correct" he said.

So, the idea that Jesus is returning is not correct, it's that people will realize that he's never left, is that correct?

(A long pause). "Yes." (Jennifer aside:) I asked about the bad stuff and suddenly got an image of Saddam Hussein –

who has not been in my mind for years; hear me out, (before I can protest that one man's villain is another man's hero) but that bad stuff is already happening... that's what I'm being shown, and that's forcing people to open their hearts to this, that's part of "the second coming," as you put it.

The reason I asked it this way – is because I want the scientists (in our class) to look at this, and Jesus and Jim to look at this all as one piece. It has nothing to do with biblical references, or religion; that's all metaphor – it's pointing to something, but it is metaphorical. I'm referring to people feeling as if Jesus was returning as we know he's not the only avatar in the game.

"Correct." I'm being shown that there is a big avatar soul group – he just showed me that. I asked, "What's the difference between you and the rest of the humans?" and he showed me that he's aware of every avatar in his soul group.

So, if someone is aware of who they were on the flipside...

He says, "Then everything (pain and suffering) starts dissipating, then your energy field doesn't make you sick; your body can recoup."

If the second coming is a revelation that he never left or that we can be conscious of all of our loved ones who passed away – including but not limited to...

Jesus.

And Mary, and everyone. Sorry I didn't mean to shift away from you Stephen.

Carl Sagan just came in.

This is the scientist who created the music CD that traveled into deep space with Chuck Berry on it.

He's saying "Like with what I (Jennifer) do for my work, music does the same thing by being in a certain lane, like in my work." He showed me music puts people in that lane, music is like a frequency going up and up.

Music is quantum mechanics and also appears to retain the memory of the moment; so, the frequency of the music also retains your experience of hearing the music. When you listen to Beethoven's 9th, you're accessing all the other performances simultaneously?

He says, "And that's related to the disk (Sagan sent into space). The Akashic memory of that event."

Carl, I need your help there is a scientist named Mino from Japan. He was a scientist, he died, and his mom wrote books about him.

What I first see is a tree in Africa or Asia. There's a huge tree that I'm seeing... then I saw that scientist with the apple... (Newton) It has to do with time and space going back and forth?

I don't know Mino's work; it could be about time and space. Let's ask. (He was a physicist).

Let me get this first. So you can pick an apple, the tree holds all the memories; it's what I'm picking up - he's showing me one tree from two different time periods. When we are there, if we allow ourselves, we can pick up

all the energy from that particular tree in that time frame, or from all the time frames.

What was Mino's work on the planet?

He says, "It was something like string theory... (Ding!). He showed me a violin... he also showed me... the guy who wrote about string theory."

He could mean Pythagoras, who really invented string theory with his thoughts on the lyre. Is that research important to you now?

He says, "Yes, because it leaps them into it. They go out of their mind and into it."

Is it related to time?

He says, "There is no time per se. We can create everything; it's already out there, we're creating it by bringing it in." Hold on. "Some people don't know they can create it, they just go and let things happen, like working on a project; you have to do it and can't expect it to be done (to get the result.)"

So, what kind of work do you want people to carry on?

"Mind focus," it feels like he's saying.

Anything specific related to my wife who asked about you?

He showed me her heart. He says, "She has a beautiful heart. Have her focus on where she wants to be as if it's happening now. If she's in a stressful place or if she's in a space where she's stressed, have her jump out of it."

Focus on what it should be like and have her turn into that?

He says, "Yes."

What's her relation to the Pleiades?

(Jennifer aside) I'm related to the Pleiades as well. (Jennifer listens). He says, "She's part of the 7 daughters; she's like the oldest daughter."

You mean relating to the Greek myth? Or are you talking about actual daughters?

I don't know either.

So, she had a lifetime in the Pleiades?

He says, "Several."

Is she visited by her friends from there?

He says, "Always."

Anything she needs to know?

He says, "Where earth is right now; they're trying to figure it out but she's so light.... – so lighthearted, everything is like nails on a chalkboard to her... They're trying to figure out if they need to come down here."

How *many* lifetimes has she had over there?

Feels like one that was a thousand years.

I've met some other Pleiadeans – I've heard there's going to be a shift in consciousness in relation to what they're doing... is that the work she's doing in her sleep?

"Yes. They want to help us save the planet."

Are they going to?

"Yes, they have to. They're checking to see if the vibration here is getting better. They want to know how they're going to acclimate."

It is getting better, isn't it?

"Yes it is."

All right, thank you class, we appreciate all your help!

*****

Physicists are interpreting music or math that is coming from the spheres.

Further we can address guides, teachers, classmates involved with the person who we are communicating with. *Accessing the "frequency" or "floppy disk" of who they are, who they were, who they always will be.*

Playing in the woods at 16.

INTERMISSION

This is my version of an intermission, with some soulful quotes about music from musicians.

"My music is the spiritual expression of what I am." -John Coltrane

"Music is the emotional life of most people." -Leonard Cohen

"Music is nothing separate from me. It is me...You'd have to remove the music surgically...Music to me is like breathing—I don't get tired of breathing." Ray Charles

"Music is a higher revelation than all wisdom and philosophy." -Ludwig van Beethoven

"Music is a world within itself. It's a language we all understand."-Stevie Wonder

"Music has healing power. It has the ability to take people out of themselves for a few hours." -Elton John

"The music is not in the notes, but in the silence between." - Wolfgang Amadeus Mozart

"If music be the food of love, play on." – William Shakespeare

"Life seems to go on without effort when I am filled with music." – George Eliot

"Music gives a soul to the universe, wings to the mind, flight to the imagination, and life to everything." – Plato

"After silence, that which comes nearest to expressing the inexpressible is music." – Aldous Huxley

"Music, once admitted to the soul, becomes a sort of spirit and never dies." – Edward Bulwer-Lytton

"When I hear music, I fear no danger. I am invulnerable. I see no foe. I am related to the earliest of times, and to the latest." – Henry David Thoreau

"Music can name the unnamable and communicate the unknowable." – Leonard Bernstein

"Music in the soul can be heard by the universe." – Lao Tzu

"Without music, life would be a mistake." – Friedrich Nietzsche

"Where words leave off, music begins." – Heinrich Heine

"I haven't understood a bar of music in my life, but I have felt it." – Igor Stravinsky

"My idea is that there is music in the air, music all around us; the world is full of it, and you simply take as much as you require." – Edward Elgar

"I don't sing because I'm happy; I'm happy because I sing." – William James

"Music is your own experience, your thoughts, your wisdom. If you don't live it, it won't come out of your horn." – Charlie Parker

"Everything in the universe has a rhythm, everything dances." – Maya Angelou

"When I am alone with my notes, my heart pounds and the tears stream from my eyes, and my emotion and my joys are too much to bear." – Giuseppe Verdi

"To send light into the darkness of men's hearts – such is the duty of the artist." – Robert Schumann

"As long as we live, there is never enough singing." – Martin Luther

"Music comes to me more readily than words." – Ludwig Van Beethoven

"Music brings a warm glow to my vision, thawing mind and muscle from their endless wintering." – Haruki Murakami

"Music is the divine way to tell beautiful, poetic things to the heart." – Pablo Casals

"Music produces a kind of pleasure which human nature cannot do without." – Confucius

"Music is the universal language of mankind." – Henry Wadsworth Longfellow

"Music is enough for a lifetime, but a lifetime is not enough for music." – Sergei Rachmaninoff

"Music is the only thing I've ever known that doesn't have any rules at all." – Josh Homme

"Music expresses feeling and thought, without language; it was below and before speech, and it is above and beyond all words." – Robert G. Ingersoll

"Works of art make rules; rules do not make works of art." – Claude Debussy

"Wake up, live your life and sing the melody of your soul." – Amit Ray

"Music is the tool to express life – and all that makes a difference." – Herbie Hancock

"Music can change the world because it can change people." Bono (U2)

"Music allows us to experience the same emotions. No matter what language we speak, what color we are, music proves: We are the same." John Denver

"Music is well said to be the speech of angels." Thomas Carlyle

"The true beauty of music is that it connects people. It carries a message, and we, the musicians, are the messengers." Roy Ayers

"Music hath charms to soothe the savage beast, to soften rocks or bend a knotted oak." William Congreve

"Take a music bath once or twice a week for a few seasons, and you will find that it is to the soul what the water bath is to the body." Oliver Wendell Holmes

"At the risk of sounding hopelessly romantic, love is the key element." John McLaughlin

"If I were not a physicist, I would probably be a musician. I often think in music. I live my daydreams in music. I see my life in terms of music." — Albert Einstein

"Music is a language that doesn't speak in particular words. It speaks in emotions." — Keith Richards

"The only truth is music." — Jack Kerouac

"There are two means of refuge from the miseries of life: music and cats." — Albert Schweitzer

"Music is the shorthand of emotion." — Leo Tolstoy

"Without music, life would be a blank to me." — Jane Austen

"Where words fail, music speaks." — Hans Christian Andersen

"Music expresses that which cannot be said and on which it is impossible to be silent." — Victor Hugo

"A painter paints pictures on canvas. But musicians paint their pictures on silence." — Leopold Stokowski

"Who hears music, feels his solitude peopled at once." — Robert Browning

"Music is the language of the spirit. It opens the secret of life bringing peace, abolishing strife." — Kahlil Gibran

"Music is my higher power" — Oliver James

"People ask me how I make music. I tell them I just step into it. It's like stepping into a river and joining the flow. Every moment in the river has its song." — Michael Jackson

"Music is the divine way to tell beautiful, poetic things to the heart..." — Pablo Casals

"This will be our reply to violence: to make music more intensely, more beautifully, more devotedly than ever before." — Leonard Bernstein

"Music is what tell us that the human race is greater than we realize." — Napoléon Bonaparte

"I would rather write 10,000 notes than a single letter of the alphabet." — Ludwig van Beethoven

"There are many ways to the Divine. I have chosen the ways of song, dance, and laughter… When I am silent, I fall into the place where everything is music." Rumi

And finally, while meeting with the Oracle of Tibet (who asked me to produce of CD of Tibetan music by his Nechung Monks) I met James Brolin and said, "I directed you in a movie, but we've never met." (I took over directing "Cannes Man" after his cameo.)

He seemed puzzled and amused. But it's true. Here's his son Josh writing about music on social media; I felt his post embodies what people on the flipside say about it.

"Something happens deeply in the soul with music. It might be as simple as birds chirping in a morning with sun rays peeking through heavy cloud cover or it might feel as if a sound, an orchestra of a repression, has come back to rage against the paranoia of a time.

Not a molecule of talent lost, these sounds come forth as a storm that raises a fire igniting us all — the wail of a strangled note, held.

Tonight (at a concert) threw me into a reverie of being a kid with my mother in some ratty old blues bar in New Orleans surround by nothing but a pulsing, almost spastic possession of the music. Transported — *Mama's home again.*

(Singers) crawl in the dirt, pull you through fields of feelings and the ghosts follow you home. Like listening to Pavarotti hit his high C during "Nessun Dorma", something *ignites in me,* and the world is suddenly full of hope. And that hope lives in the people, a remembrance of what it is to love something with total abandon. The romance of it. The insanity in it. The poetry in fully being a human fallible being." @JoshBrolin

CHAPTER ELEVEN: THEY'VE BEEN WAITING

Pere La Chaise cemetery in Paris.

In "Backstage Pass to the Flipside," Anthony Bourdain came through loud and clear and gave us notes on just about everything – how to reach out to his opera singing daughter (didn't know he had one), what kind of food I should put in my diet to help my health (string beans) and an antidote for depression; (meditation.) He's funny, charming, and always has something to add to our discussions.

Here we are at another session at Fishbar in Manhattan Beach. My questions are *in italics,* Jennifer's replies are **in bold.**

Rich: So, class, who wants to talk? Luana?

Jennifer: She has like a whole list of things; she did this her papers. (Pretends to be straightening out a stack). "They've been waiting."

Can we ask Anthony Bourdain a question?

He's here; wearing jeans, blazer and a shirt, smoking a cigarette.

I read your interview with a medium and Dr. Medhus on Channeling Erik website, anything you want to add or correct about that?

He said that *we* helped him be able to do that. He said that right off the bat.

In terms of slowing your energy down, what's the formula? How many degrees do you need to slow down?

He said, "You mean like a recipe?"

Is slow the right word?

He said "s l o wwww…"

Are you half the speed up there? Two times? More?

"Yes, it's just different." He said "It's like being on the freeway instead of a road. And on this side, we're on the dirt road. He showed me a freeway, a regular road, a dirt road; different types of paths."

So, do you slow yourself down by half? Or two thirds?

"It depends on the person; what's going on in their head."

Like with your friends, or Asia Argento; how much do you slow yourself down to talk to her?

He says, "She's not aware of him… he's been trying to – to everything to reach out to her."

Anything we can do?

"Give her the book," he said.

In your interview on Channeling Erik, you said you met God, speaking as if he was an individual.

Anthony is smiling.

My question is, was that a metaphor or a physical person that you met?

He's showing me that it almost felt like a hub. He says, "Like a frequency hub, like an electrical outlet and other frequencies come from that and we all make up the one."

Okay, so the idea of who or what God is - it's like a medium... like water or oil?

He showed me *me*.

Well, you are the medium. But I mean like paint is a medium for color.

(Jennifer taps her nose as if to say, "that's it.")

From what I understand you were talking to a medium, Veronica Drake, Eric Medhus and his mom Dr. Elisa Medhus, and in the interview, they quoted you saying that you'd "Met god and he was hilarious."

He was laughing before you asked the question – I asked him "Did you see yourself?" He said that he did.

You're looking at the source or the medium of everything. He did say that in the article, "Everyone is connected."

He showed me like the base of a power switch; he showed me that spot... it's interesting... I saw him moving with tons of glass, you know how in the film The Matrix, how everything moves together in slow motion?

The bullet effect?

Those are the speeds I'm seeing. It's the same things in multiple dimensions...

So, speed is like time?

When you asked that, I was triggered to ask, "Is that (visual) speed?" He says, "We create speed and time here."

In our dimension?

"Yes. It's all at once there."

(Note: Meaning once we are "outside of time" on the flipside, we can observe things in "all dimensions at once." We can observe all of our lifetimes.)

What do you want to talk about Anthony? You're the great interviewer.

He's fascinated about how to communicate with this side, and he's trying to reach her...

Asia?

Did she have a fall recently? He showed me her stumbling.

Maybe he's referring to her being sued by some friend of hers.

He said, "She'll get up, she'll be unscathed." It was like he showed me her getting up and wiping off her arms. He says, "That's part of her charm." He's showing me that she would throw things, she'd break things.

Anthony's interview of Asia in her home gives a sense of who she is, a complicated person.

He says, "and I'm not?" He says he was the one who complicated things...

But compared to her?

"She's a comet. Ten thousand trillion times a comet..."

Anyone else need to stop by?

My dad.

Hi Jim. Ask how's your class in astronomy with the 8-armed teacher?

(Note: We interviewed Jennifer's father after his passing, and Jim said he was "taking a class that was beyond comprehension." A class in physics taught by an 8-armed teacher. Later, I asked if she was known in India as the deity "Ma Durga" and she confirmed that obscure detail.)

When you put it like that... he says, "He's learning so much; there's so much to learn."

Like what?

"Like how to travel." He showed me orbs... "How to travel... between dimensions." That's interesting. I was wondering why you see faces in orbs; it's like an imprint.

Are you talking about orbs you see in photos? My understanding is that they're fractals that retain all the information of your previous lifetimes.

He says, "That's true."

But why do they have different sizes?

He says, "And colors. Because of your lifetimes."

So the bigger orb has more information? Is it true they pick up gunk? Because in my first deep hypnosis session, I visited a classroom where they were cleaning the fractals or orbs.

My dad says "Yes. They get gunk like cars." My dad loved cars.

Like cars pick up engine oil?

If I'm seeing this right, wow, they pick up gunk because of what we're doing with the earth... the way we're traveling whatever is happening, cutting trees, killing oxygen... causes gunk to form on them.

But in terms of these orbs... can you show Jennifer one of these orbs Jim? Let's look inside.

He showed me like a pathway, you don't feel like you're in that...

You mean opening up an orb would be like opening up a top and you look inside and see a pathway?

It's like a convertible inside.

Do they contain the emotions of previous lifetimes? One person I interviewed said they saw a holograph of themselves.

That's what I saw before... when I ask to see someone's health – I see the hologram of the person. Their past present and future.

Does one see the "perfected person?"

"Yes."

Is that a construct created by your imagination, or by the soul itself?

I would also see their etheric self, even when their self here was horrible.

Anthony who would you like to interview? Is there someone you want to interview on our behalf? Someone you're curious about.

I'm seeing Aretha again.

What do you want to know from Aretha?

(Jennifer laughs.) This is so fun. The best movie is in my head; Prince just came by, then Bill Paxton, and then Aretha came in; her voice is just so amazing. She has this perfume, it smells good. (Jennifer listens) Now she's showing me you playing guitar – like last Tuesday, you were playing?

I was.

She's trying to help you.

I was playing the original version of "The house of the rising sun."

Prince helped as well.

That's funny. It sounds weird to say it, but I'd be lying if I didn't report that I did "feel assistance" while playing it. Just noting that I did feel something.

You have not told me that – so for her to come through and tell me that...

You're right. I never told you that I perform or play anything. I don't think you've ever seen me play.

I saw piano and guitar...

That's accurate. Billy, we saw you sneak by. What's up?

He's jokingly waving Aretha away, as if she's "old news."

I was talking about you on the set the other day...

He said it was fun.

I was talking to someone of you... I spoke to Renee Zellweger.

He said, "Tell her I said hi."

You just did. Okay, Prince you snuck in?

Billy is like, "That's it?"

Well Prince snuck in – I saw that they put out some new songs for you... your thoughts on the new material?

He says, "Time doesn't matter – but it does." Jennifer aside: I asked, "Do you guys miss time?" They said, "No."

What do you miss, Prince?

He showed me the female body. He's trying to joke around. He says, "He misses being famous..." then laughs.

So, on the flipside you're not famous, just another soul?

"Yes."

But people who run into you are aware of your talent?

"Yes, all the lights that you see; you see them all together, you hang out with people who have the same frequency."

That's why you hang out with musicians for example?

"That's why there are so many in this class... and actors."

All part of the same healing light of the universe?

Jennifer aside "I asked him what color he was radiating; purple?"

We asked him that before; that day he said red. What does he look like now?

I'm seeing orange. I didn't know we asked him, I was just kidding. It's like the more you know, the higher the frequency is.

That's a good question for Anthony to ask Prince, Robin or Bill. I think we started talking to you fellows a couple of years ago.

Bill said, "Like three."

I would guess your knowledge is exponential compared to what we've learned... It was Michael Newton who turned us onto this concept or radiating colors.

You mean Morton.

(Note: When Michael Newton showed up the first time, Jennifer said "Morton is here." I said, "Who's that?" She said, "The guy you did the documentary about." Since then, Michael Newton refers to himself as Morton when he shows up.)

Yes, Morton; he said it reflected how you're feeling at that moment – someone who is purple could radiate a different color depending how their journey or path is...

That's why they can't lie.

You've said that before. But in terms of communicating with us – we've only progressed so much in the past 3 years, but you guys must grow in knowledge exponentially on the flipside. Is that accurate?

"Not all are affected in the same way. There are so many different people." By the way Rich, they're telling me you are famous over there.

That's funny. But let me ask Prince; when you're called upon by Luana to come forward – as we've heard "the light goes on that the class is happening," and people just show up... do you look forward to this, what's you're feeling about being in this communication class?

He says, "It's a lot of fun, because we (Jennifer and I) don't discount what they say." Jennifer aside; you taught me that, "Don't judge it, don't discount any of it."

(Note: Sometimes Jennifer will see an obscure image that does not make any sense to her, but I suggest she not "judge whatever comes in." It's funny to hear this from these folks, people often tell us that it's frustrating their loved ones don't believe they still exist.)

A bit like the Garry Shandling reply, when he told us that he was "golfing" on the flipside. I asked him quite seriously how he did that, to construct the courses from his experience or imagination, and I asked him specifically "How many holes do you play, is it like 36 holes?" And he said "No, two. The tees are far apart."

He's here.

How are you doing Garry? I understand Judd Apatow is making another film based on your diaries.

Garry says, "He wants him to do it."

You guys were very close friends, correct?

He says, "Yeah, he's excited about it."

(Note: In "Backstage Pass to the Flipside" Jennifer interviewed Garry about his tempestuous relationship with his former manager Brad Grey. Brad passed away at 59, not long after Garry died – so we took the opportunity to chat with him.)

Rich: I want to ask about a couple about Brad Grey.

Jennifer: I don't know who that is.

Garry, would you tell Jennifer who that is?

"They were friends when they were young, best friends, felt like they were together."

(Ding!) Brad was Garry's manager and knew each other from their early days. Then Garry got really successful so did Brad but then something happened.

"A divorce."

Brad's around he can pipe in.

What's his last name?

Grey. They did have a divorce of sorts.

"Yes, they split up."

It was over finances... money.

He's saying "It was very stupid. It was big and that's what made it so stupid."

It was battle.

"It took a huge battle; nine years."

Sounds like it; it wound up in court. Garry had to testify...

"About how Brad mismanaged it."

Garry won big sum of money.... but lost because it took a toll on his life and heart and everything else.

"It killed him." He said, "It killed him."

Well, you're not dead now are you Garry? No!

He said, "Try using that joke on the other side."

Okay, I will. So, listen, Garry you helped a lot of writers, you helped make careers, when are you going to start helping me?

"I already am," he said.

You helped Judd Apatow have a successful career and a life.

I don't know who that is.

He's written and directed a bunch of films... Directed the film about him... The "40-year-old virgin."

I loved that movie...

Judd said Garry helped him write or rewrite it, is that correct Garry?

He said, "A third of it."

In the film, they all spoke of how much you helped other people, other comedians; you're aware of that correct?

"Yes."

Garry what's your view of Buddhism now... in the film that Judd directed, called "The Zen Diaries of Garry Shandling" you talked about detachment.

"It didn't work" he said. He's laughing and said.... "He held that hot stone."

Luana can fill you in, detachment is great if it means to let go of anger, fear, stress, all the emotions you don't want to have, but you stay connected to love. It doesn't mean to detach yourself from love or positive emotion, because that's why we're on the planet.

Some people don't want to do all that.

I also noticed our classmate Gilda is in the news, her documentary "Love Gilda" is out and it's fun to see her make people laugh again.

The person that is in the film is channeling her – whoever is putting it together...

You mean Amy Poehler? She's the host of the show.

She's telling me that she's basically channeling her; then I saw Jim Carrey who did that for that comedian, what's his name.

Andy Kaufman? Wow, okay, I spoke to Jim one night about Andy because his sister moved into the home across the street from my parent's home in Northbrook. Is Andy Kaufman available?

He's hanging out with Robin Williams at the moment.

So, Andy, when I was in high school, I came across that guy "Tony the Healer" the healer that you went to see when you were ill. It must have been startling for you to realize the guy was a faker.

"Yes, he was."

Why did you choose to check out so early in this lifetime? Or was that an exit point?

"Yes."

Who was there to greet you when you crossed over?

"It was a lot of people..." it felt like it was his sister... if she's still on the planet, it could have been somebody that was like her.

You're saying it felt like a sister?

It might have been a twin that died in childbirth.

Okay. Since you've been over there, what's been your experience?

He's made everyone laugh.

You were famous for making fun of the joke or bit itself.

He's showing me that he channeled somebody else. A comedian. Someone from the 1920's...

Who?

Buster Keaton comes to mind.

Andy, are you going to come back soon?

He says, "He helps comedians." He showed me Amy Schumer.

Are you helping them with the kind of comedy you used to do – avante garde? Or just general creative tips?

He showed me Amy looking at a scene and then seeing something in the corner, "looking outside the box."

Okay, very good. Class, any questions for Andy? Luana?

They're dancing.

Andy, Luana, who's making you laugh?

I don't know why, but I got shown Tom Petty. Have we talked to Tom?

Indeed, we have. He gave us the name of the book "Backstage Pass to the Flipside." Tom, are you making Luana laugh?

"They all are."

All right Luana any parting words? Should we mention (the current President?)

She showed him tripping over his tie. They showed me (a Supreme Court Justice) with devil horns and a pitchfork.

They're saying "It's all about disrupting the norm to get people involved. It's that same frequency. There's an inner revolution without the violence that's going to go on."

Who said that?

All of them did.

*****

It's mind bending, but this kind of rapid-fire questioning – I know what's in my head, I know my journey of working in the entertainment industry for 35 years, but Jennifer does not. She doesn't have the references that I've become aware of over my lifetime, and I know for a fact, that she won't remember ANY of this conversation, the moment it finishes. And yet, it's like having an open mic or a cellphone to the flipside. Literally like she's passing around a telephone at a party, and each person gets to say "hello" or "shut up" or "where have you been?"

I know that it's problematic for many to hear this kind of rapid-fire questioning. Not everyone will get the references, or link together the dots so to speak – but in reviewing this chapter, and putting it into this book, I realize they cover a lot of territory in just a few paragraphs.

Mind blown.

Another day – another interview with class.

Anthony Bourdain showed up on the anniversary of his passing. Neither Jennifer nor I had planned to interview him. This is excerpts from that podcast.

Jennifer: Someone popped into my head today. Anthony. I wasn't thinking of him, I was taking a shower… and I'm like "Okay, so you want to say something?

There was a documentary that came out ("Roadrunner") I think I know why he wants to talk to us but go ahead.

I knew that documentary is coming out, so I went through my conscious mind; "Did I think it?" It was like, "No, I didn't really think of Anthony Bourdain when I was in the shower. It's just like "He's here and it felt like he was saying, "We got to talk about something." With what I don't know.

Listen, you and I have been doing this for so long and I happened to notice a year ago July 17th he showed up. I happened to notice the date of podcast we did around this time and, who knows, maybe this is the time he likes to show up. But I suspect it's something else, so let's ask him.

He's reminding me about the green beans comment – how you had asked him for a diet tip, and he'd given that to you. "Tell Richard he needs green beans."

Ha. Yes. The diet tip was related to fiber, of course that's accurate in general, but funny to hear it from him. But Anthony first and foremost, let's say "Welcome sir. You know how many people miss you on the planet, we miss you. I know I asked you before who was there to greet you when you crossed over and you talked about the late chef Loiseau, your friend who also checked himself out early... but let's talk about why you're here today.

He just grabbed a seat...

(Note: He has done this before, he grabs a seat and turns it around often, leans over it to chat. Smokes cigarettes sometimes. It's not something Jennifer is inventing based on his series, but is what she's seeing.)

...and he's eating something... like a piece of bread.

For those curious like how people eat on the flipside, it's reported they can construct anything that you can imagine, including a piece of French bread... but you're saying it's like baguette?

He says, "Yes, baguette." He's in Paris.

Did you get your baguette fresh in Paris today?

He says, "I made it fresh today."

Let me ask you sir, was that a talent you always had making baguette or is that something you've learned since you've been on the flipside?

He says, "It's not something he knew (over here) - how to construct that here, it was not something he had an interest in doing." He says, "Here he was more interested in Asian Thai cuisine" like that kind of thing.

Yes, but I'm asking since you've crossed over now, you're able to construct the perfect baguette? Or is it perfect?"

(Jennifer quickly) He says, "*Oh it's perfect.*" He's making me smell it – I'm reacting to it like that's really not fair as it's making me hungry.

That's beautiful.

It is beautiful like, if you could you know the crumb, like just even the crumbling part of it, like the sound of it the crunch.

I forget where I heard it (it was in the film "Ratatouille") saying that a chef knew good baguette from the sound of the bread.

I even checked, liked asking myself "Am I hungry?" I'm not even hungry but he's digging through all this stuff, and I can smell the butter.

Okay, that's a wonderful introduction, but what do you want to talk about? I have some questions - you want to talk first or prefer to answer questions?

He wants to talk first. He's referring to the movie.

It's a documentary that a filmmaker made about his life that tried to piece together why his death occurred.

He's showing me, he's saying "I did it because I was inadequately informed that you could end it all." He says

he didn't know how to enjoy himself thoroughly, saying he did a lot of things because he was told to do them, where you're supposed to do them, he because he created and produced those shows I believe...

He's saying it (the documentary) just wasn't enough. It just wasn't enough but that the way that they portrayed him... he's saying, "They got information from second-hand third-hand fourth-hand fifth-hand people, not the people close to me."

I haven't seen the film, but I've heard the filmmaker tries to point to your friend Asia as a source of your pain, your old girlfriend as being a catalyst for you doing yourself in. I know you've already told us in the past that's not accurate.

He says, "No one, especially her, could not ever make me do anything like that. She would have been a reason for me to stay."

(Note: He did say this in the past. He said his love for Asia was unconditional, he was a huge fan of her life and journey. A journalist friend of mine, skeptical of our conversation, asked me "So why didn't he leave a suicide note?" So, I asked him.)

Why didn't you leave us a note about the reasons for leaving early?

He says, "I didn't even know them myself."

You said you were under the mistaken impression of "ending it all," but that's not what happened?

He said, "Yes. It's not what happened, and in fact it got way more complicated afterwards."

How so?

He says, "I had to hear all the people that were hurting because I left."

You experienced all the trauma that they went through?

He says, "There was no logical explanation, there was no reasonable explanation into why I left so… for those people who now they're making a mockery-of-a-movie claiming that they know when I didn't even know why I left."

So, your review of this movie on a scale of one to ten…?

(Jennifer puts both thumbs down.)

Two thumbs down? Do we even get into the numbers or are we in negative territory here?

He says, "It's a five."

That's generous of you.

He says, "Well only because part of it is based upon the information that was known, stuff that had already been filmed and shot."

What's your opinion of this filmmaker taking artificial intelligence and recreating your voice? He took some text out of one of your books and had an algorithm create your voice?

(Jennifer aside) He's just laughing. He said, "I found it not as amusing as I thought it would be." Sounded like a robot. Like that's supposed to be you but it's not you – there's no like "jiving" (tone) there's no like, you know,

because there's no movement with it… (the tone of his voice) He says, "Run, Run, Run - it's Charlie!"

(Note: I didn't note this in the podcast, had no reference for it (nor can I imagine Jennifer does.) It refers to the song; "Run Charlie Run" by the Temptations (about racism) originally written during the slave era about people hunting down slaves. An obscure reference Jennifer could not know, and I didn't know it either. In his last published interview he pulled no punches, "imagining Harvey Weinstein's death in detail and slamming former US President Bill Clinton as "rapey, gropey and disgusting" (News.com.au Anthony Bourdain)

I haven't seen the film, but it was just revealed that the ending of the film was faked. An artist distraught over Anthony's death had said he thought of "defacing his portrait of him" to the filmmaker had him create another portrait and defaced it on camera. What's your opinion of that sir?

"Shitty," he said.

Okay, well there's Anthony's quote for the movie poster.

He says, "Because that guy has anger issues."

Who? The filmmaker or the painter?"

"All of them." He says, "When you're trying so hard (to tell a story), so you make up shit, you make up "This happened, then that happened" or "That's what I did to (cause me to) leave…" He says, "None of it is true. None of it is real. None of it is real."

You're saying that even the reasons that you thought you had to leave were not real?

"No, no, those were all mind-made - mental constructs - mind made thinking (that) I was going out on top," he said.

I happened to notice Asia Argento wrote something on her Instagram about her love for you, eternal, beyond measure.

He says, "She is the reason I would have stayed."

Do you have a message for her?

He says, "She listens to me. She talks to me. She's not consciously aware of it."

She talks to you while sleeping?

He said, "Yeah actually. Like dreams... because she's not talking directly but she's listening." He says, "I told her that everything's okay." That he's okay; he's reassured her in the dreams that none of this other stuff is real that they're gonna say (about him and her in the film).

I think people have seen loved ones in dreams and heard things from them and then wake up and dismiss it like it didn't happen. So what would you like to say to this filmmaker other than "he has anger issues?"

"Amateur," he says. "He just got it wrong. He tried to put a round peg in a square hole or vice versa."

(Note: I'm a filmmaker. It took me a year to read Ebert's pan of my film "Limit Up." When it was published, I asked Luana to read it to me over the phone and "edit out the negative stuff." She read "Richard Martini... (long pause) directed Limit Up." Not here to critique, just reporting.)

But let's assume the filmmaker had good intentions, "I'd really like to make a film about my hero Anthony." But if you can give people some insight into how to prevent people from leaving the planet early to prevent this from happening.

He says, "Meditation."

Jennifer let me ask you, did you hear that or see that? Like a monk meditating?

Heard it. He just says "Meditation."

We've talked about this with him before.

He says, "That's what I should have done." He says, "Take inventory of your loved ones. Take inventory of people that don't even know you that love you. Take inventory of the ground that you walk on, the air that you breathe. You know that it's the best that life has to give. Like keep doing it over and over and over again. Gratitude for your dog or your cat or you know, whatever it is. You can find something you can look at a leaf and find it beautiful and being grateful for the tree that provided the air in our space."

(At that moment, Jennifer's dog comes in at the mention of "being grateful for a dog.")

(Jennifer continues) That idea of having gratitude.

A meditation on gratitude?

He says, "It's literally thinking about what's really going on. It's an instant energy booster so you can find something to be grateful for whether it's just your skin or find gratitude for anything. If you find gratitude in

anything you'll have a less likely chance of leaving." He says, "I was humble, I loved what I did for work. I couldn't have asked for a better career. I just didn't know how to take it all in and feel it."

In terms of your drug use as a younger person; did that affect your brain physiologically? Affect the ability of your brain to regulate emotions? Once you got back to the flipside did you see this as an exit point or was it a mistake? It's hard for people to hear that but it is in the research.

He said, "It's not a mistake. It is part of the journey."

As traumatic as it was for many, was this a way for you to help people address depression on the planet? Could this also be like a lesson that you can give from where you are now?

He says, yes absolutely." He just showed me going here and going over there (home), that it's an exchange. The fact that they could go through us to give advice helps tremendously if everyone knew they can hear their loved ones or hear people they don't even know from the flipside as you would, say the world would be automatically elevated because everyone over there wants to help everyone here.

Thank you.

(Jennifer aside) I'm asking him, "Do we look like dumb idiots over here compared to over there?" He says "no, what you look like," he's speaking generally, "Is that you do look like you can be wasting time in living your life."

Like kids in a sandbox arguing about the sandbox, and the adults walk by and observe how we're stressed over nothing?

"What is the saying? Youth is wasted on the young."

Like kids in a sandbox arguing about toys? Adults say "Gee, I wish they would just get along because they're so much more to enjoy." Is it something like that?

He says, "It's exactly like that. It's interchangeable stages. One day you're in Europe, the next day you're in America, the next day you're in on the Indian reservation…" He uses interchangeable just like time is interchangeable.

Thank you. I would hope filmmakers in the future would come to you directly, use mediums or hypnotherapy to access the person. Ask them directly what they wanted to express.

He says, "The filmmaker just didn't know me."

(Jennifer notes that Robin Williams has shown up.)

Rich: It's his birthday today. Happy birthday Robin.

Jennifer: Robin says "Thank you for all the birthday wishes." He says, "They (He and Anthony) had a lot in common with not being able to feel and some of it had to do with the early drug use."

Robin, did that early drug use affect your amygdala and serotonin release later in life?

He says, "No."

Okay, always happy to be corrected.

Robin is speaking, he says, "If you're on heroin you're gonna die. Yeah, it's gonna affect you. It's gonna affect your amygdala too."

(Note: Something I heard years ago. A single dose of heroin can trick the brain into thinking there's an outside source for euphoria; a person can lose the ability to ever feel joy.)

Robin, your son was talking today about the misdiagnosis of what was happening to you, how that affected you because they gave you drugs deleterious to your mental state.

Robin says, "Don't take them! Don't take those drugs!" (Jennifer aside) He is laughing about that. About his son he says, "I'm really proud of him and I know he struggles with his own mental health as we all do, with emotional issues." He says, "(I'd tell him) Thanks for bringing your mom through it, into believing that I really cared for her." He's saying people feel bad when someone leaves the planet early – they think, what did I do wrong? What else could I have done? When it had nothing to do with them…"

And now Anthony is saying "That stupid movie ("Roadrunner") making it out like it knew why I left early, as if it had something to do with my girlfriend, because that's the very reason why I would have stayed."

Now Robin is saying, "They misdiagnosed what was going on." How they gave him drugs that made him lose his ability to focus rather than get better." (Jennifer makes a face). Well, he's saying his honest opinion about them doing that, and I can't even repeat what he just said.

Robin the most powerful thing we've heard you say from the flipside was when I asked Jennifer to ask you directly for a quote. I asked him for a blurb for the cover of my book "Hacking the Afterlife."

"Love love."

Love what love is, could be, the idea of it. The act of it. It's a verb, it's a noun, it's... Superman. It's everything, all there is. If you can love love, you can love yourself.

(Jennifer laughs) He just said, "It's kind of like the f-word but nicer."

Robin, are you hanging out with Anthony?

"Yeah." Anthony says, "there's a big celebration for his birthday up there."

Oh, by the way, Robin have you seen our friend Charles Grodin who introduced us?

Robin says, "How could I not see him?" Charles is holding a microphone and says, "I'm still doing a better job than you guys." Charles says that you had a dream about recently.

I did.

He says, "It was a really cool dream." He showed me you two younger the way you looked together in the film "Hacking the Afterlife" on the Merv Griffin show.

Oh, by the way, Chuck, I spoke to your friend Paul Simon, as after our podcast with you, I'd asked you if you had any message for your friend and you said "Tell him not to worry about his last song, because his last song is not his last song." I wrote Paul and he wrote back "It's uncanny that you would say that, and you have no idea how accurate that is, Richard."

(Jennifer aside) I win! Oh no, Charles says "He won." Prince just showed up.

It's a quorum.

He's talking to you about changing your guitar strings.

Indeed. Yesterday I gave my son a pair of strings for his guitar. But Prince if I may, is this about tuning oneself up?

He's saying, "We all need to change our strings. We all need to be in tune with each other getting rid of the old ones that no longer serve you because you've grown. Your fingers have grown, your heart has grown."

That is the subject of the next book "Tuning in to the folks on the other side" and talking about music and talking about resonance and frequency and how if we open ourselves up to them, it helps us to communicate and navigate our lives.

What he showed me is sometimes those strings are so tight they're just going to break. Like they're so tightly wound and that if you keep on holding on, they're gonna break. "So, you need to loosen them up."

I think we've talked about that - a middle way, not too tight, and not too slack... but some kind of resonant way you can access people...

He says, "By tuning into those you love with those strings of love."

Thank you.

*****

OUR FLIPSIDE CLASSROOM TEACHER

Class moderator Luana Anders circa 1965

While Jennifer and I had been meeting regularly to "talk to whomever showed up" this is a flashback to the first session where the idea of a *Flipside classroom* came up.

For those unfamiliar with the concept, I initially heard about "classrooms in the afterlife" from my friend Luana. As she was dying, one day she said, "I think when I die, I'm going to another galaxy." We had never talked about death openly – it was just a topic neither of us would discuss. But in this instance, she opened the door for me to ask, **"Why do you think that?"**

She told me she had a recurring dream where she was in a classroom, everyone was "dressed in white" and speaking a language "She'd never heard before, but somehow completely understood." I thought *"Oh, that must be from the morphine drip"* (that she had helping ease her pain from cancer.) But the day she passed her close friend Sandra Stephenson called me from Hawaii and said "I had the most wonderful dream about her last night. She was in the 4th dimension, and she was in a spiritual classroom where everyone was dressed in white."

I asked the hospice nurse Charmaine about it, and she nearly fainted. **"That was her recurring dream!"**

I moved to New York City to work on the Charles Grodin show with her good friend Charles, and while there I had an out of body experience where I felt I went to see her. It was fairly dramatic, as I've had the experience of "floating around the room" in the past, but in this case, it was like a "blast off" where I left my bed in the upper west side of Manhattan, shot into deep space, tumbled through a worm hole or black hole, and found myself traveling with great speed to suddenly screech to a halt; Luana standing in front of me.

It was Luana as I knew her – but with her eyes closed. She opened them as if to say **"You were wondering where I am. This is where I am."**

At that moment, a truck driver hit his horn – but I had the experience of "traveling back" to New York, like the Charles Eames film *"Powers of Ten"*[1] – hurtling through deep space, back to Manhattan from above to suddenly sitting up in my bed – all before the driver took his hand off the horn.

It was as if she was saying **"Not only do I still exist, but this is where you can find me."** I thought, **"Well, if she still exists somewhere off planet, or off universe, and she can come and visit me, how can I go and visit her?"**

---

[1] https://youtu.be/0fKBhvDjuy0 "Powers of 10" by Charles Eames

Some years later, when I began to research the topic of the Flipside, I found an account in Michael Newton's book *"Journey of Souls"* where the person under deep hypnosis said, "I see myself in a classroom and everyone is dressed in white." I chill went up my spine and I knew if I was looking for Luana, this would be a method of how to find her.

The first time I did a between life session, I went to visit *two* classrooms. (Hypnotherapist said, "Where would you like to go?" I said, "To find my friends.") The first classroom was fun, welcoming – the teacher seemed to know me well and introduced me to her young students. I did not consciously recognize this "teacher", but she seemed to know me and praised me to her class, who all were "turned in their seats" in my direction, as if to say *"Oh, teacher's friend is here!"*

However, I later said, "I want to visit Luana's class," when I arrived, I had the impression I was interrupting her class, mid lecture. It was the polar opposite of the journey to the first class.

Imagine yourself sitting in a room with fellow students and suddenly this hologram appears saying *"Okay, I'm here visiting a class in the afterlife!"* The students all turned to look at me, as if they were not used to interruptions. The teacher stopped his lecture, and everyone went silent. I shut up for a few seconds, and then said, *"I get the feeling I'm not supposed to be here, but since I've come all this way, I might as well continue."*

I saw Luana sitting in the back of the classroom looking at me as if saying *"What the hell? What are you doing here?"* and I explained (to the hypnotherapist, knowing I was filming this session) that this was a class in *"Accessing the healing light of the universe, and these students learn how to help healers, doctors and others to connect to that energy to heal people on Earth."*

At which point one student turned in his desk and mockingly said, *"You don't know what the hell you're talking about."*

I was startled; obviously I was interrupting them and not welcome. I said to the hypnotherapist **"Okay, a student just turned and corrected me. What I meant to say is that people in this class learn how to help doctors and healers to access the "healing light of the universe," however not all people sign up for a lifetime where they will heal everyone, and likewise people may sign up for a lifetime to experience an illness, so they can learn from it."**

To which the student said **"Well, I guess you do know something after all."**

A very weird exchange. My conscious mind was thinking "If I'm making this up, why am I making up this unhappy student challenging me? If I'm not supposed to be here, then have I broken some cardinal rule by coming here?" It was so foreign to me that when the session was over, I literally felt as if the axis of the Earth had shifted slightly – like "everything I thought I knew" had to be rethought.

Two years later with a different hypnotherapist (first was with Jimmy Quast, the second with Scott De Tamble[2]) I decided to "revisit" the classroom, not knowing if I could be able to return there. (I.e., "what if it was all a fantasy I had created?" and the second "between life journey" sent me elsewhere?)

---

[2] Jimmy Quast EastonHypnosis.com Scott De Tamble LightBetweenLives.com

But after a few seconds of Scott De Tamble "walking me down a stairway of time" *("You're getting younger now")* I interrupted him to say, "I'm already back there." It felt as if the garden gate had been left open, and it was like walking back to where I had left off two years before.

When I "arrived" back in Luana's classroom, it was as if *only twenty minutes* had gone by, even though it was physically two years after my first "visit." I was aware I was now standing in front of this huge classroom, Luana apologizing to her teacher for my rude behavior (from two years earlier but felt like twenty minutes earlier) trying to explain what it was that I was doing. After her explanation the teacher turned to me. **"So, what did you want to know?"**

So, I'm familiar with the concept of "seeing a class" on the flipside. In this following session with Jennifer, it was the day after the musician Chris Cornell had apparently committed suicide. When someone "shows up" in a session and claims to be Chris Cornell, or David Bowie or someone else that neither Jennifer and I have met, I report what they say and try to search the facts to see what might be accurate.

My questions are in *italics*, Jennifer's answers are in normal type face, **answers she's getting are in bold type**.

*****

Rich: I thought we'd see if we can access someone neither one of us knows. We're going to try and dial up Chris Cornell. Let's ask Luana if she can dial him up?

Jennifer: Luana just goes and grabs him.

Rich: Oh! That was easy. Chris did a sublime cover of Prince's song "Nothing Compares to U" and since we've had

Prince show up in our conversations before, I thought maybe they might have known each other. Chris? Say hello to the guy who wrote this song.

> (Note: Prince, or someone who appears as Prince Rogers Nelson is a frequent visitor to our class, as we'll see in ensuing chapters. He appears in *"Hacking the Afterlife"* as well.)

Jennifer: I just got chills.

Rich: Well, if anyone can talk to him that we know, it would be The Purple One. Can you help be a conduit for us?

They said, "Yes." I keep getting Robin Williams. Some group they're dealing with.

Robin was awarded a "Comedy Chair" today at USC.

(Jennifer applauds.)

Who wants to help us talk to Chris?

They're like dragging him over, he's hands are out like, "No, I don't wanna go on camera!" They're all laughing.

Can we ask you questions?

"Yes." (Jennifer aside) It's funny; I was going to talk to Chris tonight for a radio call in show.

> (Note: Jennifer does a number of shows where people ask her direct questions about people on the flipside.)[3]

---

[3] For an account of Chris Cornell's last days: https://www.rollingstone.com/music/features/chris-cornell-david-fricke-on-soundgarden-singer-final-days-w484560)

Think of this as a preshow for Chris. What does he look like to you?

He has his hair back.

Can Prince and Robin help us with him? Perhaps their presence would give us credibility with Chris.

Luana just said "Don't forget me" and that guy... the one who had the song "Don't you forget about me" in his film.

John Hughes?

Yeah.

> (Note: John Hughes came through during a session previously. I had met him on the set of *"Pretty in Pink"* and he went to my high school. He had some specific messages for friends that know him, including his wife, Nancy. Nancy and John eloped in high school; the same high school depicted as Shermer High in "Ferris Bueller.")

Rich: Well, what about John? Is he accessible?

Jennifer: He's showing me a huge tombstone.

That's correct. He has one in the cemetery in Lake Forest, a gorgeous piece of cut marble with only his last name on it.

(Jennifer, to me:) Do you have a sister? He says he's in love with your sister.

I don't have a sister, but I know who he's talking about. One of my sisters-in-law was his close pal, she and my niece were hanging out with John and his family the day he passed in Manhattan. He went to the same high school as I did.

He says both he and his wife loved your sister-in-law. They were very close.

> (Note: *(ding!)* This is one of those **"bells of verification."** Jennifer could not know that my brother and his wife were pals with John, or that my sister-in-law was a light in both his and his wife's lives or that John had known my sister-in-law since high school.)

Does he have any message for his widow?

He's showing me an image of her running. He says, "Tell her "Don't run from your feelings."

What's that mean?

He says "Tell her to not run from her feelings. She likes someone. She's afraid to show it."

Well, I think both my sister-in-law and John's wife are skeptics about talking to the flipside. What could I tell his family that only they would know about him?

He's showing me that he had a previous heart attack. One just prior to the big one, like a few hours and then another one six years earlier. He said, "She'll know about that one."

Okay. Hey, whatever happened to the copy of "Limit Up" that I gave you?

> (Note: I sent a copy of my film "Limit Up" with Ray Charles to John in hopes of working for him someday. I try to keep these conversations light so that it's not

only about the loss of an individual, but minor details help us verify it's really them we're talking to.)

He showed me an image of it being tossed into a box. It was VHS, right?

*Yes, it was. (**Ding!**) I accidentally left the note from Oliver Stone telling me he enjoyed the film in the VHS copy.*

He's showing me that he wasn't well at the time. Sweating, out of breath; heart issues. He was in no space to look at it at the time. He says, "Tell your sister-in-law not to hold back."

What does that mean?

He said, "No one has ever come over from that side to this side saying, "Gee I wish I had held back more during my life." He says, "Don't hold back."

Oh, Robin (Williams) is bringing forth John Candy. They're both saying, "We need to bring back Old Hollywood."

John Candy, one of the all-time greats, thank you very joining us.[4]

It's like they are all sitting in a classroom.

Are they in rows?

---

[4] I did see John Candy perform with Second City in Chicago, while the Toronto company switched. I met him in a bar on La Cienega in LA, and got everyone in the place to give him a standing ovation. He was flattered and laughed about it.

They keep coming up one by one, they showed me it's a classroom. Luana is in charge of this classroom – not in a hierarchy way, but in a moderator way.

What are they learning in this class?

"Translation."

It's a class in translation of the ethers in some way?

"Yes." Someone else just came in.

I'm sorry, who just came in?

The airplane girl.

Oh, Amelia. Are you part of this class or are you just sitting in?

She says, "She's helping them too."

> (Note: When Jennifer came into my life, I took the opportunity to "interview Amelia" extensively, to confirm or deny what 30 years of research had shown me.)[5]

Okay, so this is a class in communication, is that correct?

"Yes, they're telling me about the future, and how this form of communication will grow over time."

(Trying to stay on track) Guys, we're here to talk to Chris. We don't care about the future.

They said *"bullshit!"* They all laughed.

---

[5] As recounted in "Hacking the Afterlife." Createspace publishing 2016. https://www.goodreads.com/book/show/31280554-hacking-the-afterlife

I hate to herd cats, but we've got a few folks to talk to here today. The question at hand; Chris did you check yourself out? And if you're aware of it, "Why?"

He showed me his blood stream, an imbalance. He said it was regarding a breakup, "but not the way you think." There was a possible divorce... it wasn't public knowledge... He's saying that on a certain level he knew he was checking out.

Was it like an "exit point?"

(Note: "Exit points" are shorthand for a moment when people might have left the planet, but did not for whatever reason, or in this case, chose to "take an exit.")

I asked about the method of his passing, and Robin jumped up and made a face. *"Drugs!"* he said.

Class! Behave.

They're making fun of us. Hold on; Chris is talking. He showed me 5 pm last night. I feel like he just didn't think he would survive... He's showing me veins.[6]

---

[6] His wife reported, "I noticed he was slurring his words; he was different," she said in a statement issued May 19th. "When he told me he may have taken an extra Ativan or two, I contacted security and asked that they check on him." Soundgarden bodyguard Martin Kirsten kicked in the hotel-room and bedroom doors – both were locked – and found Cornell "with blood running from his mouth and a red exercise band around [his] neck," according to a police report. https://www.rollingstone.com/music/news/chris-cornells-wife-issues-statement-w483179

I know he had a drug problem before... Chris what was your experience like crossing over to the flipside?

Wow. He says **"Music. Beautiful music."** He said, **"At first he was scared."**

What was the music? Classical, ethereal? Rock and roll?

Music he's never heard from before. But the first person he saw was Prince. And then David Bowie.

Chris, did you know David?

He met him a long time ago, at a benefit, I guess. (Jennifer; aside) I've never seen David Bowie before.

> (Note: Jennifer would have no clue that Chris had met Bowie. Chris reportedly met David at a Vanity Fair photoshoot in 2001 celebrating their November "Music" issue and posted about it after Bowie passed: "I was part of a Vanity Fair music issue, where there were a lot of pretty amazing people there for a photo shoot. He (Bowie) was one of them... he saw **I was uncomfortable and went out of his way to alleviate that discomfort and make me feel happy about it. It was a compassionate moment.**")[7]

Well, can we talk to you for a second, David? What was it like for you crossing over? Who was there to greet you and what did you feel?

He showed me the music video he made.

---

[7] https://www.facebook.com/chriscornell/photos/a.116887764686.94354.505 2659686/10153873077954687

"Black Star?" (David Bowie's last music video which was about crossing over to the flipside.) Was that what the experience was like?

He's laughing. He said it (the video) was a "100th of that, of what it really was, and it was related to the kind of beauty that can't be expressed, or colors that can't be expressed through this dimension, so many lights of all the people he's known or felt." He says, "His father... was the first one that came forward."[8]

Okay.

He's showing me a letter... a love letter to his wife... I don't know if he wrote it before he left or if he hid it. (Pause) He says, "There's a few of them that he's left."

Letters that she'll find or has found?

"That she'll find."

I think he has some more music coming out.

My interpretation of what I'm seeing is love letters, but that could be a reference to music as well. I'm asking him, "Are they love letters or music?" He said, "It's a combination."

---

[8] David's father; Haywood Jones. His mother Peggy said: "The midwife said, 'This child has been on this earth before'. I thought that was rather an odd thing to say but the midwife seemed quite adamant." David wore a cross given him by his father throughout his life. https://www.thesun.co.uk/archives/news/100710/i-think-i-have-done-just-about-everything-its-possible-to-legend-david-bowies-cosmic-life-remembered/

Anything you want to tell your fans, people who love and miss you?

"The music lives on. We've all heard that, but we should know that, as well."

How about you, Prince. Why did you show up to help Chris when he crossed over?

He was up there with the orchestra.

The music Chris was hearing. How is that created?

He saw him playing his song "Nothing Compares to U."

> (Note: Chris did record a version of that Prince song. We'll hear more about "frequencies of music" in subsequent chapters.)[9]

How is that image and sound created? How do you create music for Chris to hear?

He says, "It's instantaneous; it's a frequency that just goes "zoom" together at once. A frequency that goes back to his own unique frequency and then he magnifies his (own) frequency."

Is that something you've always been able to do or something you learned over there?

He said "Yes, he's always known how to do it, but not consciously." He showed me being here, how he pulled the frequencies in here, but now, he realizes that he can do

---

[9] https://www.youtube.com/watch?v=IuUDRU9-HRk

that up there. He now knows how to amplify and draw in others."

Anything you want to impart to us, Chris?

Chris wants us to talk about suicide... He says he was "playing Russian roulette" and not realizing it... doing things that were like playing Russian roulette; he didn't think he would die from it.

Chris is asking me something... Okay. He wants me to talk (more) about suicide. "It's not the way to go, it's very challenging for people over there to get through to people over here, and they're trying to figure out the best way to communicate... to talk them out of it."

You're suggesting Jennifer should talk about suicide; what should she say?

He just said, *"Weren't you listening?"* He said, "Whether you're playing with drugs, even though you're not thinking that playing with drugs or things that can kill you, (from cigarettes to whisky to heroin) is about suicide, it is a form of suicide."

How do we tell people to stop doing that?

He showed me my friend Dr. Drew.

Therapy?

He says, "What it (drugs) does, is make your heart grow small, it makes your heart harden, your heart closes – there are drugs people use that make them feel more connected, but these kinds of drugs make it harder (to do so)." The first thing he said is "Your heart has the answers."

Best drug in the world is to have your heart open?

"Best drug in the world is you. Life."

How can we get people to stay away from drugs?

"They're not going to be able to hear it. Family members might hear it and help them, they're going through everything as well."

But Chris, would you have changed if your family had told you to stop toying with drugs?

He showed me the breakup was from something else... not about a relationship. He showed me... an imbalance. But now they're laughing and saying that they're all "chemically imbalanced." Except for David Bowie. He said, "He was not."

David, what did you learn from going through cancer, that journey through that illness to the flipside?

He learned how much he loved his wife and friends... He says "It made me learn to love life. The more you're connected to source, that's what opens up your heart."

Connect to source... how?

"Singing, acting, being creative. You make your heart fill with love and compassion, do things for other people and your heart slowly opens up."

Thank you. Okay, Robin, let's lighten up this mood. Can you tell us something funny? Maybe a flipside joke?

He says, "There are two blondes walking down the street. (Pauses. Listens) And they find an exit sign and they say, "No thanks, we don't want to leave."

Ha! Okay, a flipside blonde joke.

(Jennifer aside) Why are my ears burning suddenly? He said "It's the frequency... Please express that people who stay here (on the planet and don't commit suicide) experience so much more than leaving.

(Jennifer listens) Chris says he "No longer gets to give his daughter a kiss anymore." He's saying, "I don't get to breathe anymore." Or that he doesn't get "To worry about what's going to happen. That he doesn't get to play. It resonates. It's fun to be on the planet, to experience life. Don't be in a hurry to exit."

Does Luana want to step in?

She says she's herding them. She's saying, "This class is going to change things."

This class that she's officiating?

She says, "This is a class in communication between this side and that side."

Is there anything that you miss Luana? About being on the planet?

She pinched your cheek. "She misses you, but then she doesn't because you're here." Um. Did you guys have a convertible or something?

I had a 1965 Mustang convertible when I met her.

She misses... "Driving in the wind, driving in a convertible and not giving a shit..." She showed me her cats... her cats are there with her.

*(**Ding!** A bell of verification.) Anyone else? Oh, what about Jan Sharp? The Australian film producer.*

She's very elegant. She's holding a cigarette, a long one, like in a holder.

Last time we spoke you said you were flying around having great adventures. How are you doing? I know her family might not be open this information.

She says, "Whatever they think is right."

You had so many pals, what do you do during the day?

"They're all over there." She says she writes. She shows me like making her own garden. She's showing me the sound of the birds, the way things smell, she's out in that garden writing. It's hard for them to manufacture all those things over there. We have nature and all of it, but they have to work at it.

Can we access your writing?

"No." She told me "It's for her future self."

Anything I should tell members of your family?

Oh, good luck with that one. "Try to give more love."

You think they'll listen to me?

That's why she said, "Good luck with that one."

Well, thanks Jan. I had a lot of fun knowing you, you were such a dramatic and wonderful person.

She was an actress too. She just showed me Nicole Kidman.

Really? (Ding!) Nicole lived in their house.

Did you ever tell me that?

No, when Nicole first started in the business she lived at Jan and Phillip's home. When she made her first film "Dead Calm" with Jan's husband Phillip Noyce.

(Jennifer aside) I had nightmares about that film.

Any last words from anyone up there?

"They love you."

Who said that?

Who do you think? Luana.

Okay class see you next week.

*****

I put this chapter in here because even though it was among the first that demonstrated how we can speak to our loved ones on the other side, it gave us context to how that was occurring. If we spent time judging how this process works or might work, we'd never get to the answers to the questions.

After doing this for six years, hearing Jennifer time and again say something that I'm later able to verify as accurate, I'm able to set aside my *jaded Hollywood disbeliefs.*

CHAPTER TWELVE: ONCE MORE WITH FEELING

A mirror in a mirror in Rockefeller Plaza with Luana

The previous was the initial discussion of Luana moderating a class. Luana had shown up before, Prince and Robin Williams before, and we had various conversations with others.

But this was the first time the idea of her moderating a *"Translation class"* had come up. From this point forward, it became the structure of our conversations. If someone "showed up" we directed them to speak with or participate in some form of orientation – to see what it was that we were doing in the class.

All I can report is what Jennifer heard from her dad on the Flipside; **"It's not your job to prove that there is an afterlife. It's your responsibility to be as accurate as possible."**

Which is what we're doing. There are authors who "channel" celebrities, I've met a few people who claim to be "channeling" musicians. My thought is always to add the caveat, *"It feels to me* like I'm channeling this person's music. I have no idea if I am conversing with them or not."

The same goes for this book. It *feels* like Jennifer is communicating with these people, and when I hear contrary information, I include it. I try to see if what they're saying is accurate – especially **"new information."**

Like Chris Cornell saying he met David Bowie briefly a long time ago, something I didn't know, but turned out to be accurate. Little things Jennifer and I could not have known but are later proven to be true.

I know how odd this format is – *really*. I come from a world of formal storytelling, writing for magazines and editors as well; "How can we fact check this?" Or movie studios poring over scripts to pass "Errors and Omissions." I toyed with the idea of making these conversations "anonymous" – *"This is a person who was a famous rock star but had eyes different colors"* - but **they** insisted **I not do that.**

Very odd to have someone on the Flipside say, *"It's important you report what you're hearing verbatim."* Some will reject it outright – but the people who need to hear it, will. If by reporting what they say offends any family members; I'm sorry for doing so.

Believe me – I know how many at this point will want to return this book. **I beg you, please do!** Give it back to whomever gave it to you or get a refund. We're not here to upset anyone's apple cart, or eBook "cart." **Ultimately it's the answers that are important. Not who is saying them.**

If we can just focus on what is being said consistently – I've done this with a few mediums, while talking to people who are under hypnosis, or just asking questions while a person is fully conscious – it doesn't really matter what the method is *if we get the same answers.*

On one hand, I suggest trying to ignore "who" is speaking. See if *what they say* has any resonance with you. Try to "unfreeze your mind" about who *these people were* – and focus on what they're saying. How it might relate to our own journey. That is the value of listening to things that may seem crazy; the only way to verify crazy things is how you feel when you hear them. *"Welcome to our class!"*

Luana Anders in another class; "Reform School Girl"

Jennifer: (aside) Prince showed up at the end.

Let's talk to him. Hello Mr. Prince Rogers Nelson. Does Prince have anything he wants to say on the "Beyond Belief" show?

Tell him that it's a "sound note..." he showed me the matrix... tell him, "It's a *sound* note."

> (Note: Funny word play as well. A musician giving us a "sound note." It's a note, just the way Michael was taking notes, but it's also a musical note, and a spiritual one as well.)

What's that mean?

I don't know. Hang on. "It's not how you look, (*I think he's referring to me worrying how I "looked on the show" which I did not express to Jennifer but was on my mind*) it's not what you say, (*it's not the content of what I'm saying on the show*) it's how you vibrate in your awareness. Awareness of one another."

(After a pause) "In your awareness of the accumulation." So like, he's showing me that in your awareness, it's a note... – so if your frequency is clear, that's how you attract someone. Because when you're in the consciousness of the higher level, where there is no hierarchy... and if you're bouncing (broadcasting) on a certain level, then that gets through with more potency.

When you're bouncing on a lower level, its fragmented. If it's fragmented, you're not able to connect, which logically, you can't connect." He's showing me "You don't connect well when you're out of mode of vibration -- but when you're not afraid of vibration, you're able to then send it out and then receive that higher vibration..."

A bit like we were saying earlier, when you strike a chord, all the guitars in a room start to vibrate at that same tone. You hit a note and all the guitars resonate on that same string?

"Yes."

So, the idea being not higher or lower, but stronger?

"But not all the same – *high* frequencies can sound low." He showed me the song "Every rose has its thorns."[10]

Higher -- meaning the place they're coming from?

Right. "You can… but if you have a higher (stronger) frequency, you'll still connect with the people that will come. It's a matrix."

My question for you Prince, since we last spoke in this same restaurant two months ago; what does that feel like to you in terms of time, comparatively?

"A millisecond – even less than that…" He just told me, "It's continuous." So like he was here and it's a continuous dialog. It's a continuous "dialog with God." He just showed me a goddess, but he's kidding around with that. (looks at her watch) I gotta go.

Prince, thanks for stopping by, we'll have to get back to you!

*****

---

[10] Every rose has it's thorn, Just like every night has it's dawn, Just like every cowboy sings his sad, sad song, Every rose has it's thorn..." by Miley Cyrus

Okay let's shift to Jennifer's dad Jim, the only Bishop in the room.

> (Note: Jennifer's father was a Mormon bishop who passed a few months prior to this conversation.)

"Thank you," he says.

I appreciate you stopping by Jim.

(Jennifer turns red, can't speak.) He's laughing because I have a lump in my throat... He says, "I wanted you to know how much I love you and I hope it's not just one sided." That was something my grandfather would say...

Can you take a hold of your dad's hand and send him some radiating love, so he can feel it?

He always loved driving fast, he always takes me into the ether when he appears. I feel like he's taking me for a ride.

Can you do that now?

He says he's learning (to navigate the afterlife). Shows me falling on his elbow... so funny... "It's endless," he says. "The universe is endless."

What's the best way to connect to someone no longer on the planet?

"Through the heart; putting the awareness of your loved ones in the heart." They're all laughing. I just asked, "You mean like a cell phone?" They said "Yes, your heart's a cellphone. You have to put your intentions into your heart, that's your cell phone. It's how you connect with them."

Anyone else in the room who wants to come forward?

Prince. He's saying, (communication) **"It's like the frequencies of music. Your heart is like a guitar, in that it has strings, and those strings vibrate, and they call or connect you to the others who are connected to you..." that awareness because it takes you places.**

"Music reminds you of things you've done in your past, memories, music and words mean something to your heart. The strings are the strands of the matrix, like a guitar that connects you (plugs you in) **to the matrix."**

Listening to music is a way of connecting to your heart? A way to connect to a loved one no longer on the planet would be to play their favorite song?

"Yes. And ask them questions," he said.

Mr. Nelson, Prince Rogers, everyone's excited your music is coming out since you've crossed over; people are playing it everywhere. That must be a kick for you.

He says "It connects him to everyone. When somebody sends his music to others." He's showing me - you know how they show a stadium with all the lights? He showed me that it's like that for him - everyone playing his music and they all connect back.

I know we've talked about the meaning of Purple Rain...

He's saying, "It was seductive phrase."

But I wanted to mention how in Newton's work, he found that people connected to certain colors on the spectrum...

He's saying Michael already explained that to him.

Michael asked "If you looked in a mirror, what color of light would you see?" And the older ones would radiate in that purple end of the spectrum.

Prince is saying, "It was (just) his favorite color and he looked good in it!"

Okay. Let me ask you the same – if you looked yourself in a mirror what color would you see?

He said, "Red." (Jennifer blushed, said "he's flirting with me.") "He's more grounded into it and so that's the color he's at now; red."

Okay, we've got to go, class, thanks to everyone for showing up. Jennifer is not quite my cell phone, but my Dixie-Cup-On-a-String connection to the flipside.

*****

A friend recently asked me *"Do you actually believe you're talking to these people?"*

I said "I try to leave the concept of *belief* out of my work. I have the *experience* of talking to someone who makes me feel as if I'm talking to these people, and I ask my questions accordingly."

Once we have an "experience" of talking to someone no longer on the planet our paradigm shifts. As mind did when my dad "visited" me the night he passed with the names of his friends on the flipside I had never heard of, but my mother confirmed were his "friends who died in World War II."

Or when James Van Praagh quoted Luana as saying I had a photograph on my refrigerator that was the "essence of our relationship" – a detail no one but me could know.

I've dropped the idea of "belief" and focused on the content of what they're saying. I have no idea if it's actually Prince talking about frequencies and music. But being a musician and someone who used to sell stereo equipment, I know about tuning, frequencies that are limited, blocked or filtered, or how and when they resonate with each other. If it is or isn't Prince, the metaphors he's using, the concepts he's offering, are equally worth noting.

As Luana's pal Robert Towne said; "My whole life I was convinced that the afterlife didn't exist. And now I'm convinced that it does. What happened?"

It's experiential.

Luana reaching beyond the veil with her gaze.

TOM WILBURY

From "Backstage Pass"

In general, we've found that this process is easiest when either Jennifer or I knew the person that we bring forth to interview. It's almost as if "our frequency" is familiar with "their frequency" so inviting them to come and chat with us is easier to do.

Needless to say, whenever we think of someone we knew, we are accessing the files that we have for that person. Those files contain frequency information – because everything we see, hear, touch, feel – is a wavelength that comes to us, and our mind translates that wavelength into information or a memory. When you remember something, you're accessing that frequency of the memory.

So even when we think of a loved one who is no longer on the planet, we get a mental image of them, or we may get many senses involved; hearing their voice, smelling a perfume, remembering a meal, etc. Their ability to "*ping*" or get our mind to remember them is a matter of activating a frequency or "sending a signal" to get us to recollect our memory of them.

Apparently, it works the same way with dreams. It's reportedly easier for them to "enter our dreams" because we aren't blocking frequencies while we're asleep, we're more open to other information.

In the between life studies of Michael Newton, many discussed the process of how once they were no longer on the planet, they went about "implanting" a dream into someone's sleep. They claimed that they chose a neutral setting, so as not to freak out their loved one, and often said or did something in the dream that they could remember when they woke up. (Note: The same way that Paul McCartney's mother Mary appeared to him in a dream and said *"Let it be"* – which he turned into a song.) All memory is frequency, all visitations from people on the flipside is also a matter of frequency.

But occasionally someone shows up in our class that neither one of us knows. In this case, the singer songwriter Tom Petty had just passed away. (A founding member of the "Traveling Wilburys") I'm not aware of any connection either I or Jennifer might have had other than being fans of his music. It's only later in this book that I realize my brother Jeffrey had a relationship with Tom; they played softball together at George Harrison's house. I was not aware of that until a year after this following interview.

It's like "six degrees of separation" or as we like to call it *"Six degrees of Kevin Bacon."* I may know someone who knew someone who knows the frequency of someone else. Because I am connected to the person next to me, etherically I have a connection to everyone they've ever met or know. It's also a bit like the admonition of the 80's when people realized when they were "sleeping with a stranger" they were sleeping with everyone that person had slept with. Well, it's kind of like that – but in a positive way.

Everyone you've ever met is connected to you etherically in some way.

So ponder that for a moment; everyone you've ever met is connected to each other. And everyone they've ever met is connected to you. Fun thought, isn't it? So if I've met you in this lifetime, I can track you down on the Flipside, and interview you, *even if you won't want to be interviewed. (Scary thought!)*

*****

Jennifer: Luana is telling the classroom to "be quiet." They're doing an experiment is what I'm getting... Tom Petty is in the back of the classroom.

Rich: Cool. So how does the class bell work? How do they know when it's "time for class?"

It's a frequency, they know a certain time - it's a frequency that's sent out to everybody...

How many are in the class? Is it whoever shows up with the frequency?

There are some people with her, but it goes out to hundreds of thousands that are connected. They don't need to be physically here to be present.

Like a virtual class for the ethernet. Set the classroom visual for me – how is our professor attired?

(Jennifer fans herself) She is mentioning how hot it is. Hold on – it's interesting to hear they feel the heat...

How does she look to you?

It's down - she's wearing white – I think I always see her in white. She's changed her lipstick to orange, like a summer color.

Okay, Luana, what's up? You're here, we're here; let's talk.

She just touched my shoulders. (Jennifer listens) So I'm getting... She's saying, "Tom Petty wants to know something about his death." I'm saying to her "But he's with you – wouldn't he know about his own death?"

How can we help him?

He shows me like a computer, googling the answer.

> (Note: I did not "ask for Tom" to come to our class today. This was an example of him passing on, and "showing up spontaneously in the class." In terms of his passing, the results of his autopsy, which showed that he had a massive amount of pain killers in his body from a broken hip, had not been released by this recording.)

What would you like to know, Tom? Can Tom come forward?

"Yes."

I didn't know you Tom, but I likely have friends who knew you.

Luana touches her nose. "That's why he's here."

What would you like to know about your passing?

(Jennifer aside) Does Tom have a daughter?

I think so. Yeah.

It's about someone getting the paperwork. Like whatever help you can give them – they or she - needs to find the paperwork or whatever it was that's necessary for her estate.

But people will handle that, right Tom?

"**Yeah.**"

Who greeted you when you crossed over?

His father.

> (Note: I didn't know Tom was physically abused by his father, which led to his heroin addiction. For those who might balk at this answer, as I've reported in "Flipside" people claim that those who abused or molested them may have asked or been asked to participate in a difficult lifetime to teach or learn the hard lessons that come from that difficult choice. Suffice to say, everyone who knew Tom's dad will reject this concept, but I can only report what people consistently say about the journey; once we "return home" we drop the negative aspects of personality – no matter how cruel or bad – and appear as we exist between lives. People report consistently that "everyone agrees" on what role they're going to play in a future "performance" including the ones who play "the bad guys.")[11]

What was your experience crossing over? Were you startled to cross over?

"Wouldn't you be?"

Were you at home?

He said, "A couple weeks before; his energy was drained," he said he kind of... He said he "felt he knew."

---

[11] https://www.thesun.co.uk/news/4601250/tom-petty-childhood-marriage-breakdown-heroin-addiction/

I read an article about you being exhausted. How exhausted were you?

That's what he's saying, "He kind of knew." He said, "He told one person that he had a dream about it." It's like he saw it before hand and told someone about it... he saw a face, from the place where he is now... but it was not the way he dreamt it.

Did Luana invite you to class to help process this?

"Yes." He looks at Luana. "It (this class) helps both here and there. It gives it a sort of process... we eventually process everything. An eyewitness."

What was your experience crossing over, did you see hear or sense anything?

He's showing me smells... of the concert... whatever is in the concert... smoke...

From pot smoke?

He says, "He quit drinking... 25 years ago."

> (Note: He thought I meant *him* smoking pot, when I meant the usual aroma from a concert. However, this is accurate. In his biography, it's noted he went into rehab for heroin addiction in the late 90's, was saved by his wife Dana.)

What point did you realize you were in the afterlife?

"I saw my dad; he wasn't saying anything, but I could hear his thoughts."

How did he appear? Younger?

The age he last saw him.

Tom, when you look around this group that Luana has assembled, are there other people that you know or a fan of, or surprised to see?

"Yes, really surprised." He's showing me the heart, he was showing me that he knew something was out there (on the flipside) **because of the information he was getting from his songs... he was connected back to the place** (on the flipside) **where he "downloaded" the songs.**

Beethoven talked about that as well... he credited his music as coming from another universe, or a space beyond time.[12]

(Jennifer aside) I've never heard that.

I have an off the wall question for Luana from someone we know... from a physics professor.

She just rolled her eyes.

If there is an equal amount of matter and anti-matter in the universe, why is there more matter than anti-matter in the universe?[13]

First thing she showed me... she showed me black holes.

---

[12] As did Einstein: https://www.nytimes.com/2006/01/31/science/a-genius-finds-inspiration-in-the-music-of-another.html

[13] This is the same question posed by Forbes Magazine: https://www.forbes.com/sites/startswithabang/2018/01/27/ask-ethan-whats-so-anti-about-antimatter/#1b05583c17f0

Do black holes have anti-matter in them?

She says, "Yes."

So that's why we don't have the same amount of matter and anti-matter in the universe?

She taps her nose (as if to say "correct.")

(Laughs). *If you're correct, then we just won a Nobel prize.*

She was showing me the black hole and the anti-matter inside of it as being more translucent.

This question came up today with physicist Michio Kaku; why there's more matter than anti-matter, because when they meet they explode. But when they measure anti-matter versus matter... it's identical – so they were trying to figure out where the anti-matter is... so your answer is...

"Black holes. They consume the anti-matter."

Kaku said the person who answered this question will get the Nobel.

"Tell him. (She pauses) It's one black hole in particular, not just all of them."

One black hole in particular? Is it the one that is considered to be in the center of our universe?

She's showing me one further out.

Where is it? There's reportedly one near the center of the universe.

She showed me light years...

It happened light years ago?

"But we're now feeling it."

So the anti-matter went in one black hole, for the most part?

"That is correct - to the black holes, but predominantly just one in particular."

On the other side of black holes, would we find anti-earth or just matter in some other form?

I got somebody breaking... "physically we'd break apart, going through a black hole." She used Tom Petty for this question.

(Note: I know this doesn't seem like the proper forum to ask questions about physics, but it popped into my mind, so I asked it.)

Tom, welcome to our classroom. So Luana, a mutual friend of ours told me he was driving behind a car and saw something that reminded him of you.

She applauded.

Why?

"In reference to what you're about to say."

Okay. So this friend was driving behind a car and saw that the license plate said "Luana." He emailed me the photo; what was that about?

(Note: He says he's seen this same plate three times.)

"They try to give you information that way. It feels like coincidence, but it's more about energy and synchronicity."

I told this person that I'd talk to you today, and that we are in a "all hands-on deck" situation with regard to saving the planet.

That's why she fanned herself.

> (Note: Meaning "global warming" causes the excess heat we're all feeling.)

Well I guess if we lose this planet we won't lose ourselves.

"Right. But it takes a long time to become a civilization again."

> (Note: This is in reference to the idea that we "don't die" even when our planet explodes. We just go somewhere else and begin again – but as she points out, that will take a "long time.")

Why isn't everyone on this side and the flipside trying to stop the destruction of our planet?

"It *is* an "all hands-on deck" situation."

People on the other side are trying to solve it?

"Yes."

Earth is trying to solve it? Humans are trying to solve it?

"Yes."

How can my friend help me get that message onto the planet?

He showed me. (to them) I don't know what that means.

Jennifer specifically or people like Jennifer?

"Intuitives, mediums." But I'm "the front" she said.

The idea of Jennifer leading this research in this fashion? So if I did a book just about our conversations between Jennifer and the class, that's a way to go?

(Jennifer hits her nose again.)

> (Note: This term "a front" is common in the film business and was the title of a film made by Woody Allen that Luana and I saw together. She's identifying Jennifer as a "front" for those on the flipside who want to express themselves, the way the "front" in the film was a mouthpiece for blacklisted screenwriters. I would understand this reference, but methinks Jennifer would not.)

Jennifer: I'm seeing that Amelia Earhart tapped you on the shoulder.

> (Note: As noted elsewhere, Jennifer and I have had "conversations" with Amelia. I call them that because in all three cases she verified research that I've gathered over 30 years of working on a film about her and this research is not in the public domain.)

Rich: Amelia, I know your father was incarcerated for being an alcoholic. Did he physically abuse you?

(She pauses) I'm not getting a *not*. He did when she was younger. It's why she didn't like men. She liked certain

men because she knew they'd get her places (she wanted to go) ... **but she didn't like them in that way.**

I guess that was part of your journey and path. So how long were you imprisoned in Saipan?

"Seven years."

Did you get to go out around the island ever?

(Jennifer pauses) **"First four years she was able to move around; the last three years she was locked away... but the islanders were trying to help her ... she was well liked by the natives there."**

Was she sick?

"Yeah. Dysentery."

Jumping around a bit. What does Tom Petty think we should call this book?

"Backstage pass." Because we are getting unlimited access to the flipside.

That's what Luana's doing – giving us a "backstage pass?"

I would never ask that question, and she put it in your head... Luana and her friends can also access information you wouldn't think they could.

We can have these "conscious conversations." Like "How do we exist?"

I just saw that the more people know about who we are or where we came from... she showed me a thing going from translucent to matter - the more we understand what's going on, the more fulfilled we are.

And learning this information from them helps us to become more solid or full of understanding?

It comes from (both) **here and there.**

But how does it affect you guys?

She just showed me an earthquake... wait. That scares me a little bit.

Okay, Luana, please give her a different image because she's used to predicting earthquakes... use another metaphor.

(Jennifer smiles) Thank you. Wow, she showed me a light so intense, it blinded me. Thank you for that; she's sorry about the earthquake thing. She meant "It jolts them out of complacency." Whatever we do here, in our class, communicating with them, it helps them, like a loop. Luana just showed me the symbol for infinity.

A sideways 8. What would be an example of something we speak about that would help people back there?

She shows me Tom Petty. (Like Tom) **People who just now stepped off the planet... so Tom will be able to believe that he can access friends.**

I would think it would be annoying for someone on that side to wait for months or years to be able to speak to their loved ones, and even after entering their dreams, the loved one says, "I don't believe it was them, I made it up."

My dad has shown up – he says "hello."

Hi Jim.

Thank you. My mom is worried about something to do with my sister and brother, he showed me a whole force of attorneys up there helping them.

So Jim are you telling us attorneys continue to work on the flipside? Just kidding. How do they wind up choosing that occupation in the first place?

"It's a frequency – it always comes back to frequency; music arts, movies, literature, the second we get here, we distort it and we forget we have access to it."

So Luana, who is your guide?

"You are."

So when I want to talk to your guide I gotta talk to myself?

She's not kidding.

Luana, during one of my hypnosis sessions, you introduced me to your teacher in your healing class.

Morton just came in... hang on. (It's that) **"You get information from all of them and from the teacher Luana had."**

He's referring to the teacher I met in Luana's class during my second hypnotherapy session. It was a class in "the healing light of the universe."

Luana had to introduce him softly to you... to have you understand it, because it might have been too abrupt.

I was just thinking about this teacher, and I would say that all the teachers out there – perhaps they're all connected somehow, and it's just the time element is off.

They're all laughing. It's about the time effect you're talking about. My dad just came forward and said, "I love you Jennifer." Then he told me to "stay away from Prince."

Very funny; a little late now.

(My dad) says "your buddy from the Titanic says, "Thank you." Then he brought in Harry Dean (Stanton). He said "You made it so much fun at the wake..."

Buddy from "Titanic" is Bill Paxton. You mean Harry Dean's memorial? I think people are still talking about it.

They are, trying to figure it out. You sent out a wave they only know; Luana showed me the shock wave that you provided from him. It's so powerful they can't stop thinking about it.

> (Note: As mentioned, I passed Harry Dean's comments along at his memorial service to the individuals he asked me to speak to which blew their skeptical minds, as only he could have known what he told them.)

It's a way of deepening it.

I was writing about a Tibetan meditation, the "Jewel Tree Meditation" where you imagine throwing love and it comes back as a loop.

The infinity figure 8, yeah, the loop. It keeps going, it's going to keep coming back to you over and over again. Luana just high fived me (for that observation.) Luana just appeared dressed up like a nurse.

That's funny. She played a nurse in our last film together; "The Point of Betrayal" with Rod Taylor.

That was her way of showing me what that means, giving nursing advice to her pals back here.

Jennifer has to run. Tom, welcome, the people in this room can help you in your transitioning.

He says, "They already have."

My problem is, as soon as I mention someone of fame appearing in our sessions, (like Tom Petty) it sounds like I'm selling something. I didn't know Tom, but they're telling you that they did.

They say, "F*ck it."

Does Tom have anything specific he wants me to impart?

He wrote out the word "Spirit." He said "If anyone had any idea how amazing it is to be – not just here, but that's what gives *you* life here – like having backstage passes. But backstage is... they have it backwards... (The) backstage pass is being alive! That's the pass.

I like that.

Being over here (on the flipside) **is like being backstage but observing everything that is happening – over there on our side.**

So once you're on the flipside, then it's like having a backstage pass?

We get to experience everything immersively. The people outside in the audience; that's the afterlife, those are all

the souls watching us perform here on stage. We both have passes; they're just for different dimensions. But the "all access pass" is for all dimensions.

Once you're on the flipside you're observing the stage... back here on the planet?

I would say that people tell us that over here (on the flipside) **we can have "a lot of fun;" you can zip around.**

But they can't feel tactile things or the hard emotions like we do. But they can feel love through us?

"Yes. They feel love through us. Our strongest core, with our heart at peace, is with yourselves. You have to love yourself - that frequency of love is so elevated that they get to feel it; that's the shockwave from them... I think of anger – how anger stops everything... but love allows it (the energy) **to go everywhere."**

Okay, thanks class. See you on the flipside!

*****

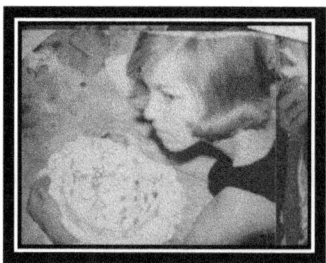

Cake for "blu" – the nickname Jack Nicholson gave her

P. ROGERS NELSON

"Surfing the Ethers"

As noted, Prince has shown up a number of times during our conversations. I mentioned the following conversation in *"Hacking the Afterlife."*[14]

*Richard: So **why is the veil thinning?** Why is that thing between us becoming easier to access?*

Jennifer: (Robin) just showed me Prince.

Prince the musician? What about him?

(Jennifer shrugs) I don't know.

He's in the new book. (I was still working on it.)

Is he? Give me a second… When you said, "why is the veil thinning," he showed me Prince. (Pause, listening.) He said, "Prince just wanted to go home."

What?

"Prince just wanted to go home."

Okay I understand. I include an interview with him in the book. In the interview, he talks about what it was like when he got home.

Yeah.

Are you guys friends? (Robin and Prince) You guys hang out?

---

[14] Reprinted from *"Hacking the Afterlife"* Createspace publishing 2016. With permission from myself.

(Laughs.) They're both laughing. "We go way back." They're laughing about the whole concept of "way back." Like *what does that mean?* In their world, where they're at, way back is like… (laughs).

Let me ask Prince a question. Are you aware of your (chapter) in my book?

…. He's showing me reading a book. Page 149. (or 49).

What's he reading?

I don't know. (pause) He says you're at not taking things out. He's laughing; he says, "It's a good thing." I asked (him) "Is it a good or a bad thing?" And he gave me a look, said "It's a good thing."

You mean not taking things out… you mean like I'm allowing everything to be in?

Yes, everybody else takes bits and pieces out. …. He says, "Love is what it is." Now he's playing his guitar.

Prince what are you and Robin up to?

"Surfing the ethers."

Surfing the ethers? Cool. Do you go around and check out your fans, reach out to them? Or do you guys hang around and do your own thing?

(Listens) No, what? (Laughs. Nods. Smiles.) They're both teaching (the class) "How Not to Leave the Earth Early."

Excellent, well that's a great class. I'd like to take that class. I know a few people who need to take that class.

He says "Music hurts too much;" it hurt his joints. He said, **"It hurts." .....** They said, **"Thank you for not questioning our existence… from your guides."**

Prince, any last words?

"Live and let live." [15]

*****

So it's not an odd thing when Prince Rogers Nelson shows up in our conversation.

Rich: Ok, so we had a question for someone in our class. Who's here?

Jennifer: Prince is here. He really wants to answer the question. By the way I'm asking, *"Is this really Prince?"*

Okay, that's good, because I know this woman who had 3 near death events, and when I told her about our conversations, she said she wanted to ask Prince a question. I was watching him dance a few days ago.

Jennifer: "That was old stuff," he said.

> (Note: That was accurate. Footage from him rehearsing "Purple Rain.")

I think it's cool they're finally putting out your work.

He said, "It's about time."

Well you were "Mr. Secretive..." So what do you think about them releasing your new old material?

---

[15] Excerpted from "Hacking the Afterlife"

He said, "They're not going to get the ending right."

Do they ever?

Everyone's laughing.

There is no ending.

Everyone's laughing when you said that. They're reminding me of the flat tire – how Harry Dean thought the afterlife was a dream, but then when he got the flat tire realized he couldn't be in a dream.

Okay, I need us to give Jennifer a recap of the stop sign conversation we had before... Kind of confusing. How does slowing things down help us access the flipside?

"First you can't text and drive." That's funny (To the class: "I heard you loud and clear." Jennifer puts up two hands) Originally, it was like I didn't know when my dad was communicating with me, he showed me going to a stop sign and consciously stopping your thoughts so that you can access new ones.

You know how we go around driving unconsciously, it's a meditative state? He's saying... "When you arrive at a stop sign it slows everything down and it's then you ask, "Who's here?" And see what comes in."

This woman I met at a dinner party had a question for Prince. She says she felt she had a conversation with you the day you died. Was that accurate or imaginary?

"It was not imaginary but..." he's holding up his finger – "She was tapping into the matrix of what was happening. It wasn't that they were having a conversation - it's not

like he came to visit her - but it's like there's a big bandwidth and she tapped into the bandwidth.

It's such a big bandwidth, whoever is dialing in can get into the same phone call... so if something is happening and she's dialed in, she can access that matrix, she was online with what was happening with him."

Not because she's tuned into his frequency, but because she's a fan of his, and was able to access that frequency?

"Her subconscious accessed what was happening to his frequency."

Sounds as if whoever is tuned a particular way can feel "there's a disturbance in the force." She says she asked you questions, wanted to know if it was really you answering.

He showed me the matrix of him; the frequencies of who he is.

She wondered if it was important information for her future...

He said, "Don't try to make something out of it, just allow it."

Does he mean me or her?

"Her. Her subconscious made that event, where she felt herself in an enclosed space, her mind made that seem as if that was the elevator where they found him." I had something similar when I got an image of something bad happening to Prince, and then saw a plane going down... saw him in a jet.

That was a few days before, when they had to land his plane after his Atlanta performance for a drug overdose. Okay, let me ask Prince, this... we spoke 6 months ago, what does that feel like to you in terms of time?

A thousand years. He showed me a vast sea of lights...

When people pray or think of you, do you respond to everybody? Are you enjoying that or is that work?

He just hit you upside the head like that was a rhetorical question... He says, "He's not helping them; he's igniting them."

Igniting?

He showed me a flame, getting it to spark; that's what I'm seeing.

Like literally lighting their "inner matches?"

He showed me a musician, putting in their mind they can work, they can play, sparking them.

Is that something you learned to do over there; is this a new quality?

He did it before but didn't know he was doing it – it's always been his role to spark people; he didn't know it was the case when he was here.

You're inspiring people to be creative?

It's a combination – but he's saying, "a more powerful word than combination." He's got a powerful connection with the people who consider him a spark. He's showing me Whitney.

Houston? You're hanging out with her?

He's calling it "the *black brat pack.*"

Who else is there?

He's saying her daughter.... and Sammy Davis Jr.

Do you guys perform together?

He says, "They're practicing for their next lives." Hold on. Okay, from what I'm getting: "You create your life up there. You're busy talking to people, working with people, and you come down there and you're supposed to remember it." (What you practiced.)

Let's say you're training to be an athlete, a football player, sniper or surgeon. You're honing your craft before you come here and you get to a point during your life, hopefully, where you get to practice your craft. Is that correct?

"Yes."

Very cool. Anyone else?

They're all raising their hands.

Who wants to talk?

Robin.

Hey there's a documentary coming out about you – someone who loves you made it.

"Magical," he says. His family is really involved in this, feels like.

So your review is "It's magical?"

"Magical but not the beginning. It builds up the story."

What's the beginning about?

"His parents."

They're trying to rationalize why you took your own life?

"**They talk about cocaine** (in the show)."

Is it inaccurate or not the whole picture?

"**Just not the whole picture. They shouldn't emphasize the struggle as much.**" Robin showed me the homeless guy.

"Radioman?" The character he played in "The Fisher King" with Jeff Bridges?

"**Hollywood's like that; they just do that.**"

"Conflict is the essence of drama..." we could ask Aristotle to come in and give us that lecture, but we won't.

He's giving me goose bumps. I love that... "Conflict is the essence of drama." An "OxyMormon" my dad just said.

OxyMormon? That's hilarious.

My dad said to me "You are conflict." How everybody is in conflict with themselves, you have to give people permission (to be who they are) – **that's what I learned from him.**

Your dad is calling you an Oxymoron or an OxyMormon? Nobody laughed at that?

Luana did.

Thanks Lu. Here's my question... I've been telling people that based on our research we only bring about a third of our conscious energy to the planet, roughly, and when we access the other two thirds, can we ask them questions like we ask you?

Your higher self?

Yes, but the higher self of someone who is currently incarnated on the planet. In other words, someone I know - can we ask their higher-self questions? Is that possible? Or inappropriate?

There has to be a connection of some sort.

Sure, someone we know.

I could ask if I can bring them forward. (A pause) "For medical reasons, (they're telling me) Yes."

But not for the "Rich Martini show?"

"Yes, but within reason – they'll give us the idea to do it or not."

I'm asking because it could be helpful to people, could be a health issue. Like asking "How can we help you recover from the illness you have, whether in real time, with us, or by way of information?"

Hang on... (Jennifer listens). It's the same with me getting something physically; "As long as there is a connection." It's what I do... they're showing me "that's a possibility."

By me asking questions...

As long as they are open to it... hold on. "You have to ask permission." I'm asking, "Can we do that, speak to their

higher self about an illness?" and they're saying, "No, you have to ask permission."

Some things are not permissible to pass along, as it would interrupt or disrupt their path?

I always ask for permission when it comes to passing along information about someone's health. Just because they say it is, doesn't mean I should pass it along. For example, I had a friend's relative in a coma, this person told me details about everyone in the room. I asked if he was going to make it, and he said "My spirit is fighting but my body might not allow me to come back in." So I told them that.

I'll ask the person in a coma to give me a visual of "where you are when you're not struggling." And they'll say, "I'm in a forest, near a waterfall," and then the family can always think of them when they see that.

Luana, I need your help bringing someone forth. Both you and my mom knew her.

They're showing me the fish Dory.

Well yes, that's her name; Doreen. (ding!)

She's already here. She's fixing your hair.

She was close to my brother.

> (Note: Doreen Tracy, one of the original Disney Mouseketeers.)

Did she have breast cancer?

The adorable former Mouseketeer Doreen Tracy

Yes. (Ding!) She passed two or three weeks ago, has a son.

He's tall.

Doreen, tell Jennifer about the woman who gave you some money, this young girl you helped...

I saw Monte Carlo... when this girl was younger, her parents weren't around so Doreen kind of took her in.

(Ding!) Can you show Jennifer what your occupation was?

Somewhere in California, I'm getting... like an agency...

> (Note: That's accurate, she worked as an agent and as a secretary at Warner Brother's music.)

She was part of a troupe of performers... that's when Doreen helped this young girl who later helped her.

And then I get troops. Did she perform for the troops?

I don't know.

(Note: Something I was not aware of; I found online that she had toured extensively in Vietnam. *Ding!*) [16]

She was a performer.

On TV?

Yes... associated with a group...

Disney? Oh my god.

Yes, she was a Mouseketeer. She also worked at Warner Records, worked with Frank Zappa and others... a generous soul. Anything you want to pass along to my brother?

She says that "He sees her. She said that everything's gonna be okay."

He told me he had a dream about her before her death.

They were holding hands, there was a flower involved, like he gave her a flower. She showed me they were very happy; I don't know if there was a truck or a barn or something in the country.

(Note: My brother says this is accurate.)

Any advice for my brother?

---

[16] "Doreen Tracy ...toured Vietnam with the USO. Trading her formerly demur Mouseketeer sweater & ears for a skin-tight t-shirt, white go-go boots and mini-skirt, Tracey was choppering from base to base as she entertains the troops. Performing covers of then-popular 1960s songs like "Hold On, I'm Coming" and "We've Gotta Get Out of This Place" with her band, Doreen and the Invaders." https://www.huffingtonpost.com/entry/looking-back-at-the-colorful-show-business-career-of_us_5a5d36aae4b01ccdd48b5ef6

He's right about already seeing her in person, and to not discount that. Bill Paxton just came up to my ear.

What do you want to say buddy?

Bill says "Tell Rich that I'm working with him. Finally."

Okay guys, thank you. Nice chatting with you. Thanks Doreen. Thanks class.

P. R. NELSON PART II

"Don't lose the attachment."

Luana with her pal Michael Gough

This photo above was *kismet*.[17] Luana and I were backstage at Michael "Mick" Gough's Broadway play "Breaking the Code." We asked to see him, but no one gave him the message. So we wandered backstage, and while walking across the pitch-black stage, Luana bumped into him in the dark. Pitch black and he and Luana found each other. I took this photo moments later.

---

[17] Arabic word for "Fate"

They had been friends since they both appeared on Broadway when Luana was a teen (with Rex Harrison in "Der Luberlu" directed by Peter Brooks) Mick and Luana remained the best of pals over the decades.

Seven years after her passing, I was in Tibet camped in a tent on the side of Mt. Kailash. I heard Mick's voice, clear as a bell in my tent saying "Richard, I think what you're doing is fantastic!" I was startled – I had no idea if he was alive or dead, but clearly it was his voice.

I said in my head "Mick? Is that you? Are you dead?" And he said, "No darling, occasionally I take trips with Luana around the universe and I just stopped by to say that what you're doing is simply marvelous." I had the impression that our friend Luana was hovering some distance away as to not interfere.

When I finished the journey around Kailash, I found an internet cafe in Darchen, a small village at the foot of the sacred mountain. I emailed Mick's wife Henrietta... "How is Mick? Is he okay?" The email I got back from her was "Oh, he's fine. He's napping right now." I couldn't figure out how to write what had happened in an email. It took me a year to get him on the phone so I could pass it to him directly. I was in transit in Heathrow when I rang him up.

I told him the story, and asked "Have you ever had a dream where you were traveling around outer space with Luana?" And he said, "No darling, but it sounds absolutely fantastic!" After Luana passed, I had made a point of visiting him and his lovely wife Henrietta and scattered some of Luana's ashes around the bench in the back of their home that overlooked the English countryside. I like to think that he's continuing his adventures with Luana, as he's no longer on the planet.

Something I'll have to explore in a future session with Jennifer. But this photograph reminds me that we "never lose the connection that is between us."

*****

Rich: We were going to talk about healing... so Luana, as we all know, I've been in your classroom and I've talked to your teacher in your class about the healing process... I've asked about the healing process which includes altering the future – there is no such thing as healing unless there's illness?

Jennifer: Correct. Morton just arrived.

Okay, Michael Newton – Morton - we were now going to address the topic of healing individuals here on the planet.

He's showing me so many...

Including how to heal people who may not want to be healed so they can learn that energetic lesson.

I was just shown something that actually hurts. I was shown my dad. That if he would have lived longer we wouldn't have been able to work together with him the way we are working together now. I wouldn't be able to learn from him on the other side. Because it's a different learning when it's coming from him on the other side.

Are you saying it's impossible to alter others' paths without their help?

No. They just showed me a quick preview of when my dad, when he passed... Now they're trying to make me laugh...

showing me the baby Jesus, which was my nickname for him (As in "He could "do no wrong."") He was an only child, perfect in everyone's eyes... He's showing me that, yeah, the power of prayer, the power of that frequency is the power to heal.

The power of prayer is the power of that frequency to heal?

"However that looks; to the gods, goddesses... you have to call on it from all lifetimes."

For example, if you were going to pray for some individual we perceive as ill, unhappy - how would we call upon the healing light of the universe in order to assist this person we think needs help?

"We have to change the way our hearts view him or her in order to help them."

So the first order of business is we alter our perception of reality as to who we think that person is?

"Correct. We make him or her just a human being."

Think of him or her as a person with a soul. Then how do we call upon the healing light of the universe to help?

It's important that you have to believe in the power of prayer, and I'm seeing as an example, Dwayne Johnson's avatar in the film "Jumanji" – in truth we are all much bigger elsewhere. And we can send that frequency from all parts of it to the person in need of healing. We can call upon the angels.

So if you're going to ask for the healing light, shift your perception of that person, then connect yourself to your higher consciousness?

That's key. Take a "bad person" for example; it's the attachment we have of him as a temporary being. We have to lose the attachment to who they are in order to give the medicine to them. We don't know what they're like elsewhere.

So when we unlock or open our hearts and connect to our higher consciousness?

They showed me... if I'm giving medicine for this place or person, but I detach from that, open my heart - then I can give medicine through prayer. And whatever I do in this process, it becomes medicine for him or her everywhere.

There are the two thirds of his higher energy we can access... (seeing her wince) What's the matter?

Ow, this hurts. It's really weird.

Are you getting some kind of download? Or is someone disagreeing with this assessment?

Hold on. Wow. (Jennifer laughs) They're saying you don't have to do a detachment, that is a metaphor – it's (just) to realize there's so much more.

Who disagreed with you?

My dad.

So Jim you put a pain in your daughter's head to get her attention?

He didn't do it, it's the frequency of not getting it right. That really hurt by the way – normally it's a high pitch, they put a high-pitched pain on my side... Our friend Prince just showed up to weigh in on this; showed me the film "Coco" and said, "Don't lose the attachment."

Because in his case, Prince's music is everywhere and people access him that way... it's not about our detaching ourselves from someone else, or about an attachment, they want us to know that there's so much more, infinitely more. Nobody is really aware of that, because they're looking at just this life.

To recap; it's a bit like the Tibetan meditation called Tonglen which means "Give and take." You picture your loved one in a happy state, then imagine their illness as a color or smoke, pull it out of them and into you and then to ask the healing light of the universe to transform that into a healing energy before you breathe the healed energy back into them. Something like that?

The whole class is behind you on that... but your heart has to be clearly immersed without the attachment to the outcome. Meaning, even if someone dies here...

They don't die over there.

Hang on. "Even though you might die here, it doesn't mean it didn't help them elsewhere – they might die here, but their energy might be rebuilt (healed) elsewhere."

They may not be healed here, but they are healed on some level somewhere else?

Luana is saying "yes" and showing me my muscles – we don't know how powerful we are, because we don't allow

ourselves to realize how strong we are. **Bill Paxton showed up.**

So Billy – you appeared in Jennifer's consciousness – as the film she just saw "Call Me By Your Name" is dedicated to you... your agent's husband produced the movie, and Bill had gone to visit the set in Italy, and the director decided to dedicate the film to him.

He's showing me the guy, the guy that the boy fell in love with...

Armie Hammer.

He had a connection in helping with his character –

Ok.

But it was unanimous that they dedicate the film to him.

What else, Billy?

He's showing me the anniversary of his passing is coming around. I don't remember.

It's coming up, yeah, February (this is January.)

He just showed me the 14th or 24th of Feb.

(He passed on the 25th) You want me to post anything?

His voice is so great. Hang on. **"That they're working really hard over there. They're in charge of the coincidences of everything happened here – they're the master minds of that."** Why did he show me the film "Avatar?"

He knows the director.

Right. He's making you meet him. And then you'll know. That will be interesting.

Do you have any message for Jim Cameron?

There's a dream he had in November about Bill. They played football – he showed me a movie with a football, something to do with that sport?

Does Jim remember the dream?

It will be "foggy," he says.

Is there anyone that you know Billy that would help Jim know it's you?

It felt like Jim mentored someone close to him, who was like a son to him, who passed away, feels like cancer... I got something way long ago – 1989.

That could be very specific – someone Jim knew, felt like a son, died of a cancer in 1989, Bill brought that up so that Jim would know it's Bill reaching out to him?

"Yes."

Anyone in our group who wants to speak up?

Your mom.

Hi mom. Anything my mom wants to tell my brothers?

"Love. Know that they're loved. They don't always feel that way. You are loved, you can't feel that way about yourself but know you are loved." She's showed me like a shooting star, tons of pink light, it's a loving color.

"Love yourself because..."

"You'll be able to feel love. If you don't recognize what it feels like you can't know it." Your mom is a calming influence. She says, "Thank you."

For what?

"For opening up your mind. Your heart has always been open but opening up your mind..." – the whole class... it's like they're giving you a standing ovation.

Take a look at Mom. How old does she appear you?

I want to say 89. That's what comes up.

That's correct. (Ding!)

She was 89, she says. Bright eyes, same as your son, same kind of intensity, not color... – did she work in the garden a lot?

In her youth. I once asked her to describe heaven and she described living in a "comfy home with a garden."

She's making everything grow.

Anyone else in our class? How about Prince? People were posting videos of him playing "Auld Lange Syne" at a New Year's eve party.

He's really busy... He's showing me Switzerland, but I feel like it's a metaphor for him being everywhere.

Like a neutral country?

A neutral state of being. But he's currently helping people cross over.

I'm sure that's fun for people crossing over the Flipside. "Oh my god, it's Prince!"

Purple Rain!

*****

This podcast from summer 2021:

Speaking of Janis

Monterey Pop festival - 1967

This is from a recent podcast where Janis Joplin stopped by.

Rich: So Luana... Who wants to speak with us?

Jennifer: What was the last question you were asked on Quora?

(Note: Quora.com is a website where people ask questions about the afterlife in my forum "Hacking the Afterlife.")

I was asked about why we don't interview "so and so." Luana, do you have someone on your list related to that question?

She says, "Yes."

As we were just discussing, it helps for Jennifer to have a name. Her first name is "Janice."

(Note: I said it like I would say the name of someone named *Janice*. Not even a leading tone from my voice.)

Janice? Okay is she a musician?

Yes, she is.

I just got a visual of like the Mamas and Papas, but I don't know who it is.

Very close, that gave me a chill. This person performed with the Mamas and Papas at the Monterey pop festival that Luana attended.

(Jennifer aside) Just for the audience, if someone asked me a song from the Mamas and Papas, I wouldn't know one.

It's not in your reference. It's also a point that we've made before; (the image you saw) it's in reference to my awareness of it and in my documentary "Hacking the Afterlife." There is a section about the Monterey pop festival. This musician was at that festival (but was not mentioned in the film.)

I feel like she attended it three times...

There were a few days and they had to perform a couple of times, but she may be referring to some of the other festivals she performed at. Let's just focus on this musician named Janice. I want to ask you some questions about your journey.

She's smoking a cigarette sitting down wearing a velvet dress feels like velvet it's probably the time period that I'm being shown… and I almost feel like somebody's there wearing a hat.

That was her signature style you just described. Many in the audience know who we're talking about, but Jennifer does not which is fine. Janice, I would like to ask some questions about your journey but first of all let's skip down to the most important question; a friend of mine is making a film about you. Is anything you want to say about that?

Did she do a lot of drugs too? I'm getting that sometimes she did.

That is correct.

Also, is there a question about how she died? I'm seeing that there could be multiple reasons. It feels like it's related to drugs. That's what she said. I just asked her. (Jennifer aside) I'm sorry I'm like doing sidebars while you're talking. I asked her "Please how'd you die?"

She says, "Lots of drugs and alcohol…" She said, "That wasn't what killed me though…" I don't know if it was a blood clot or an aneurysm.

Okay, very interesting to ask that question because people talk about her in reference to a particular drug but that's not what's important because we're talking to this person now.

It feels more like heroin.

That's exactly the drug people talk about in reference to her. I was just reading in your bio…

She just showed me Amy Winehouse, so something similar?

Yes, very similar. It's actually the same age Amy died, at 27.

(Jennifer aside) That's too bad.

Yes, it is sad but it's this idea of we're talking to somebody who still exists, so I just want to repeat we're not talking to a dead singer.

Right.

She was a singer.

She has a raspy voice too.

Yes, correct – she had a very raspy voice. Are you sure you don't know who this person is?

(Jennifer shrugs) I have no f*cking idea!

Okay, I just want to keep saying that.

I'm trying not to swear…

She was known for her raspy voice, known for her ability to sing, but I just want to ask you some questions...

So she showed me the range of scenes; she showed me her raspy voice and then she hit this high note that just... I have chills... like just whacked it out, like instantly!

Unbelievable. Her range was prolific very good. But you grew up in Texas, and I know that you...

(Joking) I just told her "I'm sorry."

I know that you went out to San Francisco when you were a kid, you hitchhiked out there, but you went back home.

When she was 14?

A little later, but young, like 19. She hitchhiked out to North Beach in San Francisco, was introduced to drugs and eventually became a meth addict. She then moved back to Texas and cleaned herself up.

She says, "Yes."

She met with counselors in Texas who told her "You can be a musician and not get involved with drugs" which of course didn't turn out to be true.

(Jennifer aside) What was interesting is... so when I when I apologized for making fun of where she was from, she said "I got cleaned up." She was saying what you were saying about her going back to Texas to clean up.

Well, Texas was home. She was able to go back home to her mom Dorothy and her dad Seth a Texaco oil man in Port Arthur. But then she recorded at the University of Texas and went back to San Francisco. She joined a band and became world famous.

Why did she show me Slash? Oh okay, she was in a band.

I'm not that familiar with all the members, but they toured quite a bit.

She said it was like "Guns and Roses."

(Note: "Guns and Roses" was obviously many years later, but she's using visual references in Jennifer's mind.)

Well she had a relationship with a guy named country Joe McDonald who had long hair and a headband. I'm sure you Jennifer has no idea who that is, but anybody my age would know. She played at a number of festivals with her band, two of the most famous ones were Monterey Pop and Woodstock.

Did she change her name?

No, but why are you asking?

Because I still have no idea who she is.

Janice... do you want me to tell Jennifer your last name?

Is it Blondie? No, Blondie's still alive. I have no idea.

It begins with the letter J.

Joplin!

I'm sorry for laughing but I love to watch Jennifer discover things on the flipside.

She said her name at the beginning, but then I heard the Mama's and Papa's, so I went in that direction.

(Note: Jennifer likely doesn't recall that we interviewed Mama Cass as well.)

I did say they performed at Monterey. The guy the guy who started the Mamas and Papa's (John Phillips) created the Monterey pop film festival with a music producer (Lou Adler)

(Note: In the film "Hacking the Afterlife" there's a discussion of why Luana and her pals went to the festival together.)

Oh my god, now it's rushing back. Janis Joplin!

That's great but people tuning in to our podcast think we're making it up anyway so it doesn't matter it's fine.

If the audience could see our text messages before the show... "Dude, what time are you available? Will I see you?"

Well, yesterday talking to this woman on Quora, I said I might want to talk to Janis because of my friend is making a movie about her and I wanted to know what she thinks about that. Is that a good idea?

She says, "Yes. Anything, as long as I'm center stage... and focus on the happy parts."

He found an actress and showed me a clip of her performing. I asked "Where'd you find this footage of Janis?" He was like, "No, that's our actress." It was like she channeled her. Let me ask; have you come back to the planet, or are you thinking about it?

It was really cool what she showed me. She showed me like two or three versions of her coming back. She says, "I was way too big of a spirit to return as one person - I just kind of exploded at 27."

I saw a clip of you in a documentary about Clive Davis.

She said, "By the way, she's waiting for her soul group to get their asses back home so she can come back with them."

(Note: People report that we all have "groups" that we tend to incarnate with, or wait on until everyone gets back home before planning their next adventure.)

For people not familiar with the concept, if you want to figure out who our soul group is look around and see who feels like you've known them forever. Janis, when you got to the flipside, who was there to greet you?

I feel like it was a little brother... that might have been... hold on. Oh. She's showing me that she was pregnant

once... or she had a miscarriage. When she was younger... it feels like when she was 18.

She did have a guy that she was engaged to marry but didn't marry him was that was that the father or

Feels like it.

(Note: I don't know Peter de Blanc, and this may or may not be accurate. Don't mean to tread on memories of this era, but sometimes we hear things that right on the money.)

I read in your bio that Bessie Smith, Ma Rainey and Lead Belly were all huge influences on your career. Have you talked to them since crossing over?

She said, "They were right there to grab her. They just went "foop" (pulling gesture.)

What was that like?

She said "Amazing." God, she's so funny... just "Amazing balls!"

(Note: While "Amazeballs" is a colloquial expression of late, people on the flipside use whatever words they've heard since crossing. Jennifer says "amazing" as it's not her term.)

Cool.

She's um... kind of laughing. She says, "You kind of never grow up here (on the flipside). We learn a lot, (but) we don't really grow up. She's saying, "Like her same essence is just like when she left!" That's what I'm feeling right now.

(Note: Someone asked, "I thought when we crossed over, we became wise from all of our previous lifetimes?" That may be the case, but Jennifer is reporting verbatim what she's hearing. Based on her reply, I ask the following.)

Can you recall your any previous lifetimes? Is that something that's been shown to you or that you've been able to access?

She says, "Yeah." Hold on… (to Janis) What century? She said, "She was a courtesan… like in the 16th century. So that's where she learned music apparently." She says, "She used to like be a servant…" and it's interesting, as she says, "She brought her interests forward, and it was like it didn't take her a long time to figure out who she was, but it took her a long time to figure out what she liked or what she wanted in her life."

Clive Davis told a story in his documentary when he signed you at the Monterey Pop festival what's your memory of that?

She's showing me just all this excitement… (at being signed by him) but she didn't want anybody to own her, so it was kind of like a little battle, it feels like.

Fascinating, as he was a straight-laced Harvard businessman and attorney.

She said, "She fully nailed down what she wanted." She says, "She had no hesitation to tell this person what she wanted. She was not going to be subservient to some label or whatever." That's the feeling I'm getting from her.

Anything you want to say to Clive Davis?

She says, "Thank you." She's like a little bit emotional about it. She says, "She feels like she let him down by leaving so soon." She says, "You know, she's eternally grateful." Which has a whole different meaning when they say it from there. She says, "Eternally gratefully that they found each other."

Have you kept an eye on him?

She says, "It's a full team up here keeping an eye on him."

Quite a few of the artists we've spoken to were part of his world. Aretha, Whitney. Are you singing are you performing with anybody on the Flipside, or how does that work?

She says, "We're making new chords like new frequencies. We're trying to invent different versions. She's showing me these different decades, the 60s, 70s, 80s, 90s, 2020s. "That's what we're into. Different frequencies within it, like a different tone. So, if you take like disco or whatever and you just change it a little bit… it's new again."

Do you mean like strumming a chord on a guitar? Making new versions of that sound?

She says, "Yes, but it's not a guitar. It's a different type of instrument that produces similar sounds." She wants me to say this, "Your knowledge, everybody uses knowledge to "Go to Mars" or whatever and they're just laughing over there about it.

And it's like everybody over here is in a race to invent an instrument, something that sounds way more spectacular than the last version." She says, "So it's like you're putting all those musical minds together and you say "Well what's a sound that we can create to do that? Who's good at that? And all these musicians come forward, and you look around at the crowd, and it's everyone, from the guy from Cars (Ric Ocasek) and then Eddie…

Do you mean Eddie Van Halen, one of the greatest guitarists?

(Jennifer laughs). Eddie says, "He's like number one even up there." And she says, "I'm f*cking number one and it's like he's still giving the music away!"

So, are all these musicians on this level?

She says, "There's no hierarchy and you meet some great musician, like Beethoven. It doesn't matter (who) and now you say, "Hey listen to this!" And then they participate… (Jennifer aside) I just asked, "Can you touch someone and get all their information?" and she said, "Yeah."

She says, "But you can't really tell if you already knew that (information) from before or wherever. She says, it's just different but way cooler than that, because you're mind reading as well."

What are you doing over there Janis besides creating music?

She said, "What do you think I'm f*cking doing? Philanthropy? No, I'm making excellent music excellently." She says, "I'm doing all of it." She said it again, "All of it."

Can you still create a taste? Like Southern Comfort?

She said, "I'm making it better, okay?" And she just showed me Ryan Reynolds, is he making some kind of alcohol? Some kind of whiskey? She says she's helping him.

Okay, that's funny. I think he has a gin. So, you have a Janis Southern Comfort?

She says, "Something like that. It's like people come by for a visit you and they say, "Can I get a sip of that?" And then you present it to them. She says, "You can do that from anywhere, it's like it's on tap it's not that they need her to pour it."

But do people get drunk? That would be physically hard to do.

She says, "You can make an imitation of that, yes, because you can remember the times you were drunk. But then you're like the only person doing that, like no one else is doing it but you are. No one does that because it doesn't really work."

She says, "We treat ourselves (by) coming back to earth to do that again right? In other words, that's a reason you might come back." She says, "Like I miss being drunk, so I think I'll come back!"

Anything I should pass along to the folks making a film about your life?

She says, "Her relationship with her mother, how she didn't get along until later, but it all worked out. Like she ended up getting signed, she ended up coming back home to get treatment." She says, "So even the most difficult of relationships might not be bad when everything works out despite the way it ends."

What was it like to see your mom Dorothy when she finally came over? (Passed in 1998)

She says, "I couldn't wait to get her and then I told her she was going to rehab."

Rehab in heaven?

She says, "I told her it would cost a gazillion dollars to send her there." (Laughs)

Anything you want to say to your fans because no one's going to believe we're talking to you?

She's saying, "Keep listening. Make your own music. Take certain sounds from different eras or different albums or records or whatever you want and make your own music." She just showed me an image of Dua Lipa, how she's taking all the like frequencies of everything and mixing it." She says, "The combination of a lot of artists are much better than just one. No one works alone (because) it's challenging to work alone."

Have you seen Amy Winehouse?

She's like, "Seen her? I _was_ Amy."

Emotionally anyway.

She says, "Yeah, Amy was greeted with applause." She said "Everyone was applauding her when she came (home). They wanted her to know that she fulfilled her mission." (Jennifer aside) Wow.

That's brilliant. Have you seen Jimi over there?

She says, "Yes, Jimi's everywhere. He's family! She says, "He plays so many roles – he was a guitar player over there… (Over here) and now he plays every single part!" (Jennifer aside) It's like he's playing different roles for different people coming to the flipside.

She's showing me this other thing. Like they take away your awareness of something until they want you to see it. Like you're looking for your keys, they'll take your awareness from the keys and then all of a sudden you find them. They don't move them, but they shift your awareness away from seeing them. So I just told Janis thanks, because she's so great to show up and give us so much information.

Thank you, Janis!

CHAPTER THIRTEEN: MUSICAL CONSCIOUSNESS

A conversation with my concert pianist mom.

Another day, another concerto.

Jennifer and I are meeting for our usual chat. Then;

Rich: Anybody else want to come forward?

Jennifer: Your mom.

My mother Anthy. Are you playing the piano over there?

> (Note: Mom played nearly every day of her life.)

Mmhm... She's playing piano for your uncle there.

> (Note: Earlier in this conversation, we talked about my uncle Arigo "Rig" Martini who once purchased an entire music store for my mother, and then a concert grand piano to play at their estate in Ohio.)

Mom, tell me about playing the piano over there. How do you create that?

"It's the frequency, through mathematical equations. It's not nearly as fun to play here (as it is over there back on earth), but you can do it by thinking of a frequency."

By doing so, can you create a piano? All 88 keys?

"Yes."

Let me ask, what piano do you choose to create? Is it a concert grand or a spinet? Is it short or long?

First I saw an etheric image of a piano with lots of layers, and then I got shown an antique piano.

One of mom's pianos lives in a music room at Lake Forest College.

Is the piano you are playing a piano that you knew during your lifetime?

"Yes. Her first piano... the one she knew as a child."

There was a famous Cuban piano teacher who taught you how to play in college. Have you seen him?

"Yes." She's saying, "In her life music was everything." She says, "It affected all of her connections."

And we've heard that music is an amplification system to talk to the flipside, is that right?

"Yes. It's a higher frequency."

Let me ask you an off the wall question. Your father was in the office of Naval Intelligence during World War II. Was your father the source of my investigating Amelia's Earhart's story all these years, even though he passed a month after I was born?[18]

"Yes." There's someone else with your grandfather.

His wife Mimi, I imagine. I've dreamt about visiting them at their home in Chicago – a home I was never in, but when I described the place to my brother, he said "that was their home over Lincoln Park."

Edward A Hayes. Mimi Hayes, Louise Heibenstreit

He's showing me Amelia.

---

[18] Navy Commander Edward A Hayes. Assistant Secretary of the Navy to Frank Knox 1940-44. During the period when the US found Earhart's plane on Saipan, he was in "CinqPaq" the naval headquarters in the Pacific with Admiral Nimitz, who famously told investigator Fred Goerner "You're on the right track with regard to Earhart being on Saipan. Keep looking."

Okay, that makes sense. I imagine this setting is getting crowded with all these people.

They tell me, "They're learning over there."

Learning what?

(Jennifer listens) "Learning the different waves of energy to go through... (to navigate) through different dimensions, to make the energies get through to the energy to manifest here."

Okay. So you strengthen the energy to make it manifest here?

They're showing me that by coming together with a group, like family members -- they are able to sustain the connection way longer than they normally would.

So the group helps amplify the signal?

Yes. It's like a cellphone tower.

It's like when my friend Iris did a deep hypnosis session and saw herself between lives in a classroom that was learning how to lift giant objects, like slabs of rock. There were 28 students and she said "This is a class in learning to share energy as a group. It's not a class in how to lift rocks, but how to get the group to lift the rock together."

"Yes, the collective is always stronger than the individual."

So when we pray, and ask for guidance, we should ask everyone to show up?

"Yes."

Hmm. (Joking) What's an app I can use to do that?

They showed me "ancestry.com" to find names. That's how I connect – I need to get their name to get a hold of the person.

It makes sense; a person's name is a place holder of their energy; if you're searching for someone you need a name.

Having the name makes me feel more secure as well.

Like we asked Morton, "Should we say the name of the person we want to speak with aloud?" He said, "It doesn't matter."

You can think of colors as well. Like, "What's the first color you associate with that person?" And when you get that color, you draw upon that color and bring it in to you.

What about this thing of people believing they can manifest wealth through intention or prayer?

That means you have to give it away in order for it to be replaced. The more positive energy you give away, the more it returns to you.

I'm including the idea that you may have a spiritual path that may not include gaining wealth in this lifetime, so it would be worthless to try to attract money if it's not part of the path that you signed up for.

My dad Jim showed up. He's showing me how these things aren't brought to us through intent – we may have signed up to learn different lessons. Where you put your intentions, it results in things that come to you.

Once you start to redefine what money or wealth is – wealth may come in terms of health or some other way... Once you redefine what wealth really is - then whatever comes to you should come to you.

They're giving you standing ovation for that observation.

Rich: Like I asked your dad, Jim, about how people manifest "making a drink" with friends over there. They have to agree on the bar as well as the bartender.

Jennifer: They made a joke... "It's like a "party line" (over here) **A frequency** (signal) **goes out like "It's a party!"**

A 1-800 party line on the flipside. I think it's funny to hear about people manifesting objects, homes, classes, even cigars.

They don't need to.

But they do because it's fun. Am I right that some people smoke all the time over there?

"Yes."

But it's unusual to see. Ghosts smoking.

They know the frequency of it.

Even if they died of lung cancer they can continue smoking, having fun with the manifestation of it.

"Yeah."

I was thinking that by examining this stuff as we do, we can change our future by examining the past.

Morton just said, "It works."

We alter our past when we examine previous lives. Not "changing the fabric of time" but by seeing we chose those lifetimes to learn lessons, we then alter our memory of having suffered in a previous lifetime. It's not suffering if it's a lesson we chose to learn; it's learning. By changing our "past" be accessing it, understanding it, we change our present and our future.

"Yes." I just got the chills. Wow.

If you can observe your lifetime in the past, whatever it was, and see that it was part of your blueprint, creating who you are - you can see why it was completely necessary to go through whatever it is we've gone through.

"And see the love."

By seeing the love that existed in that lifetime, you've now altered that past. So this research alters your past, it affects your present and can change your future.

"It alters your frequency. It makes it lighter."

So you're not carrying that stress.

*****

Sitting by the piano waiting for mom to play.

BROTHERS FROM ANOTHER PLANET

Archangel with pals, Tiziano Vecellio

I was having lunch with a couple of my oldest friends in LA, and they were giving me the raised eyebrows about this research. I just have to get used to it – part of the reason is that they've known me for decades as a funny, goofy film guy. But they relate to this research as if it either belongs in Mad Magazine or from a pulpit somewhere. *No one wants to talk about death until they have to.*

I understand that. But when you conclude that death is an illusion – not from a philosophical religious point of view – but a literal, *"Hey! This thing that we're doing here on the planet is a stage play! There's nothing to fear because "everyone gets out alive!"* It's hard to not repeat it to your friends, but equally hard to have your friends not run from the room.

Charles Grodin for example, one of the most loyal friends I've ever known, literally would bolt from the room the moment someone asked me, "So what are you up to these days?" *Not everyone wants to hear or talk about the thing they fear the most.* I don't blame him – but there are so many of his friends that I'm talking to, it's hard not to share what I'm hearing.

Another conversation with Jennifer Shaffer.

Rich: It's funny, in our last class, we talked about your guide's "wings." He said his name was Michael, but to avoid any connotation of that famous Archangel, I'm calling him Mike the Angel. I asked him about the composition of his wings and you said, "It's composed of light."

Jennifer: "Layers and layers of light... frequencies."

But what's odd is that I know I filmed the conversation about his wings, but it's disappeared from the tape. I can't find it.

We'll ask about it again.

I remember him saying he's 16 feet tall. But perhaps he doesn't want us to talk about his wings?

He's pointing out that, "It's more comfortable for him to appear with wings... and also for the people he appears to; that's their comfort zone." He doesn't want to take that away from them. -- But you can talk about it.

I think I understand. Wings are a mental construct and as a metaphor they represent something greater than we can imagine... but they aren't related to religion or hierarchy, but related to something else.

(Jennifer taps her nose.) "For light speed."

For moving and flying?

"Yes."

People talk about non-reincarnating entities. I've heard people use that term to describe so called "angels."

He showed me like (being able to move to) other galaxies.

Do you incarnate on other planets?

He said "No." He showed me the different galaxies and said, "What we do is bring in the energies from all the different realms..." - he showed me a number of planets – "...from the constellations." He brings that energy because if you believe it then you'll feel it.

We were talking about grief being a frequency or a sound. What does that mean?

I saw a ricochet.

Do we generate that or are we tapping into it?

We generate it and also are tapping into it.

Like a water wave that goes out and comes back?

"Yes." They just showed me that we send (the feeling) out, then it comes back and it gets bigger and bigger, that's the ricochet effect. I was thinking it just ricochets, (like a bullet) but they're showing me it bounces back, comes back to us (like a loop). "What you put out comes back tenfold." It's something I deal with in my work, I deal with a lot of grief on a daily basis. I am fortunate in my work to help people, but I deal with a lot of grief and sadness.

So one way of mitigating the wall of grief it to set it aside when speaking to people on the other side. To acknowledge the grief, "Hello grief" and then set it aside like a suitcase. "I know where you are; I know how to tap into you but I'm going to put it down next to me while I examine something or talk to my loved one."

(Jennifer taps her nose.) "Detach." They're showing me that by knowing your own grief... (aside) Like, I know what my grief is... "By knowing your own grief, you know the frequency of it." Like I associate grief with my dad's passing... (Pause) Oh, when I said that, my dad said, "No! *Happiness!*" He's saying, "You should associate grief with happiness; the memory of your loved one (him) comes with happiness, *not sadness.*"

So if you associate grief with happy memories; or nostalgia, then you can alter that experience of sadness?

Instead of associating my dad with grief, he's like... showing me how to flip it.

Turn grief into nostalgia; that's a concept that contains both sadness and happiness.

It's like you said, "Put grief in a suitcase. I know you're there. I know you exist." Last year, after my dad's passing, I was one sick doctor. People came to see me to help them with their grief, it was like going to a doctor with a snotty nose when you're trying to get better. It really took me forever to get into my office, as it was challenging – but the more I do this work, the stronger I get.

I suggest people take out a photo of their loved one, meditate on it, and think of your loved one in present tense.

They just said, "Don't use meditation as the word." I just heard a collective voice.

Ha. I get it; people associate meditation with yoga, and yoga with exercise and no one wants to have to work for it. I'm suggesting trying to set aside the emotions of the memory, so when you address this person on the flipside, you do it without the emotional baggage; so you can hear them.

Baggage. That's funny. "Set the baggage aside."

A question for Mike the Angel; can you appear on anyone's council?

"Yes." He says he can be a part of anybody's council. He's showing me the frequency; your heart can access him at the same time. That frequency... can connect to an "angel with wings."

He told us he has different responsibilities on different councils.

He's referring to the higher consciousnesses.

Okay, he before that his main role was to help people "not stop." He's embodying the courage to go forward.

"To go inside."

You help drive people to the inside?

"It's a healing vehicle. It's a..."

Merkabah?

352

"Yes." That's what I saw.

> (Note: Merkabah is a word used in new age circles, I had never heard it before, but it came up in a hypnosis session. A term used in ancient religions, including Judaism, referring to a "vehicle of enlightenment." Not sure why it popped into my head.)

Jennifer: I asked him (Michael) "Do you really exist?" I can't help myself but to ask. He said "No, I don't exist without a belief in your heart." That's what makes him what he is and makes him be able to match your frequency. To that end, he just showed me Santa and the Tooth Fairy.

Rich: What you're saying is when someone sees you, during a near death event or during a between life hypnosis sessions, they might say, "I'm seeing this angel..." But do they have to believe in you in order to see you?

Jennifer: "They're connecting to their higher self; they're seeing themselves at a higher vibration. That is why they can see me."

*Rich: Okay, but you're making this argument that you don't exist unless we **believe** in you. Which is kind of weird to be making, don't you think?*

He says he exists, but "You have to believe in him, for him to appear."

I see, not believing that I'm seeing an angel would make it so I can't see you. I haven't had a near death experience...

I'm getting that you've had two. Once when you were little, when you weren't breathing, the next was in a car... like through a hallucinogen, something drug related.

> (Note: In high school, I was stupid enough to accept a pill from a stranger at a party who called it "Angel Dust." (*IRONY?*) Turned out it was PCP, a horse tranquilizer. I had no idea – but was driving the car with all my friends in it, and suddenly saw *two* of everything. I was smart enough to pull over and say "I can't drive. Someone else has to." I was sick out the window. Thankfully, my pal *(guardian angel?)* Mark Caplis washed the car, dropped me at my home, and I spent the night under a tree in the front yard. Now that I'm recalling it – I am aware that *someone* visited me during that event. Maybe a guide or angel. But I had forgotten this event until she mentioned it.)

But if I don't believe I could see you, do I see you as this sixteen-foot-tall dude with wings? You're saying I wouldn't know who you were because I'm not tuned in?

"You would recognize me because of all your past lives. Because you've run into me in some form or other during them." He's saying that "You would recognize his energy." He's showing me a fresco.

Have you ever shown up on this planet? Have you ever incarnated here?

"No."

Have you incarnated on any planet?

"Yes, but not here." He just *shot* me to a different planet – even when he's showing me, I get this enormous being. I can feel being next to him in my mind, feeling his feathers, knowing his feathers are a frequency but I can feel them.

> (Note: In the interview with Pete Smith, current President of the Newton Institute, over 35% of their clients recall lifetimes off planet.[19])

Rich: What's it feel like when you're with Mike the Angel?

I feel (as if) there's something that's both comfort and peace rolled into one.

Like unconditional love?

"Yeah."

All right class. We talked to our angel friend, talked to Luana, we talked to Tim's mom, we talked to Billy...

Bill says, "But I was here first."

---

[19] His interview in in my book "It's a Wonderful Afterlife."

What's he want to say?

"Thank you." (Jennifer listens) **For reaching out to his family. They did read your blog post about Bill.**[20]

Did they believe it?

It resonated. They didn't want to believe it, there was resistance there. He says "No, the resistance was grief." They have so much grief... but um... you did help on some level.

I understand it's very stressful that kind of loss, you were their everything.

And then some... and he showed me "and a bucket of coal and a bucket of rocks, too." That's a perfect thing to share with others... that will help them even more.

It will help people here or over there (on the Flipside)?

"Both." That's funny. He said "Rich, you're like a good hooker. Work both sides of the room."

Very funny. I noted in the post; "The only reason we're doing this is because Bill insists we put it out in a raw form."

"Within reason. But there's no boundaries," he said, "because by not having boundaries you can't limit their thinking."

Well, as an actor and filmmaker you had no boundaries.

"Better than you."

---

[20] http://richmartini.blogspot.com/2018/03/in-memoriam-interview-with-bill-paxton.html

Ha. I agree with that. I finally saw your golf movie "Greatest Game Ever Played."[21]

He made a face; "Well, it's about time."

I didn't get invited to a screening the way you were invited to a screening of "Cannes Man."

"You were out of town," he said.

Hell yes. I am out to lunch.

"Off the planet."

It was well done. Shia LaBeouf was good.

The footage you've put together about talking to him on the Flipside was raw, he (Bill) liked seeing it – he said, "now you have your (own) Bill Paxton movie."

I put together a rough cut of our chatting with him and showed it to a few people. But just as many who saw your golf movie, buddy.

He just made an X at you. Luana said "Happy birthday." I forgot to mention that to you last time we talked.

Luana's birthday is coming up.

Is it May 12th?

Why do I even bother responding? (Laughs) (ding!)

She showed me my daughter. Hers is May 12th as well.

Cool. Anyone else?

---

[21] https://www.imdb.com/title/tt0388980/?ref_=nm_flmg_act_33

Prince. (reacts to a sound) That was a loud guitar.

Tell her what chord that is.

He said, "G." I don't know what a G is.

I do.

He said like "up." *Not H minor... I don't know music... but up to next one. I don't know what that means.*

"A" minor?"

"Yes."

Next?

"Then C, E, then down..."

G, Am, C, E or E minor?

"E minor."

And then back to G? Cool. Oddly enough I was playing something like this on the piano yesterday.

She taps her nose.

You're inspiring musicians?

He says, "You have that frequency," and he showed me purple just coming in.

Thanks Prince. Next time we'll ask you for lyrics.

> (Note: Go ahead musicians; play it. Sounds a bit Prince-like when you do.)

By the way, speaking of musicians, Craig Cole is a guy who played saxophone in our band, he died while I was in Tibet.

He had a stroke?

Could be. He was ill.

Oh, he had diabetes, something that made his coloring felt off, a kidney disease, his coloring was way off had to do with his blood sugars, may have had blood cancer.

That's true. (ding!) I know my wife saw him in Hollywood prior to his passing and she said he was really pale.

His heart just stopped. You had a dream about him.

I did. How do you do that Craig?

He said, "It's an awareness."

Craig, I don't know if you've met Luana before.

A year ago. As a result of one of your books.

Are you playing music with anyone?

Hendrix.

Are you playing with Zappa?

I don't know who that is. He says "Yes, when he crossed over it was him who came to get him when he got out." (Jennifer aside) Did this Zappa fellow die before him?

Yes. So he pulled you out into the flipside?

"Yes." He went *"foom"* like, "come with us!" and they went straight into a concert. He pulled him out, put him straight onto stage, there were thousands of people. And then, when he saw his mom in the front row, he knew he wasn't alive. He said "Wait – my mom shouldn't be here."

Remember the car ride when Harry Dean realized he was in the afterlife? That was his "car ride."

Craig used to play with Frank Zappa that would make sense he would be the one pulling him on stage.

I don't know who that is. Craig says, "Your book is going to be on fire." He showed me flames. He says he didn't believe it when he died, it took him going out there and noticing something different during the event on stage.

Thanks Craig!

*****

I was in Tibet when I got an email from pal and bandmate Bruce Haring entitled "Craig Cole"; I *knew* before opening it he'd died. I wrote his name on a Tibetan prayer flag; am happy to report Craig's flag is flying high over Kailash.[22]

---

[22] Craig Cole in Imminent Disaster. https://youtu.be/mBenjE9BL4c

MUSICAL CONSCIOUSNESS: JOHN, GEORGE, JIMI

"Blue Suede Shoes"

Black and white photo, but they're blue suede shoes.

As mentioned, we normally don't try to "chat" with anyone we don't know. But based on some of the previous sessions, I just thought "What the hell? Why not try?" As we'll hear in this report, there are some things that are true, some things that could be true, and some things that could be someone on the flipside screwing with us.

"Wait, what?"

As I try to note in all of these sessions, I'm asking questions and Jennifer gets an image or a sensation or a sentence that she then translates into an answer. She may be mistranslating what she's seeing (a possibility), the person on the flipside may be sending the wrong photograph to impart how they want to answer the question (also possible) or they may be tailoring the answer to their audience (again, possible.)

In terms of tailoring an answer, I suggest thinking of three people in a room with one medium. One is the daughter of the person on the flipside, one is the spouse and the third is their business partner. In each case, a person asks a question – let's say *"How or what are you doing?"*

The daughter might get an answer steeped in love or a sweet memory, the spouse might get a different more descriptive answer that includes "flying around to the places we used to visit" and the business partner might get an off-color joke.

It could be an answer based on how they "used to feel" or an answer that describes their "memory of how things occurred" – which like *any memory* is subject to all kinds of influences – or they may just be screwing around giving alternate answers at a given moment because they're bored with the questions.

I don't have any doubt that Jennifer is "seeing" or hearing something from spirit – and that it's in a direct reply to my questions – but there are any number of variations that can come into play, including people not knowing the answer but who give one anyway, giving an answer one day and a different one the next, or not liking the question and give an answer that is contrary to what happened.

But that doesn't stop me from asking. What I'm trying to focus on here is that it is possible to converse with anyone we knew or loved. It takes some time and practice and sometimes asking the same question over and over again in different settings, but as you can see; we do get answers.

It's when they repeat their answers over multiple sessions or expand upon them we can gain insight into what their experience might be like "back home." With that in mind, I present you with the chapter where I just "shot arrows into the sky to see where they landed."

Rich: Hi class, how are we doing? Who's here?

Jennifer: A lot. Really interesting.... Keith Richards is still alive, correct? It's someone Keith Richards knows.

Yes. People joke about Keith being still on the planet when so many like him are not. We're going to invite a bunch of friends today.

Well, Paul McCartney showed up in my head. I know he's still alive...

Paul, Keith... hmm. Who else?

John Lennon.

I invited him.

You did? That's so awesome. You didn't tell me that.

No, I did not. This morning I thought, "Hmm, I wonder if it's possible..." and then asked him to join us today.

Luana showed me Keith Richards, and I was like "I know they're all alive" but then I saw Paul and John Lennon.

John, this is Luana, have you guys met before?

"Up there, backstage."

I'm going to ask you some questions John, please don't take anything the wrong way. Are you aware of this class? Has anyone briefed you as to what we're doing?

He wasn't aware of the class, but "Yes, he's been briefed."

Who briefed you?

(Jennifer asks) Who was it? (Pause). So weird. He said, "His wife."

Which one?

(Jennifer aside) I don't know.

Let's ask him. Are you in touch with your first wife, Cynthia?

Jennifer taps her nose with her finger (to signify "that's it.")

I want to ask you both some questions. I'm friends with your son, Julian, who appeared in one of my films. Anything you want to say to him?

"Tell him to stop dragging his feet."

About what?

(Jennifer aside) I don't know – Is he supposed to get married? I'm sorry, I'm just asking him myself... I'm still shocked by seeing John Lennon.

Well, we're going to talk to him as a soul, not as a famous person.

(Jennifer laughs) I know, but you've got to give me a little time to adjust.

Can I ask Cynthia a direct question, John?

Did she die three years after him? Or three years ago?

I think it was three years ago.

> (Note: That's correct. Cynthia Powell Lennon passed away from cancer in 2015)[23]

---

[23] https://www.telegraph.co.uk/news/obituaries/11509668/Cynthia-Lennon-obituary.html

Did she have cancer? It seems like it was up in this area (waves around her chest and throat). I'm hearing a thick, raspy voice. She's very funny.

> (Note: Her voice might not have been raspy at all. But that's what Jennifer is "hearing.")

Who was there to greet you, Cynthia?

Her mom. (Jennifer crosses her fingers.) Hold on. That may have been a joke. *Yes.* It was a joke; they weren't close.

Is that when you realized you crossed over?

"Yes, I realized I must be in hell," she said. (Jennifer laughs.)

So did John come to greet you as well?

"Yes. Two days prior."

What did John look like to you when he showed up and what was your feeling when he showed up?

(Jennifer looks into the distance) Oh, that's so cool. She showed me a memory, it almost feels like high school. I don't know if they knew each other in school?

They did.

It was a memory in front of this brownstone, he was smoking, she had this like... her hair was... (Jennifer lifts her hands up).

Like in the 1950's?

I'm getting... 1956?

(Note: The official record is they met in art school in September 1957).

Kind of when they first met?

"John was way too skinny," she says.

Was he wearing a leather jacket? Mr. Skiffle?

He was "just John." She's showing me that they wrote together... feels like... back then... "It's a circle," he shows me. They were writing together back then and are writing together now. (Jennifer starts to hum the melody for "I want to hold your hand.")

Was that a song written about the two of you?

No. They're both like fighting, laughing about it... hold on a second, I want to ask.

So John...

"You're bossy," says Cynthia... *(referring to me)* **She wants to talk about her son too, so give me a second. (Pause) They're saying "It was like a reverse song; it meant the opposite. That *he* didn't like holding hands, she's teasing him like it was an OCD kind of thing, she's totally teasing him." She's talking about someone named Robert...**

That could be her ex, who just crossed over recently.[24]

Felt like it was his heart. A heart attack. Okay, so they both want to tell Julian "To not to wait any longer."

---

[24] "Cynthia Lennon... In 1970 married an Italian hotelier, Roberto Bassanini, in 1976 an engineer..." (Telegraph, ibid)

He'll understand what that means?

(Jennifer touches her nose.) "Yeah." Feels like it could be a marriage with his work or an actual marriage.

John, who was there to greet you when you crossed over?

This is interesting, first thing I was shown was Jimi Hendrix... was he alive when John died?

No, he died ten years earlier.

(Jennifer aside) I didn't know that.

They were friends. So was Jimi there to greet you John?

"Yeah." I thought he was showing me like a dream he had... like he thought he was in a dream.

It felt like a dream?

Now he's showing me Woodstock.

You crossed over and then you saw Jimi Hendrix?

And Jimi said, "Come up on stage."

So John did you step on stage with him?

Yes. He's showing me the audience. Hold on a second, I just saw something really funny. "It was like a welcome home party," he says, – "Then suddenly everybody in the audience became like little aliens...

(Jennifer aside: "Kind of like the tire scene in Harry Dean Stanton's story") – that was the moment he realized he was in the afterlife, because everyone suddenly appeared

as these little robot girls – just a funny visual, and he's like "Whaaaat?" and that was like "Oh. Welcome home."

What was the song you guys were playing when you crossed over?

He showed me... This doesn't make sense. But I'm seeing shoes. Blue suede shoes?

That makes sense. The Carl Perkins tune.

> (Note: Jimi Hendrix recorded "Blue Suede Shoes" during a show in 1970 in Berkeley, John recorded the song in 1969 with Yoko and the Plastic Ono band.)

They're showing me a back-up band playing, a band that looks like Led Zeppelin, but I know it's not them...

This is a concert you're seeing with other band members?

It feels like 1969.

That makes sense, that was the year of Woodstock.

(Jennifer aside) I didn't know that.

That's why I'm here. So Jimi pulls you on stage, John, you notice the audience is not who you thought they'd be... and then you're feeling was...

"Sudden silence. Crickets..." he was trying to figure out what was going on... because I felt his – he was super high when he was shot...

You mean stoned on grass?

"Yes." He didn't know what was going on, until... yeah... it was when he heard his wife... Yoko. All of sudden he

heard her yelling and it kind of interrupted his homecoming party... he could feel her shouting.

Rich: Was this an exit point for you?

Jennifer: (quickly) "Yes."

> (Note: "Exit points" are term for how people describe key moments in their lives where they have an opportunity to exit. It shows how things are not preplanned, or that the journey is all mapped in advance. They often refer to these "exit points" as something that comes along, and if they feel they've done what they set out to accomplish or have some compelling reason for "returning home" they do so. It's not a pejorative in any way, nor is it meant to diminish a person's loss to the rest of his or her loved ones. It's just a question he could have answered "no" or "I don't know" to... but in this case, his answer came before I could finish the sentence.)

Since then, you've been doing other stuff, correct? What have you been doing, what are you up to?

He showed me channeling into someone else. A musician. Helping musicians.

Other musicians?

Yes, he showed me (a visual of) **the frequency of music – it being in his veins.**

What does that look like?

It looks like a darkish blue (energy), **a metallic blue, it's just a really deep color of blue.**

That's in your etheric veins?

"In your thread of the soul; that's what you're there for."

I've got a couple of questions for John. You told Julian how you might reach out to him.

He just showed me a balloon, something going up into the sky...

I've read that you told Julian if there is an afterlife, you'd reach out to you via this object...

(She laughs.) I'm seeing something from a bird... a feather? I'm seeing a pink feather.

Julian told the story of how his dad had said to him at some point, "If I die, I will try to reach out to you in the form of a feather." When Julian was in Australia on tour, an aboriginal Chief showed up in his hotel and said, "We need your help with getting fresh water to our people." Julian said he'd help in any way he could, and the Chief presented him with a giant ostrich feather. So, Julian created the White Feather Foundation, which helps indigenous people around the world to obtain fresh water, including the Standing Rock tribe in the U.S.

That is so awesome... he was showing me different ways to get to that (image) **and I** (had) **cut it off... he was showing me going up in the sky through an image of a balloon and then a bird...**

How do you reach out to people?

"Through the mind."

The other thing I wanted to ask about was when I was staying at Julian's house and heard a voice wake me up with "Who the fuck are you?" I looked around and saw no one, but then recognized your voice. What was that about? Do you remember this?

"Yeah," he says he does. Hold on. (Pause, listens) He did that so you would tell the story later.

Okay, well I mentioned that story in "Flipside" without using your name, but in the book "It's a Wonderful Afterlife" I did use your name. Any problem with my doing that?

(She shakes her head, no.)

I asked for some other folks to come by today.

I got Prince, but we see him all the time.

Luana, you know who I asked for. There's someone else that I asked to show up today... who was that?

I got Eric Clapton. But he's alive.

Right... but I'm thinking of someone else that John knows.

But what musician is the one whose son died? Who sings the song "Tears in Heaven?"

Oh wow. I forgot. I did ask Conor Clapton to come forward.

You asked for his son to show up?

Yeah, I did the other night and forgot about it. So let's talk to Conor. How are you?

"Awesome," he says.

How old does he appear to you Jennifer?

I feel like he's 18 now.

> (Note: Eric Clapton's son Conor passed away in in 1991. I mentioned him in "Flipside" "Would you know my name, if I saw you in heaven?" but I try to be as accurate as I can in these transcripts. We don't age the same way over there, but it was 27 years earlier than this conversation.)

Conor, who was there to greet you when you crossed over?

I feel like they had a miscarriage before – because he says his sister was there... She was like three years older. She was there to greet him.

But since then, Conor, what have you been up to?

"Playing music."

Have you reincarnated yet, or are you keeping an eye on your mom or dad?

"I have to wait," he says. He has to wait until they come back first.

Are you aware of that song your dad wrote about you?[25]

"The most beautiful song," he says.

I happened to be in the sound stage when the song was recorded. My friend was producing it and I got to hear it just after it was recorded. I saw your dad's handwritten lyrics on

---

[25] "Tears in Heaven" written by Eric Clapton and Will Jennings.

the music stand and have one of the guitar picks with your dad's name on it from that session.

(Jennifer makes a circle with her hand) That's crazy! Another story that occurred so you could tell it later.

That's why I was thinking of you while watching a documentary about your dad. So what do you want to tell your dad? Is it nice over there?

"Yes. I'm fine. I keep an eye on him."

Okay, thanks. I'll try to pass that along to him through a mutual friend. Class, there's someone else I'd like to ask John to bring forward. A band mate of his.

The one with the curly long hair? George.

Yes.

Oh, of course. "Yes, he's here."

George, we have a mutual friend. I remember him telling me that he owned a piano once owned by you...[26]

(Jennifer laughs.) He just showed me the piano not being played because he wouldn't play it.

That's funny. Luana and I were at Russ' house for dinner, I asked if I could play his piano and my friend said, "I listen to music all day long, I'd really prefer it if you didn't."

---

[26] After talking to Russ about this, he says his piano was not owned by George, but the conversation was as depicted about me "not playing it by request."

(Note: Russ tells me I have this wrong; he **did not** own one of George's piano, but owned a large stone Buddha statute of George's. I misheard him when he was talking about the statue, thought he was talking about the piano. Either way George's comment holds true, as my friend Russ requested I *not play it*. I.e.; "Do you take requests?" "Sure." "Can you play "Far far away?"")

They're all laughing over there. George said, "He had 3 pianos."

I have a question on behalf of my brother Jeffrey.

He's showing me they went out for drinks.

Could be, he was dating your sister-in-law, Linda.

Okay, I just got that as you were saying it.

George's wife is Olivia, and her sister Linda was my brother's girlfriend, and he says he played softball with Tom Petty and George. He asked me to ask Tom a question.

"It's about time!" Tom just said.

Do you remember when you played softball with my brother Jeffrey?

Did he break a window?

Could be.

"It was something that he did..." Hold on. No one was paying attention though.

Okay, he says he hit a home run... and nobody saw it? That makes sense.

He's saying, "No one was paying attention but yes, they do remember."

George – let me ask, who was there to greet you when you crossed over?

His animals. I'm seeing a bunch of them, including a little dog and a big one... a Great Dane.

> (Note: George had a number of pets, including cats and dogs. I've can't find any reference to him and a Great Dane, but there is a myriad of reasons why she may have seen a dog he didn't own late in life including a dog from earlier in his life.)

Did that seem odd to you that you were greeted by animals? When did you realize that you were in the afterlife?

He already had visitations before he left... from John... from... some comedians?

He was a big fan of Peter Sellers and the boys in Monty Python.

I'm seeing there are two people from Monty Python that he knew really well.

Well, Eric Idle and Michael Palin were close (and he produced their film "Life of Brian"). Not sure about the others.

One of them died before George?

Yes, Graham Chapman (who died in 1989, George financed the Python film "Life of Brian" in 1978 by mortgaging his house to pay for the budget).

Okay, but I'm seeing that he was in the back part of their group though. (Note: That's correct, the "lesser known one" but beloved just the same). All the memories came up all at once.

George have you met Luana before?

Feels like in a bathroom... It felt like after a concert... because they were laughing and giggling in this smaller place.

Might have been after one of their Hollywood Bowl concerts in the 60's. She told me she and her pals met them at a post-concert party. George wrote a song about a house on Blue Jay Way; "there's a fog upon L.A; up in Blue Jay Way." [27]

John says it coincided with "Lucy In The Sky with Diamonds."

> (Note: Inspired by his son Julian's drawing, "Lucy" was released prior to "Blue Jay Way." "Julian inspired the song with a nursery school drawing he called "Lucy in the sky with diamonds."[28] George lived in the Blue Jay Way house in 67, what's accurate is the two songs "coincided.")

---

[27] "Blue Jay Way" was released in 1967... The song was named after a street in the Hollywood Hills of Los Angeles where Harrison stayed in August 1967. The lyrics document Harrison's wait for music publicist Derek Taylor to find his way to Blue Jay Way through the fog-ridden hills, while Harrison struggled to stay awake after the flight from London to Los Angeles." Wikipedia)

[28] Wikipedia.

George, are you having conversations with anyone back on the planet?

"Yes." **Does he have like 5 kids?**

I think he has a son, but you're saying he has five people he's talking to that he considers family?

"Yes. Affiliated, associated, people he considers family."

> (Note: When Jennifer reports something, I consider possible interpretations; it could mean he "considers" five other people on the planet to be "like children" or it could be she's misinterpreting what she's seeing. It's not meant to offend anyone, or to claim anything different, but the public record is he has an only son, Dhani, also a musician. If this detail would prevent a person from reading further, I concur; *it's time to get a refund!*)

George, are you playing music over there?

"Yes."

Who are you playing with?

"John." **(pause)** **"And a bit infused with Prince now."**

What was your experience checking off the planet and running into John?

"Old times." **And now they're all laughing at the word "old."**

I know you're someone who understood Hindu philosophy...

I'm seeing someone greet him on the other side, like a woman on a white horse. He's showing me walking with someone with a horse on a beach somewhere...

I heard in a documentary that you used to think the manner of your death was important – you talked about the time you were attacked in your home and you had the thought you didn't want to die being traumatized. A crazed fan stabbed you in the throat... and then years later you had throat cancer... was that from..?

"Smoking too much."

Okay. But from the angle you're at now, what do you want to say about spirituality?

"It is limitless. It is a frequency that can never be right or wrong, but that's not the right terminology; whatever you believe in, is right; so how can that be wrong? As long as you aren't hurting someone with your beliefs. Hurting someone causes a ricochet in their soul – you know how you see a sandy beach, and if a bullet hits the sand it's hard and it gets stuck? If you hurt someone you hurt them in time and space and in all their environments."

Anyone that you regret hurting?

(quickly) "John."

How'd you hurt John?

He says, "He didn't want him to be their front guy."

I know that John and Paul had a financial deal where they got more royalties...

"That was fuuuucked up," he says.

But now it doesn't matter does it?

"Yes. It does." They're laughing. He's saying, "They want their heirs to get more money so when they reincarnate as one of their heirs, they will have more money to choose from!"

> (Note: This is both funny and odd. Normally we find people who've crossed over have a kind of "live and let live" impression they like to impart. I've never heard anyone say *"Yeah, if we had more money, then we can reincarnate as one of our heirs and have access to it!"* It's not the way people report the process works but of course, there's room for comedy here, or perhaps for it to actually occur. *Who knows?)*

George were you a musician in a previous lifetime?

He's showing me Beethoven...

Someone from the Beethoven era or Beethoven himself?

A musician from that era... but he says, "He knew Beethoven." He says, "He helped him in some way."

> (Note: If you're going to name drop, why not just claim you were Beethoven? But he shows Jennifer an image of Beethoven, and then says he "Knew him and helped him in that era." This is one of those details I'd have to spend weeks researching, asking questions about the name of this person, and who or what he did. But as you can see from this freewheeling discussion, I just let it slide.)

How about you John, are you aware of any of your previous lifetimes?

He's super funny. He just said (very dryly) "I like to live in the present."

Yes, I'm sure you do, but did you have any previous lifetimes that you remember?

"Yes, one in Asia."

Oh, did you and Yoko know each other from before?

"Yes, as little kids, as brother and sister and they took care of each other."

> (Note: There are reports that John believed in reincarnation, was quoted as saying "it's just getting out of one car and getting into another." However, when we "recognize" someone in our lifetime that we feel we've known forever, it's possible we did know them before.)

So did you recognize her energy when you met her?

"Yeah."

I figured you guys were likely soul mates on some level. In terms of your soul group – are you and George in that same group, or are there people in your class that we would know, or are you part of different groups?

Interesting. He's showing me there are people that are like "extras," you may not know them... (but they play important roles.)

They're people that you knew that you've incarnated with in the past?

"They all take turns."

So when you signed up in this lifetime were you aware the way it would end? Or just that you had an exit point somewhere in the future?

That's interesting. He says he had "Fears about his life ending soon" for a long time.

As a kid? Or later in life?

"As a kid; he didn't think he'd make it past 25."

Then later in life, did you have a premonition it was going to be short?

"In his dreams." He says, "He had a hard time sleeping." It feels like the drugs made it hard for him to sleep as well, but it feels like he did, yeah. "A premonition in his dreams."

Your dreams were stressful?

"Yeah."

George, did you have any premonition about your leaving? Why did you check out when you did?

"No," he says he didn't have a premonition... He said "He needed to help some people (before he checked out). **That's why it took him the amount of time it did."**

Let me ask you about that. Your son, and your wife – are you helping them?

He's like "Of course!" He's telling me that his wife was the one on the horse.

What about your sister-in-law Linda? My brother asked as he regrets he didn't ask her to marry him.

He said, "If he had, he wouldn't be a missing tooth."

> (Note: As it turns out, my brother had just lost a tooth, a funny specific and accurate reference.)

He says, "He wasn't ready."

My brother asked this question as well – "Is there auto racing in the afterlife?" He knew George loved Formula One.

"Yeah." Hold on. (pause) "Yes."

> (Note: My brother Jeffry is a racing enthusiast. Former advertising director of Rolling Stone, he's owned over a dozen cars, has raced in at least two "Cannonball Run" cross country races (came in second, 5 minutes behind.) He told me about George's passion for Formula One racing.)

*So there **is** Formula One racing over there?*

"Yes. But it's more like Mach speed... it's like racing spaceships."

Have you ever done that?

"It's how I got here today." (Jennifer laughs)

Ha. Okay, what's the one, two, three? How do people race over there? What's the math involved?

"You put the thought in your head..." He just showed me his mind, (points to her head). Jennifer listens; *No f*cking way!* **Sorry! He said, "Then you assume the feeling that you want, so you put it in your mind what it is that you want to do, then you assume the feeling, of like the wind, the speed, everything that is going on..."**

Why did you say, "No fucking way"?

Because it's the same thing a lot of "new age spiritualists" say: "Assume the feeling you want; you already have it within."

A bit like how we asked Bill Paxton about how he creates a place of rest, the white beach he likes to hang out on. So creating this sensation of racing, are you racing against other people?

"All the time."

How do they invite you or do you invite them?

"It's the frequency. It's just like the frequency of this class; you send out a signal that the class or the race is about to begin and everyone who wants to race gets involved. They show you what's happening."

Who's they? Who shows you?

"God." (Jennifer laughs.)

You mean the network? You're talking about God as the network?

Yes, "Google."

So, you have the sensation "I think I want to go racing." But does everyone agree on when the green light is going to happen, or are they just racing in their own minds? Is it an agreement to wait for the green light or is that just everyone's own personal version of the race?

Jennifer: He just showed me chariots. (She laughs). **He showed me different time and space, everyone's green light is different.**

Okay, so it's a bit like the race in "Ready Player One" – everyone shows up with their own version of a speedster - if you're a charioteer, that's your experience, but you might be a guy in a car which might be a DeLorean?

"Yes." He just showed me Seinfeld in a DeLorean. (Which he drove around with Patton Oswalt in "Comedians in Cars Getting Coffee") Interesting; so they race against themselves, in their own time period and the frequency of whoever is fastest...

How about the guy who gets the laurels? Are you creating that in your own mind that you're winning? Or are you actually the winner?

"Eh... it's a bit of both." He showed me like "trying to make a thought and it's not quite working."

So racing in the afterlife is a bit like Little League for kids; everyone is a winner, no one gets to lose.

"Yes. It's like you're winning the vibrations, bringing the frequency up, even if it's just a version of bringing the energy of horses and converting it to cars..."

I just got a thought put in my head. Can everyone play some music for Jennifer to hear? George would you play a G with a guitar? Can you do that?

Hold on. (pause) Is G the same tone or note that monks use when they chant?

Sure, could be. Is he playing one note or a chord on the guitar?

I'm hearing the same note on many instruments, guitars, violins, everyone. It's an orchestra.

Okay John, chime in if you want, Prince, can you chime in?

Wow. It jumps... the frequency is what I can see... and with so many people it's challenging to listen – I have to really focus to hear them. The other day I asked, "So why is it when I go to concerts or movie theaters, I see more spirits?" And the answer I got was "Because it's loud in theaters and concerts, it's easier for them to hear it (on the flipside), the sound is loud so they can hear more."

So folks on the flipside like go to the movies... that's funny. Anyone else want to chime in?

(Note: Jennifer's cell phone rings on cue.)

Very funny. All right so...here's a question. John have you ever met Mick Jagger's dad, Joe?

"Once or twice."

Can you bring him forward?

"Yes."

Hi Joe. Who was there to greet you when you crossed over?

He's showing me three people.

Joe, do you remember meeting me?

"Yes." He just patted you on your head. He says you met him at a birthday party.

Yes. That is correct. (ding!) It was his daughter-in-law's birthday party. Jerry Hall. How's she doing by the way?

> (Note: I met Jerry through Phillip Noyce's wife Jan Sharp, and Jerry Hall invited me to her birthday party in San Francisco where I met Mick's dad; he had an uncanny resemblance to the great comedian Stan Laurel.)

Jennifer: What's going on with her?

If he knows. She's married to a wealthy fella.

He says, "You should try and reach out to her."

Joe, you probably have better access than I do.

Is Jerry's mom over there too?

Yes, Marjorie, I met her in Austin. (ding!) Original "daughter of the Republic of Texas" she had five daughters, raised cattle. She passed about 5 years ago. She's a sweetheart.

She loved you! She's telling me, "She loved you." She's very loud, by the way.

That's funny. Texas mama. I told her I was thinking about adapting Jerry's autobiography into a film. Her mom tried to talk both me and her out of that.

She says, "You have to try to reach out to her." Tell Jerry "There's more information that she needs, there's something coming to a close; she needs information."

Hard to reach out to her these days. Any suggestion how?

I got "Twitter" and the message "Just try."

Joe? Any message for your son Mick Jagger?

"Don't forget to dot your i's and cross your t's... and mind your P's and Q's."[29]

Well, he did major in finance in college so maybe it refers to that. Hope he knows what it means. John, anything else?

He just kissed you on the forehead.

Anything you want me to tell Julian on your behalf?

"He needs to look further out... – he gets caught up in... he needs to reach further out... to reach for them."

You mean to reach for his parents on the flipside?

"Yes. Tell him to write. To write and listen."

Like the Morton method?

> (Note: We've heard this before. "Say the name of your loved one. Ask them questions. When you hear a reply before you can form the question, you've made a connection.")

"Yes."

Okay, I'll let him know. Any last words from our class? George anything you want to tell us?

"Love."

---

[29] Oxford dictionary says P's and Q's is "old english;" P is a sailor's pea coat and Q is queue, a pigtail. "1602: Now thou art in thy Pee and Kue, thou hast such a villainous broad backe..." https://blog.oxforddictionaries.com/2012/01/09/origin-to-mind-your-ps-and-qs/

Robin, anything you want to tell George? You gave us the concept of "Love love."

"Yeah."

How about you, John?

"No more guns." That's what he was trying to say back then.

Conor? Anything you want to say?

"Tell my dad to not give up. And to keep writing music. He stopped for a little while, feels like."

Anyone else?

David Bowie showed up. He said **"I forgot to mention. I'm having a ball."**

Anything you want to say?

"Live life to the fullest extent."

Tom Petty?

"Not to dream small. We can help you if you dream big."

George – your comment "Love" is related to what... love as an action? Love as a verb? A noun? Or ...?

"Love is all."

Thank you. How about you Robin?

Robin says, "He said it first!"

Very funny. Thank you. Speaking of our peanut gallery, Garry Shandling spoke to us last week, I didn't realize you were such good friends with Tom Petty.

Garry says, "I love Tom. We go way back."

Garry you were hilarious last week... Jennifer doesn't know because I haven't shown her the transcript yet.

I have no idea (what we said).

At one point you said you were golfing. I asked if you played 36 holes, you said "No, two. They're just very far apart." So class, we just want to remind everyone the reason we're doing this is to help people on the planet... or as Michael Newton can tell you...

Morton.

Morton will tell you...

He's taking notes up there... trying to help people over there help people communicate to their loved ones over here. I just got shown that frequency again, like the car example in Harry Dean Stanton's crossing over... To show that everyone who wants to talk, can; it's a frequency. He's showing me people over there who are hurting, who want to talk, who want to help the planet be better, who want to help invent things to help the planet...

Michael, how are you showing them to communicate? Do they adjust their frequency slower? Faster?

He's showing me a grid. (Laughs.) Oh, that's funny. He's saying "*We know we're no longer on the planet*, it's much harder for people here to communicate with people back there because people don't believe they can be talked to. People claim they're trying so hard to get a hold of us, that we are the ones who can't hear them... but *it's the other way around.* You can't hear us. So, there's a whole big

school trying to help. (On the Flipside) They know where they're at, we're the ones who don't. Tell Scott De Tamble that Michael is keeping an eye on him and his daughter.

Thanks. See you on the flipside, class!

****

I'm sure this chapter is filled with inaccuracies and points of contention. After all, these folks have had their lives written about for decades. I didn't know any of them closely – and I point out the "brushing shoulders" aspect of how it might be that they are accessible. Again – not trying to wave the celebrity flag here. All I can report is our attempt at trying to "talk to people we don't know" and see what comes through.

"We know we're no longer on the planet, it's much harder for people here to communicate with people back there because people don't believe they can be talked to."

Photo Copyright Russ Titelman 2018, All Rights Reserved.

CHAPTER FOURTEEN: IDEE FIXES

Jimi Hendrix on the Dick Cavett show

As noted, film director Phillip Noyce once introduced me as *"This is Richard. He thinks he can talk to the dead."*

I had to correct him; **"I don't to the dead. I talk to *people who can talk to the dead.*"**

I must acknowledge that indeed it is a possibility this is all some form of random imaginary two-step. That my random questions to Jennifer elicit some kind of random response that comes from some etheric imaginary place, within me, within her, or perhaps in the imaginations from people no longer on the planet.

But as I've noted, there are numerous times when an answer comes forth that is *new information* and later turns out to be forensically true. That does not mean *all* the answers are true, and as noted, there are a number of reasons why things are inaccurate.

But meanwhile, back to our class.

****

Jennifer: My introduction to you was when I sent you a Facebook message.

Rich: I talk about that (in the latest book) too... Whatever you want to talk about – it's up to you.

Jennifer: You've helped me gain tools. You ask questions I've never asked... Like what just happens when a song runs through my head, you ask not only who was responsible for putting it there, but *how* they were able to get it into my head. I would have never asked that question before... You've given me the gift of asking questions to spirit.

When I asked my dad, "How'd you do that?" Prince showed up.

We know what Prince does; helps people with musical frequency. I was wondering who to ask to write the foreword to the book ("Backstage Pass.")

Robin Williams jumped up, and I need to ask why Luana just stepped in front of him! (Listens) Luana says *she* is going to write the foreword to the book. ("Backstage Pass") She thinks it's important for a collaboration from both sides – I think she wants her own foreword.

Great, you'll be the conduit for her. (And the foreword to that book is directly from Luana). Okay, so we wanted to invite someone who has appeared in a couple of other sessions. Someone who helped pull one of our subjects on stage.

Jimi Hendrix?

Wow. That's who! **(ding!)** *Can we call him forward?*

(Jennifer aside) Did he die young?

He's part of that 27 club, Jim Morrison was as well. Hey, he showed up last week, can Jim Morrison and Jimi come forward? Who wants to talk first? Oh by the way, the image you saw of John Lennon a few weeks ago? Was he young, middle aged, older?

I saw him when he had long hair and glasses. He is looking out a window, light is coming through.

Okay, I was just curious because John, you put that image in her head, you found the file in her memory and then you dinged it and that's why you came to mind. Is that correct?

"Ding, ding, ding." Jennifer taps her nose.

So Mr. Hendrix – you've helped a few of our classmates into the flipside. Can we ask you about this? Who greeted you when you crossed over?

Feels like his grandmother.[30]

From Seattle I'd guess?

"Yes. She was there."

What was the feeling when you crossed over? Was this an exit point for you? Was it an accident or an overdose?

"It's what it felt like yeah. An accident."

I think had taken some sleeping pills, didn't realize he'd thrown up; asphyxiated.

---

[30] His maternal grandmother was Clarice Jeter (Lawson) who died March 15, 1967 at 75 from TB. Buried in Seattle.

"Yeah." (Jennifer, aside) Odd, that's the second time I've heard that in my work today.

Were you startled by that sudden exit?

"Pissed off. He wasn't even high," he said.

Who greeted you besides your grandmother?

He says, "A little girl."

Who was that? Someone you knew or lost?

Feels like she was his little girl.

From a miscarriage or...?

Felt like a girl who drowned.

> (Note: I can ask questions about this, get a rough outline for an answer, and then do the forensic research into how he might have known this little girl. Jimi had a couple of children "out of wedlock" but in these stories of life journeys, nothing happens by accident. However, when we return "home" we are outside of time, we may run into loved ones we knew from a previous lifetime, from our soul group, even people who normally don't incarnate – could be anyone. All I can do is ask questions and try to figure out who that person might be. In this case, I have no idea.)

Someone he knew as a kid, someone from your soul group?

"Yeah," he says. Like "his little girl."

He had a little girl who drowned at five we're not aware of?

"Yes, she was five when she drowned."

No one knows about it?

"No, they don't."

Jimi, you met my sister-in-law, my brother's wife Jeanne backstage in Sweden in the 60's. She has pictures of you.

He said, "She smelled good."

(Funny comment – never heard it before, but sounds accurate. John Hughes loved my sister-in-law as well as my brother Robbie, his wife was best friends with John and his wife Nancy – they all went to the same high school outside Chicago where I also went.)

Jimi, why are you the guy pulling people on stage? Is that part of your gig?

He said, "It helps him."

How?

(Jennifer aside) Show me again? (Listens) "So they don't get sad." It's like that car ride... that Harry Dean Stanton talked about. (A way of helping them have a "soft landing" on the flipside.)

A distraction so they aren't focused on the fact they're no longer on the planet? So you pulled John on stage to play "Blue Suede Shoes?" I found you recorded it in 1969, and John a year later. Why that song? Because John knew it?

"No." He says "They were making fun of Elvis..." That's what they're saying.

When John recorded it he says on the recording, "I chose a song that everybody in the band knows." Is that why you used that song or were you just teasing Elvis?

"It did two things... homage to Elvis and picking a song John knew." (Jennifer aside) When he pulled John Lennon onto the stage, I wanted to ask what song they played!

We did; we asked him what song it was and instead of giving you a title, he showed you a pair of blue shoes.

(Jennifer aside) I don't remember.

It's an old Carl Perkins song Elvis made into a hit, and both of these fellows recorded it. Okay fellows let's turn to the guy from the Doors.

Yes, he's sitting on the couch.

Jim, why did you check out at 27?

"Second death event," he said; "There was another one at (age) 19."

At the age of 19. Who greeted you when you crossed over?

"His sister. Felt like."

Sister from this life or a previous life?

I think it was a sister from a previous life... that's interesting... (to me) why would you ask that question?

> (Note. I didn't know, but it turns out Jim Morrison has a sister born in 1947, Anne Robin who lives in Albuquerque. I felt he didn't mean his sister from this life, hence why I asked the question "from a previous

lifetime." Again, his sister is alive, but for some reason, that's the impression he gave Jennifer. Could have been her "higher self" that was there to greet him, as reportedly the majority of our conscious energy is "always back home.")

Because it just popped into my head. I know your dad was very controlling and a military guy.

"He beat the shit out of him," he said. He showed me somebody whacking his ass.

Now are you guys reconciled and do you understand why you chose him as your father?

He says, "Yes."

As a poet you talked about really unusual things. Why did you choose such interesting topics for your songs?

He showed me LSD.

The band was named after Aldous Huxley's book "The Doors of Perception." LSD is a door of perception... but why were you so into alcohol? What pain were you carrying that you had to dull so much?

"He felt alone."

Did you have a mental affliction or something? Were you bi-polar? Or just hated fame?

He says "Just depressed; couldn't get himself out of it."

So why did you choose this lifetime to be famous and depressed?

He said, "Just to try to figure it out – tried to balance (it) and it didn't work."

I was in court with the surviving "Doors." They fought over who could use the name "The Doors." They were all these old grey-haired dudes. By the way, Jim's attorney gets a signed postcard from someone posing as you every year on the day of your death; signs your name. Who's doing that?

He said, "It's somebody..." (Jennifer aside) feels like a company.

I don't think the attorney ever told anybody about it.

Feels like someone he knew, someone who is part of a company that's doing it.

I have a friend who took a photo in Per Lachaise cemetery – a photo of her friend, but it looks like you in the background; how'd you manifest like that?

(Jennifer aside) What cemetery is he in?

Per Lachaise. In Paris. Edith Piaf is buried there... People come from all over the world to leave poems for you, are you there sometimes?

He showed me a bunch of people playing guitars. He said, "They make that energy happen."

I took a pic of your tombstone, when I got home, there was a photo with like an upside-down vortex - a weird light in energetic bands. That too?

He said, "Like a prism ... there's a vortex there. It's easier to access him because of it."

Oh great, now everyone will want to take a photo. But who creates the vortex? The people coming to visit or is it you? My guess is that it's related to people depositing emotions at your tombstone that creates the vortex.

He said, "Yes."

I experienced it in Anne Frank's home in Amsterdam. Like a vortex of sadness. It also happened at the Vietnam memorial even though I knew no one on the panel. Are people depositing their sadness and that's what I'm feeling?

He said "Not only are you feeling that, but you're also feeling the sadness from the other side... at that moment."

How can we bottle that in terms of positive energy?

"You can separate it, away from you." He's showing me a suitcase... like the metaphor you used. (Put emotions into a suitcase while accessing a memory).

Thanks for talking to us, Jim. Come back soon and make some more music.

He said, "He's *done*. He's helping people here from over there."

Who are you helping?

(Jennifer aside) I just got the chills. He said, "He's helping musicians in like punk bands... helping them with the energy of being in a punk band."

You mean helping musicians to play?

He said, "No. To not fucking die."

(Note: It's a sentence I've never heard from Jennifer over our six years of sessions. Novel concept.)

*****

Now these two fellas can chat when they want to.

Another day, another classroom conversation.

Jennifer: My dad came in.

Rich: Hi Jim. I was going to ask about how you put a song in your daughter's mind.

He said, "He learned that from Prince." I'm asking, "What was it like for you to meet Prince?" and he said, "It was amazing." He said, "These classes allow us to finally get to know each other."

When Jennifer and I are not here, are you guys hanging out?

They showed me by their consciousness together... the group raises their vibration which makes it higher, stronger... it's conducting, changing the frequencies... Stephen Hawking just appeared in his wheelchair, and I said to him "You don't have to use that anymore (to identify himself)"

He says, "The vibrant part of the book is what they're saying, these words whether you believe in it (the Flipside) or not, the words still hold the vibration."

He's saying the frequency of the words themselves will help people to figure out how to communicate to people over there?

"It increases the frequency on your side." He showed me like a room opening up and growing bigger. It's like "Their minds open up, so people (on the flipside) can talk to them.

The best thing about the frequency is that this book is going to hold a frequency which they can use to open (people) up – so they can talk to them." That's funny. They're calling it "ghost stories..."

All right, thank you. Is that it for now class? Other folks from the flipside have to come and talk to Jennifer.

*****

INTERVIEW WITH AN EVERLY

The Everly Brothers (Wikimedia)

Let me tell you the story of how I met Don Everly, and how that led to a gig playing on a yacht in the Caribbean.

Not to be confused with the gig I took playing piano in St. Martin in the Caribbean when I was 21, being flown down to my friend's hotel on the Dutch side and how my run in with the shyster manager led to my early dismissal. That's another story.

Some years ago, when playing in our band "Imminent Disaster" I got us this gig playing at the trendy nightclub Les Deux in Hollywood. We played Saturdays for about six months, and the back room with its Yamaha baby grand was packed each night..

One day the owner said "The people in your band, who come to see your band, can't get a table in my restaurant. Your band is drinking me out of profits." (Free drinks for the ten-piece band – that's a lot of drinks.) She said "I'm firing your band. I want you to play solo." I begged Craig Cole to stay – play sax with my piano. Craig was the consummate sax player, I was thrilled that he said "Yeah, sure man."

One night, as I was starting to play "Knocking on Heaven's Door," I heard this angelic voice in my ear singing harmony. I recognized it instantly, even though I'd never met him. It was Don Everly. I couldn't see him, only hear him leaning forward into our shared microphone.

"Mama take this badge from me, I can't use it anymore. It's getting dark too dark to see, feels like I'm knockin' on heaven's door..."

That led to a regular gig at Les Deux. Then another night, I was dining with film director Phillip Noyce and his pal Bob

Shaye, the founder of New Line Cinema. Over dinner Bob told some pretty funny stories about his career while complaining about the cruelty of show biz. The owner of the restaurant asked if I'd play a few tunes.

The actor Billy Zane stepped up and we did a duet of "Sweet Home Chicago." Afterward, I improvised "The Bob Shaye Blues" which turned everything he complained about over dinner into a blues song, mocking him to the delight of the crowd and Bob as well. "My name is Bob, I'm a millionaire, but I can't get Harvey Weinstein out of my hair…"

After the tune, thunderous laughter and applause from the crowd, Bob came up to the piano. "That was great. Whatever you want, it's yours!"

I said, *"How about a three-picture movie deal?"*

He said, "You got it!"

(Really? Grab the brass ring! You can't get it unless you reach out for it.)

A few months later, I heard Bob had rented a yacht for an eight-week millennium cruise in the Caribbean celebrating the new century from 1999 to 2000.

I sent him a cheeky fax saying "If you're looking for a keyboard player for your cruise; I'm available" and named all the nautical tunes I knew. "Beyond the Sea" "Sitting on the Dock of the Bay" etc.

Lo and behold, the man who brought us the "Lord of the Rings" trilogy thought that was a good idea. I got a call from his secretary "If you can be in Caracas on Tuesday you can join the trip." Off I went to Venezuela to meet the boat.

Bob Shaye somewhere in time.

For two legs, about a month, I played tunes in the bar on "The Levant" yacht. About new 25 celebs would board in different ports; I was on the last two. "Movie stars! Billionaires!" Francis Coppola and his wife. Ted Turner and his girlfriend. Every night people were asked to perform for the passengers – read from their novel, do a scene from a play, sing a song or tell a story.

I played backup piano for Penny Marshall who did a parody of "Hello Dolly" for Bob and Ava Shaye, famed record producer Richard Perry sang Johnny Cash tunes, and Luana's old pal Francis had me participate in acting improvs.

It was a legendary cruise, I did the same thing I'd done at Les Deux Café', listen to what people whined about on the boat and turned it later into their "blues song." But when it came time for me to do "my own 30 minutes" I wrote and sang a song called "How I got on this boat."

In 12 bar blues, I recounted how everyone on this boat had a hand in my life, like an idee fixe – either career wise or personal experiences – I'd done a Laverne and Shirley but was cut out, how Luana Anders and I spent 8 years going to the Coppola house at Thanksgiving and how after Francis saw my short film and told me "go into porno," how everyone on that boat including Bob Shaye had some oddball connection to me, but had also expressed dismay that they didn't really know how I got on the trip of a lifetime.

I told the story of my dozen or so oddball connections, Peter Tunney, Ron Silver, Michelle Phillips, Mathew Modine, Rennie Harland, Dana Delany, Phillip Noyce, Jan Sharp - literally some wacky memory with everyone on that boat. Of course none of them knew each other, but all of them had crossed my path. And I sang of how more than one demanded to know the trick, the ruse, the scam I had pulled to get on this champagne and caviar cruise of a lifetime.

I realized how all had met me in some oddball fashion, often related to Luana (perhaps *always* related to her) and that night when my showstopping mockery of Bob Shaye got him to promise me a fairy tale "three picture deal!"

I sang, *"Looks like I lost that three-picture quote, but I did get my ass on the on the motherf**king boat."*

Making "Limit Up."

It took me years to understand there was no coincidence to my being on that boat. I had Luana's ashes with me, scattered them across the Caribbean. Luana was, and always is, with me when I travel, because when I asked her what she wanted me to do with her ashes she said simply; **"Take them wherever you go."**

But what are we to make of this idea that we are all frequency, we are all strings vibrating in quantum fashion, all of the universe is music?

From another session with Jennifer:

Rich: So, shall we ask our pal Luana, who is "the holder of the clipboard" for whomever she wants us to speak with? Is it somebody that I've invited or somebody who shows up?

Jennifer: Well, it's James Dean again. I had a blank slate then I double checked (with Luana) but that's what's coming through.

Well, Luana knows I did invite somebody today but if James has elbowed his way in, that's fine.

It could mean that this other person you invited could have been an associate or a pal or have the name James.

I'm not going to give James the "bum's rush" out of his chair. We've had a couple of conversations with James; once in our book Backstage Pass to the Flipside and then recently Jennifer and I had a session where we talked to James and connected him with somebody who for lack of a better term is traipsing around the planet with some portion of his conscious energy in him.

(Jennifer aside) What's interesting is the last couple days I've seen James everywhere. I was driving in Hollywood

and looked over and there's that huge mural of James Dean.

Well, let's ask him because he's elbowed his way into the front of our class. What do you want to say Mr. Dean without giving away who this person is that is aware of your presence in his life?

He says, "To keep believing…" And "Who cares if it's going to make you feel a little crazy?"

What do you mean? Crazy by the person we're talking about or being someone like Jennifer?

Well, we all know that we're crazy, so it goes without saying… That's a good question. He's showing me the pictures in my mind of the mural in Hollywood or the other ones I've seen recently over the last few days. He says, "That's just me saying hello."

Let's talk about the process, how'd he make you aware of it?

What he's saying is, "It's a bigger issue. The reason why he's coming through is to show us about the process. How we can connect with our loved ones, and they do that to us all the time. Our awareness to things that we normally would not be looking at but find ourselves suddenly seeing.

So it's the equivalent of looking for a necklace you can't find? But then your loved one on the other side changes your awareness so that you see it and then you realize "Oh, they must be here. They obviously put that in my path?

He says, "Right."

So how do you guys do that?

He says, "For some people it's like trying to crack open a brick or break into a brick.

Because of the filters are thick?

"Yeah." He showed me this little kid in school looking up. Like in kindergarten; looking at the sky and being able to daydream because they're not so focused on every single thing that's going on around them. That they're actually missing out on what could be given to them.

So the process would be to get out of the loops that are in your head and then it goes back to meditation it goes back to allowing yourself to just kind of daydream a little bit and see what pops in?

"Right."

On your side, is it that you guys are sort of generating a field of energy in our direction and then we're allowing that to pop in or are they specific about driving down this particular street because there's a photograph of me on this corner?

He says, "It's everything. It's everything from getting someone out the door at this precise moment where the stoplight appears for you, and you are able to look to the left."

He says, "There are millions of things happening." He showed me this kid tying a shoe in the morning, like you're going to be late somewhere when really that's exactly what's supposed to happen. (Timed) "So you'd have that butterfly go across the car go across the car windshield."

James for those who aren't aware of what we're doing we've had you come by before, this idea that it's starting to happen more often is because we talked to this friend (who recalls being him in his previous lifetime)? We opened that door?

He says, "Yeah you opened the belief structure." He's showing me it's a rippling effect. It's something that sets off a chain of events that can't be explained.

Like what we consider coincidence, but it literally is blueprints converging over a certain field?

Right and then he just showed me what happened for me to see that wall. I was going to a place in Hollywood, I never go. I was with my son, and suddenly thought, "We could drive down the block," and I turned and there was James Dean looking at me. He's showing me all the process that it took to get me in front of that mural.

James I did invite someone today, you're always welcome here and of course we're going to have more conversations with you. I just want to thank you for allowing us into this kind of introduction.

(Jennifer aside) Did the person you invite sing?

Yes, that's correct.

I'm hearing music and I'm hearing I'm feeling the brat pack (or that era of the 1950's) and I'm hearing... it almost feels it might be Tony Bennett, but I know he's alive.

Well, it's in the era, but I'm gonna tell you his first name it's Don. Luana, is Don ready to talk to us?

She's like, "Let me go find him." (After a moment) Yes, he is. He was talking to someone else. I believe it's the person that asked for us to talk to him.

(Note: My friend Craig Cole introduced us, so it may be him. We'll chat with him in a minute.)

I met Don, but I didn't know him – he may or may not remember me, but I was playing piano in a nightclub in Hollywood.

He just showed me the piano. He also showed me Laverne from Laverne and Shirley... So was that related?

That's pretty good Don – because Penny Marshall is related. I did perform with Penny on that Bob Shaye cruise. But there is a mutual friend of ours that brought you in to the club one night and I was singing a specific song. Do you want to put that song in Jennifer's mind?

It feels like an Italian song...

Actually it was a Bob Dylan tune.

(Jennifer aside) But I'm seeing you play it in Italy.

(Note: I can recall pretty much every time I played a Dylan song in Italy. Once was with guitar on the Spanish Steps as a student at the Rome Center. The Romans chanted "play Bob

Deelan!" and I sang "Tangled Up in Blue" which has just been released in 1976. I have played "Knocking on Heaven's Door" many a night in Cannes.)

I was playing a gig at Les Deux Café when I heard Don's voice in my ear. Don was a member of a famous duo, and sang harmony to "Knocking on Heaven's Door." I instantly knew who he was but had never met him. Don is this you? That same fella?

He says, "Well, who else would it be?"

Do you mind if I interview you?

He says, "I'd love it."

Who was there to greet you when you crossed over?

I'm seeing a mother.

Your mom, okay, Margaret Embry. And what was that like for you to see her?

(Note: Don's mother is still alive. 103 thank you very much. But we bring a portion of our conscious energy to a lifetime and the rest stays home. People often report seeing someone greet them during a near death event, or on the flipside that is still on the planet.)

(Jennifer aside) They showed me the video someone took of me greeting my son at O'Hare airport after being away from him. That kind of embrace, unbelievable love.

Do you have any messages for your wife Adela? I see that you guys were married like 24 years.

(Jennifer aside) What? I can't say that.

Sure, you can. He had like three wives.

He's saying, "she needs to move on" and I'm saying, "You can't say that." He's saying, "She'll know what I mean."

Are you saying, "It's okay to move on?" "She needs to move on" might seem a bit early if you mean "It's okay to move on."

"Yes," he says. "That's correct."

I want to ask you about your brother Phil. What was it like when you ran into him or how was that experience?

He snapped his fingers, he said "Just went like that." He said, "It took a little bit (of time) at first," because I'm seeing him look at his watch, and he says "You guys are talking about being late. Because it felt like I waited forever for him to show up."

Please describe that. His brother passed away before he did...

He's saying that was seven years ago.

That's correct.

Give me his brother's first name?

Phil.

He says, "Phil let my mom come through first" and he said, "Phil was singing."

He's showing me like hearing his harmony (before seeing him) and knowing who it was. Like he was singing in the background, which made it a "soft landing for him."

A soft landing to the flipside. We've heard that before.

There was a harmony when he saw his mom, so he knew that feeling, he was encompassed in love. That's what it feels like to me.

Don, can you talk to us about harmony? The harmonies you and your brother did were famous, all the great bands learned from you, The Beach Boys, the Beatles. You're quoted as saying "It was like my brother was in my head." How does that relate to what we're talking about frequency on the flipside and music?

He said, "Prince said it before."

(Note: Don is referring to an earlier conversation with Prince – a conversation he could not have heard, because it was said on the Podcast previously, a conversation that Jennifer does not remember, but because I'm filming, I do. It's an odd thing to say, because the observation from Prince happened years earlier on the flipside.)

He says, "The frequency that you call the flipside…" (Jennifer aside) He just laughs about that term in general. He says, "Like the other side of the record, but it's better than being (called) "dead," right?

(Note: That's the first time anyone on the flipside has made fun of the term. Who better than someone who had 100's of hit records? The Everly Brothers hold the record for the most Top 100 singles by any duo.)

(Jennifer aside) I asked him, "Do you get mad when people say you're dead?" He said "Yeah, because you're not."

He said the frequency is like… he showed me like pulling a rope, "You're pulling that person into you and when

you're in harmony it's easier to pull the rope faster (closer?) So if you live with harmony within yourself…" (Jennifer aside) I know you're asking about music…

No actually, that's what I'm asking about. The word harmony – what does it mean?

He says, "If you're living in harmony with your heart, you're more open to accessing the other side."

With regard to Phil, did you guys know each other in a previous lifetime before?

He says, "Yeah." (Laughs) Then he says, "I want the stage all to myself next time."

Can we ask Phil a question?

"Good job," he said. "Good job."

I know you guys were interviewed often together, but there was the famous breakup that happened at Knotts Berry Farm on stage. Do you want to show that to Jennifer?

(Jennifer aside) Was it over a girl or a band member?

I think it was over a girl because I heard them talking about it at the Hollywood bowl one of them said it was over a girl

He says, "There were many girls."

(Note: An acquaintance of Don's called me after the interview and told me that both Don and Phil had a relationship with a friend of hers during the swinging sixties. The friend lived with Don for two years and Phil lived with her for two. And then one day the girlfriend let it slip that she also had a fling with one of the band members, so they fired him.)

I'm feeling like Janis Joplin is here. Could it have been her?

Might have looked like her or been a singer. But then Don, you brothers reconciled, came back together

He says, "They realized it was stupid."

You toured with Paul Simon and Art Garfunkel for the "Old Friend's" Tour and that brings Luana into the mix because Luana was pals with both Paul and Artie. But I have a question for you – I'm seeing in your credits you worked on the film Tequila Sunrise with our pal Robert Towne (who directed the film). Were you in the film or contributed a song?

He showed me like a cameo part in the background... but also that he was on the soundtrack.

Yes, that's accurate. On the soundtrack was a Beach Boys song sung by Phil and Don with The Beach Boys. Do you want to tell Jennifer which song that was? It might be hard since she doesn't know your music.

(Jennifer aside) I'm not getting it.

Don and Phil sang with Brian Wilson on "Don't Worry Baby." But back to your journey, Don, so you're seeing your mom and brother on the flipside, but at what point does your dad show up?

He says, "My dad will tell you... I can't tell you because they're talking (which each other) He said, "It was not that it would have been hard to recognize them, but it just wasn't... my mom had to take on the responsibilities."

He says, "My mom was everything, and then I saw my brother, but then I saw my dad – and he was really proud. You know, we took care of our mom."

Phil, what was it like when you crossed over; who greeted you?

He's saying his wife... that's what it feels like. I don't know how many wives he had but like I think it's like three.

That's what his bio says.

(Note: His first wife Jacqueline, a songwriter, is still on the planet. I didn't ask him to clarify. Again – a portion of our conscious energy is here, and the rest is always "back home" so we can "greet people" even if we're still on the planet.)

He said, "It was kind of groovy." He said, "They did a lot of work getting me over." He's saying, "They put a lot of work into making it a softer landing."

We've heard that about soft landings, helping people as they arrive in an unfamiliar place. Phil what was it like for you to see your brother Don?

He says, "He heard his voice first, before seeing him... and that was super exciting."

Are you guys singing together now?

He says, "We're writing more music." He's showing me visuals as well, like writing music for films that are not out there yet...

Let me clarify. We heard from Carl Laemmle, founder of Universal who passed in 1939, talk about how you can create any kind of creative construct on the flipside. Are you saying you are creating music for other people's adventures?

He says, "Right."

Don, I have a question about our mutual friend Craig Cole who brought us together.

Don said, "He was right behind me" (when he crossed over.)

Craig, what was it like for you when you crossed over?

He says, "It was serene... and the experience was even better and greater and more vast than I expected."

And what was that like?

He showed me pictures. He says, "It's like stepping out of one room and into another. Let's pretend we're in a room that's very colorful." He says, "It's like stepping out of that room into the same room but it's just more magnificent and just it comes alive... and you are (still) you, but you become everything in the room."

Wow that's beautiful.

He's showing me, I'm seeing butterflies coming out of the walls. He's saying, "It's like whatever you feel like your heaven is, *your heaven is.*"

Craig you played with some pretty famous people like Frank Zappa... did they show up at some point or how did that work?

He says, "I had a concert in honor of me making it (home.)"

Cool.

(Note: You can listen to Craig Cold on the track "Point of Betrayal Theme" on YouTube or Amazon)

How about you Don, what musicians have you seen since you've been back home?

He says, "Michael Jackson. Prince. Elvis." He says, "Now I get to talk." He's showing me Aretha Franklin… and somebody you would know but that I don't know that also plays piano. He's showing me Tony Bennett even though he's still on the planet.

Well, his higher self is back there.

Somebody else… who plays piano. I can't quite get the name. Nat.

Nat King Cole?

Yes… (Jennifer aside) Was he a piano player?

Yes, was famous as a piano player before a singer.

He's showing me John Belushi.

John's been with us before, also a musician.

Don says, "He's very entertaining."

Don, are you familiar with Luana?

He says, "Let me just put it this way, "Everyone's familiar with Luana."

What's your impression of what she's doing on the flipside? We act like it's normal saying our pal who passed in 1996 is conducting this class over there with her VIP list.

He says, "It's fantastic because you guys are talking right now (because of her)." But he's saying people get to access it from all different dimensions, spaces and times.

But is she helping you guys to learn how to communicate to us?

He says, "Not exactly. She's helping us…." (Jennifer aside) I think they're making fun of me. He says, "She's helping us understand why people can't get all the information correctly. That it's better to show (people on earth) signs and symbols." He says, "We're very rare (to converse with) but says, "If we were to bombard people, they wouldn't be able to move on."

What does that mean?

He says, "Meaning that it's one thing for us to communicate all the time to them via people like me (Jennifer or a medium) but it's another thing for them to constantly talk to their loved ones because then they would be bombarding them. They would not move on - they would hold on (to grief).

You're saying, "Be judicious about how much contact you do between here and there?"

He says, "To move on with their lives. It's harder for people to move on if they're always trying to connect."

He says, "It's a fine line because otherwise we would never let you screw up and then what's a life worth living for if you can't have the chance to make things right?"

It's a philosophical point, but to clarify; Don, you're saying "it's good for people to realize their loved ones can communicate but not get stuck by needing constant emotional feedback?" Because then they can't move on?

"Right."

We heard this from Jennifer's father on the other side, the idea the grief is only sad memories, but nostalgia is both happy and sad memories. Jim said, "When you can move grief to nostalgia you begin the healing process."

He says, "That is correct. They have all the knowledge of all their lives when they go over there."

Jennifer doesn't have your music in her head but is there one title you can give her? Something that goes with "Bye Bye?"

"Baby?" Oh. "Love."

"Bye Bye Love."

(Jennifer aside) Janis Joplin wants to talk to you.

Okay, please.

Janis has come through a couple of times today; it's like "I just really want to talk to Rich." She says, "Don't give up on creating…" I think it's one of your movies.

Are you saying one of my films I'm trying to get made or is it something else?

I don't know. Like something to do with musicians.

Well there is the book I'm working on about musicians on the flipside, is that what you mean?

She says, "Yes. That's it."

The book is excerpts from all the musicians we've interviewed talking about frequency. Like Don mentioning Prince talking about frequency – or Aretha stopping by. Oh, by the way, Aretha, what did you think of the Jennifer Hudson film about you?

She gave it a thumbs up and thumbs down.

She's a tough critic. Sorry, I had to ask. Janis, you're suggesting I continue pursuing this book about music?

Hang on. Look who's calling. (Jennifer holds up her phone and Robert Towne's name is on the phone. The fellow who hired Don to produce a song for his film.)

Wow. That's funny. Don probably got him to call us during our podcast. But is what you mean Janis? To talk about music in terms of frequency and how you guys are still creating music?

She says, "Yes. For future projects. Like those jumping up and getting them. Like "Who's gonna get them first in the next lifetime?""

But also because you're creating music over there? Are you saying you get to create them for the universe, you and your pals?

"Yes."

You're creating music over there so billions of souls can say "I saw Janis Joplin last night!" Is that correct?

She says, "Yep. That's correct. I just want people to know, to be aware of what it does… it gives people more room to daydream. Instead of being so caught up with "What's unattainable." It gives them more room to daydream within it."

Do you mean people on that side, to create over there?

Both sides.

It goes back to the initial thought that James Dean expressed, about the child daydreaming, looking around and observing the world as it is. To daydream our loved ones are still with us, to daydream that my life has meaning even if I don't understand what that is?

He said, "Yes."

It's like Craig Cole said, "It's like you're walking to the next room and you are everything in the room."

He says, "Yeah."

On that note; "Bye Bye Love."

*****

Thanks Don.

CHAPTER FIFTEEN: CELESTIAL MUSIC

Kutenla, The State Oracle of Tibet. Photo Sanjay Saxena

Back in the 1990's I had the chance to study Tibetan Buddhism with Robert Thurman. I've told the story elsewhere, where he turned me down to auditing his graduate philosophy class, but I had insisted because I felt it was something that was important for me to learn.

Plus I'd read an article about him where he had met his old teacher, his former Geshe who had reincarnated as a small boy living in Dharamsala.

How Robert had gone into the boy's home unannounced, sat on a bench and watched his former teacher doing donuts on a tricycle. But then the toddler had rolled up to him and stopped at his feet. As Robert put it, "He scrunched up his face at me and said in a voice I recognized "Thurman, why did you leave the monkhood?"

Robert was startled – no one knew his name or why he was there. And this toddler had the same look of disappointment he'd seen before in the monastery. Bob explained that as a teacher he thought he could bring the dharma or teachings of Buddha to the west, and that seemed to mollify the child who rode off.

One thing that Robert noted was that he had reconciled with his former teacher after leaving the monkhood – that his teacher had accepted that he had shifted gears. Yet, this toddler was aware of it, and focused on that aspect of it.

Like hearing an old song, and then focusing on the lyric of that song and not what may have happened after it was written.

Outside of time, outside of space.

But Robert let me audit his class – not because when he asked me "how familiar are you with Hegel and Kant?" I had said "They play for the 49ers." That's the joke I wished I had told, and now it's too funny not to repeat. But he let me audit his class at Columbia for PhD candidates.

I loved it. Just like surfing in a meteor shower. So many words I'd never heard before. Concomitance. But I stuck it out – read everything Robert wrote about Tsong Khapa and then leaped at the chance to take someone's spot who couldn't make a trip to Ladakh with Robert's tour group.

So off I went.

And it was on this trip that he introduced me to Kutenla, Thubten Ngodup, the Oracle of Tibet. We became pals on that trip, something about him just made me want to make him laugh. Yes, I was aware that he was a unique person, unique in the pantheon of Tibetan holy men – but only vaguely knew how he got the gig.

He told me that he was a Nechung monk when it happened. That the old "State Oracle of Tibet" has passed away and they were earnestly looking for his replacement. It's not normal or necessary for that replacement to be a monk – could be anyone.

But one day, while saying prayers as a monk, Thubten Ngodup fainted. When he awoke people were standing around him in shock. Apparently, he'd said some pretty outrageous things to everyone around. Which is part and parcel of this fellow's modus operandi.

Basically the State Oracle is a channel – for a Tibetan warrior who speaks on behalf of the deity that is in charge of predicting the future or unusual events. The warrior speaks an old dialect of Tibetan and not many understand it – but a few do. Also he tends to swear or curse the folks who are asking him questions, especially if he finds the question wanting.

He's kind of notorious for chewing out the Dalai Lama. So actually the Dalai Lama was the one who gave him his test – and for those keeping score, the Dalai Lama knew the last Oracle who saved his life by telling him the exact day and route to take out of Lhasa to escape the Chinese onslaught. Literally told him to "straight through the Chinese camp of soldiers" the next morning. Of course everyone was horrified when he did – but as the Dalai Lama arrived at the camp, the Chinese invaders had suddenly left.

So he knows the fellow, or at least the former channel who channeled the fellow.

But again, I was meeting him for the first time in Dharamsala. And I was thoroughly entertained by him, and we made each other laugh. So when he showed up in San Francisco a few months later, visiting the home of my friend Sanjay Saxena, the intrepid tour maestro who took us through Ladakh and later Tibet, I went up to his home to see him.

Kutenla visiting Santa Monica Beach

At the end of his visit, he said he was going to visit Los Angeles in a few days, and perhaps I was available to give him a tour?

And I did – he was staying at the home of Goldie Hawn and Kurt Russell, two really unusual and cool people, neither of whom I'd met before. I spent the day driving Kutenla around Los Angeles, took him to Paramount studios ("Look! Reality! Non-Reality!") and showed him the sights.

Later that night, there was a dinner for him at Goldie's home, and I was exhausted by our adventure. So when he told me he was going to go to Disneyland the next day, and that he wished I would come along, I deferred. I assumed he was going with Goldie and Kurt; I didn't want to intrude – and said my goodbyes at the end of the evening.

Until about 3 am when my doorbell rang. Kutenla had come to my apartment in Santa Monica earlier in the day, and he looked around it like he was memorizing it, then said a prayer of protection in my apartment. I recorded it with my DAT Audio recorder so I would have a copy.

But at 3 a.m. the front door to the apartment rang. And I got out of bed and went downstairs and opened the door. And there was Kutenla in the hallway wearing his robes. But he was glowing... I mean like sparkles around his body, that kind of CGI effect that one sees in the film "Twilight." And I looked at him and said "I'm sorry that I can't come to Disneyland with you tomorrow."

And he went into the apartment, again, like he was looking around. He turned to me and said "Richard-la, I would really appreciate it if you would come to Disneyland with me tomorrow."

It was then I realized this was a dream.

It wasn't a dream per se – because those are all over the map. This included a doorbell, and a stairs walk, and a hallway visit. But I realized this was not reality. And this was a version of Kutenla speaking to me, but I could see him sparkling as well.

I laughed and bowed, saying "Of course I will come to Disneyland tomorrow." And he disappeared.

The next thing I knew the phone rang and it was his attendant Tenzing. He said "Kutenla thinks he left his camera bag in your car, could you bring it to him at Disneyland?" I said "Tell him that I got his message last night" assuming he was aware of the visit.

Inside the monastery in Dharamsala

I got to Disneyland and he had a couple of monks with him, he was dressed in his maroon robes, and everyone at Disneyland assumed he must be part of a ride. The monks were beside themselves with glee, work Mickey Mouse hats and generally were having the best day in the happiest place on earth.

Over lunch I asked him if he was aware of the visitation the night before.

He was not.

Not at all. No clue as to what I was referring to. But he never did ask me for the camera bag, and it wasn't in my car.

I remember as the day was about over, he looked at his watch and said, "If we run we can make Indiana Jones." And we did.

The next time I saw him is the reason for this chapter.

I went to visit him in Dharamsala and he said "I wish you had brought your DAT machine because I'd really like to make a CD of my monks for the monastery." I opened my bag and brought it out. I set up a microphone stand and covered it with small microphones – I think it was 8 – and put that in the center of the monastery. And the monks did their prayers and played their instruments.

The CD is called "Traditional Chants of Tibet."

Whenever he comes to the US I make sure that he has a number of them so he can hand them out to people who come to see him (like Barbra Streisand who has a copy.)

It's produced by yours truly and can be found at online websites, including CD baby and the one that rhymes with Babizon.

I've heard from people all around the planet who say that they put the CD on and go into a trance themselves. A peaceful one.

Which is unusual, because these are the monks who pray and chant and make music which puts the State Oracle of Tibet into his trance. This CD has made me a music producer.

Just an aside, I just got off the phone with Robert Towne, the screenwriter, friend of Luana's and he wanted to repeat a story that happened during a phone conversation with our mutual friend Jennifer Shaffer.

Robert had an Asian nanny when he was growing up in San Pedro, California, and he wondered about her. Jennifer was able to access her, and she expressed a detail only she could have known. That is, she was concerned about a tree that grew in Robert's backyard in San Pedro, and how he climbed it all the time and was worried that he "took too many risks."

What makes it unusual is that he'd forgotten about that tree – and the last time he was driving by his old home in San Pedro he saw it. And here was his nanny, whom he hadn't seen since he was five years old (when she was deported to a camp for Japanese people during World War II) reminding him of a detail he'd long forgotten. The resonance of who we were stays with us, like echoes of strings on a guitar vibrating in another room.

I realized I'm not really making the connection here – the one that goes unseen, despite my affection for Kutenla and Tibetans in general.

Let's discuss that resonance for half a minute.

While auditing classes at Columbia in Robert Thurman's PhD candidate course, I was invited to meet Diana Takata, the head of the Students for a Free Tibet. We became pals, and she told me about this young fellow who was a Fulbright scholar who went to Tibet to record some music for his doctoral thesis. Ngawang Choephel (there's a page on his life on Wikipedia.)

And while he was there he was arrested and thrown into Drapchi prison. I didn't know much about the politics of the situation at the time, but I could empathize with a musician being arrested for filming dances.

So I did what I could, showing up at protests in front of the Chinese embassy, getting a film crew from CNBC to cover it and share the footage with Diana. Tiny ripples in a pond.

That eventually led to Diana and her husband Don inviting me to see the Dalai Lama in Wisconsin. Later, I would learn about Richard Davidson's work there, showing that meditation can cure or alleviate symptoms of depression, but at this moment in time, I was just someone who wanted to see the Dalai Lama speak.

And at some point we were invited onstage to take a picture with him – I've never seen that photo, but I took my own selfie, which was awkward and unusual. Just my eyeball and the back of his head.

Then some years later, when making the CD for Kutenla, he said "Some refugees have just arrived from Tibet, maybe you'd like to interview them."

And I did – I made this documentary called "Tibetan Refugee" and filmed people telling their stories. People who were tortured for years for having a photograph of him, chained to walls – one guy lost his foot from frostbite. I tried to be non-partial in the documentary, asking everyone the same questions: "Why did you leave, what did you hope to find here? What's your impression of the Dalai Lama?"

I filmed in the Tibetan Children's Village, met some of the children who were living in a building donated for them. I interviewed dozens of children who had just arrived, whose parents, hoping they might have a better life, or a life where they learned about Tibetan Buddhism, sent them through the treacherous hills of the Himalayas to Nepal, and eventually to Dharamsala. The film is free and online – Youtube has it under "Tibetan Refugee" by yours truly.

But I filmed people singing their songs and that of that fellow trapped in Drapchi prison for filming these same songs. Oddly enough some years later, Diana sent me an email that Ngawang Choephel had been released, and wanted to know if I knew of anyone who might help him financially because he was in India with no funds whatsoever.

And I had met Goldie Hawn with Kutenla, so I called her up and she said "Where do I sent the check?" She gave Ngawang five grand on the spot to help him out. Since then he's become an award-winning filmmaker, and I loaned him some footage from my film in Tibet.

Which we're getting to.

So now I've spent time with Robert Thurman in India, Ladakh, and then I invited myself to accompany him to Tibet. I said I'd shoot the trip, wherever they went, and would donate the footage to Geographic Expeditions and Tibet House so that they would have a record of the trip.

And to my surprise he said yes.

I'll not that Nena said it was a bad idea; "People on a spiritual pilgrimage don't want you and your camera in their noses!" But for some reason, he thought it was a good idea.

I was making a Bollywood film, something called "My Bollywood Bride" a story I had written about the last trip to India where I found the one person I knew, who had been with me at USC film school – Manjulla Nanavati – and like magic, someone at the dinner table in Mumbai knew her.

So I'd written a script about "kismet" or falling in love from afar and the lengths an American would go to find his true love. And then I turned down directing it, but agreed to shoot second unit (the shots around Mumbai) and do the rewrites in return for a trip to India.

And it was there I got an email from Robert saying "If you can be in Katmandu on Tuesday, you can join our trip around Mt. Kailash and Lhasa and film it."

Imagine my chagrin!

I bid farewell to the blisteringly hot sound stages in Juhu making "My Bollywood Bride" and hopped on a plane to Nepal. Bob was leading a tour group of 25, which included George Lucas' secretary, a doctor, and others who had save up a lifetime for the trip.

And we landed in Lhasa without going through the proper channels. The tour company had to pay a hefty fine – and as I sat on the tarmac in this Air Nepal plane, I had the distinct impression "I was home."

Home. As in "Back in Tibet where I used to live."

It had happened once when landing in Rome, Italy, a place I'd never been and then again, the first time I landed in Mumbai. "I'm home."

Since then, having done 6 hypnotherapy sessions I understand why I felt that way – I was "returning" to a place I used to live.

But not from the visuals – which were new to me. But some kind of geometric memory, the frequency of the place, or its geographical place on the magnetized planet. I don't know. All I do know is that I felt like "I was home" in places I'd never been, never dreamed of visiting.

And we traipsed across Tibet. Spent a week in Lhasa, went through the Dalai Lama's old digs at the Potala, where I surreptitiously snapped a photo…

And then after Lhasa, drove across the land of the snows, all the way to Mt. Kailash in Western Tibet, where I've mentioned some unusual tales, including hearing Michael Gough speak to me in my tent (and he wasn't off the planet, just somehow visiting me on one of his trips around the universe with Luana Anders). And I've mentioned how my son claimed that he "found me" on Mt. Kailash – which reminded me that I had stood on that sacred mountain and in the midst of making a "wish for a million dollars" instead said "I want a son."

Tibet is a land of magic. It's also a land of resonance.

To think that I would meet the Dalai Lama at his home, and film him, and then a few years later be at his home in Tibet – what are the odds? And then some years later to have a past life regression where I saw myself living as a monk near Lhasa ("A day ride by donkey" I said) where I worked as a librarian, collecting books, and how I had lived to a ripe old age.

What made that memory poignant was the fact that I could remember how "lonely it was being of old age" – not because of the decrepitude, but because all of my pals who got my jokes were no longer on the planet. I'd say something funny to my attendant, a pun perhaps, and he'd nod like "Yes, the old man just farted again."

And I had those pangs of "everyone being gone" and no one getting my jokes. Which is not something I could have conceived when I accessed it.

Or remembering the moment when I finally keeled over, after hacking and coughing and hearing my coughs echo in the chambers of the monastery, and how when I finally left my body, I went to my attendants room, patted him on the head, and then blew out his candle to make him aware that I was gone. **But not gone.** *Clearly not so.*

Clearly here writing this sentence. Saying these words. That same fellow. Not back from the dead – but just continuing on the story. Life as life can only be. Part of being home, part of being here. Part of the journey we all take.

Author, Luana and Dave Patlak in Hawaii

CELESTIAL MUSIC

(Excerpt from "It's a Wonderful Afterlife" Book One.)

"When in the evening I contemplate the sky in wonder and the host of luminous bodies continually revolving within their orbits, suns or earths by name, then my spirit rises beyond these constellations . . . to the primeval source from which all creation flows and from which new creations shall flow eternally. . . . The spirit must rise from the earth, in which for a time the divine spark is confined, and much like the field to which the ploughman entrusts precious seed, it must flower and bear many fruits, and, thus multiplied, rise again towards the source from which it has flown." -- Ludwig Van Beethoven, *Letters, Journals*

How does music fit into these visions of the afterlife?

During LBLs and NDEs people often report "hearing" music that's not of an Earthly nature. In a number of LBLs I've heard people report that music and healing come from "related" places in the universe. But there are many musicians who claim to hear music when composing.

When we study the great composers, like Beethoven, we find that they spoke often of "hearing celestial music." Oliver Sachs, the renowned scientist, considers this "hallucinatory music." As he notes:

> True musical hallucinations are experienced by those who have them as unprecedented and deeply disquieting. There is insufficient awareness among physicians of musical hallucinations, in part because

patients are reluctant to report them, fearing that they will be dismissed or seen as 'crazy'. But musical hallucinations are surprisingly common, affecting at least 2% of those who are losing their hearing, as well as patients with a variety of other conditions. Working with a population of elderly patients (though I have seen it in younger people as well), I am often given vivid descriptions of musical hallucinosis, and I think it is by far the most common form of non-psychotic hallucination. I related two stories of musical hallucination in my 1985 book "The Man Who Mistook his Wife for a Hat," and since then have received hundreds of letters from people with this condition. With musical hallucinations it is common for several voices or instruments to be heard simultaneously, and such experiences are almost always attributed, initially, to an external source. Thus in 1995 I received a vivid letter from June M., a charming and creative woman of 70, telling me of her musical hallucinations:

> "…Most of the music I hear is from my past—many of the songs are hymns, some are folk music, some pop up from the forties and fifties, some classical and some show tunes. All the selections are sung by a chorus—there is never a solo performance or any orchestration. This first started last November when I was visiting my sister and brother in law in Cape Hatteras, NC, one night. After turning off the TV and preparing to retire, I

started hearing 'Amazing Grace.' It was being sung by a choir, over and over again. I checked with my sister to see if they had some church service on TV, but they had Monday night football, or some such. So I went onto the deck overlooking Pamlico Sound. The music followed me. I looked down on the quiet coastline and the few houses with lights and realized that the music couldn't possibly be coming from anywhere in that area. It had to be in my head."

It was not clear why June M. started to have musical hallucinations, or why she still has them, 11 years later. She has excellent hearing, is not epileptic, has no known medical problems and is intellectually quite intact. With her, as with many other patients, the most searching examination may fail to pinpoint the cause of musical hallucinations..." [31]

There is another possible explanation for the source of her music that Dr. Sach's hasn't explored: that it is not created by her mind.

A speaker can sometimes pick up the vibrations from other sound waves and reproduce them, but the sound is not being created by the speaker. Sometimes our radio picks up bursts of short wave radios from police scanners, but it's not that the announcement is created by our stereo.

---

[31] "The Power of Music" by Oliver Sachs. Oxford Journals *Brain* Volume 129.

438

In Eben Alexander's NDE he heard "celestial music." "I heard… the richest, most complex, most beautiful piece of music (I've) ever heard." It's also one of the hallmarks of NDE's according to Bruce Greyson's research.

> "As a high school student, Burt Bacharach always had trouble getting to school on time: he couldn't sleep at night because he kept hearing music in his head. Throughout his life, Bacharach would never stop hearing music, because for him music would always be about sounds rather than ideas." [32]

In David Bennett's interview ("Voyage of Purpose") he talks about hearing a "canyon of sound" during his NDE. He gives specific details on what that music sounds like.

Pete Townshend, legendary member of the band, The Who, heard celestial music as an 11 year old boy. "Townshend tells of hearing the music while on a boat with his Sea Scout troop. "I heard violins, cellos, horns, harps and voices, which increased in number until I could hear the threads of an angelic choir. It was a sublime experience. I have never heard such music since and my personal music ambition has always been to rediscover that sound and relive its effect on me."[33]

Stuart Sharp heard celestial music when he was a young man. The experience was similar to Townshend's: he first heard the

---

[32] "Self-Portrait of an Experimental Songwriter" David Galenson, Huffington Post 2-19-14

[33] "Who I am: a Memoir" by Pete Townshend Harper, 2013

angelic orchestra in a dream as a boy in 1956. Years later he heard it again after his baby son Ben died at birth. He explains: "In my dream I was back at Ben's graveside staring down at his tiny white coffin. I heard distant angelic music with choirs, violins, cellos, horns and harps that grew in intensity and I gasped as Ben's spirit rose slowly through the coffin. I couldn't bring myself to see him in the mortuary. I didn't have the courage."

He was so haunted by the music he quit his job as cook in a Leicestershire country pub, left his wife and two daughters and moved to London and into a homeless shelter. He taught himself to play music after he bought a battered guitar from a second-hand shop which, by an amazing co-incidence, happened to be owned by Townshend's parents. Eventually Stuart Sharp met someone who was moved by his story and helped him record with the London symphony – the result is an orchestral piece called "Angeli Symphony."[34]

I've found other accounts, just from searching them out on the internet. From the NDE of "Jeanette Mitchell-Meadows": "When I went for surgery the operation took nine hours. During the operation my spirit left my body, in the time it takes to blink an eye, I was in Heaven and saw the light of Heaven… There were musical notes I have never heard on Earth. They were so clear and flawless, and the tone was so beautiful. It is the most wonderful place to be. [35]

---

[34] "Homeless man turns haunting noises in his head into symphony" The Express May 2, 2013

[35] http://www.bibleprobe.com/mitchell-meadows.htm

Or the account of an NDE from Canadian musician Gilles Bedard: "All day long, I went in and out of a coma... Then I saw myself from the ceiling. I was nine feet higher than my body and I was looking down at the people around me.... My vision expanded and I went into a place like a cosmos where there were twelve people standing in a half-circle. They were all pure white lights and they had no faces. I somehow knew these people although they weren't family or people I could recognize. It was as if they were waiting for me. I asked them what was happening, and they told me, 'You are not going to die. You are going back to Earth. You have something to do.' I asked them what it was, and as soon as I asked it was as if I knew the answer... What I remembered most is the music I heard when I was out of my body. It was fascinating.[36]

MY IDEE FIXES

In 7th grade, winning the State Science Fair.

---

[36] Gilles Bedard's Near-Death Experience and Music Research by Kevin Williams
http://www.near-death.com/music.html

What is an idee fixe?

Idée fixe, (French: "fixed idea") in music and literature, a recurring theme or character trait that serves as the structural foundation of a work. Britannica

It's a musical term, refers to the "main theme" or a series of notes that are repeated in a symphony. A "structural foundation" of the work.

Watching the 1960 version of "The Magnificent Seven" recently, I heard the theme repeated throughout the film. Elmer Bernstein used movement of horse to bring in the symphony and drums, but conversations were buttressed by the main theme, or the "idee fixe" of the story.

Dimitri Tiomkin did the same for the film "High Noon" with his recurring theme "Do Not Forsake Me, O My Darlin." Modern culture refers to these musical memories as "ear worms" or "memes" – not thinking of the Goddess referenced.

You know. The Goddess of Memory. C'mon. Already forgot her name? It was mentioned back at the beginning of this book. So famous that said a prayer to her before every Greek play, so actors wouldn't forget lines. You must remember her name, it's where the word memory comes from – meme as well. *Give up?*

Well we have her to thank for the whole conundrum. She is the Goddess who gives a traveler a drink of water when he dies, so he can "remember all of his previous lifetimes." But we should be able to remember her name, as she's the same Goddess who shows up when we're born, gives us a drink so we forgot "all those previous lifetimes."

She's the one responsible for the "filters." She's the one we need to speak with about bypassing the filters, one would imagine. And where does that drink come from? (Hint: Her name sounds like *"Nemazani."*)

What does it have to do with idee fixes over many lifetimes?

One of the most famous is in Berlioz's "Symphony Fantastique." The notes sometimes float over the action, float under the story, sometimes weave in and out. It's 6 notes. Some can refer to "Jaws" theme or perhaps "Close Encounters of the Third Time" as memorable idee fixes. The idea being when you hear the notes, you know what the musician is referring to.

Beethoven uses them throughout his music, sometimes the Ninth has the haunting notes from the first movement repeated in the fourth. Sometimes people look at the idee fixe as a repeated theme in a painting – something that makes the artwork jump out to the viewer. The movement of grass or stars in a Van Gogh painting, the placement of light in a Hopper painting, the chiaroscuro of a Renaissance master, the delicacy of a finger or hand in a Michelangelo statue perhaps, knowing that Michelangelo would first sculpt sometime perfectly – a hand, an arm, a knee, and then work out the rest of the sculpture, releasing the "figure within" to be seen.

The point is to focus on the *themes* in an artist's work. And we can do so with paint, with sculpture, with music. With writing, with pretty much anything.

It's a bit like having a frequency that identifies an individual.

I often ask people to recall the "first conscious moment they knew they wanted to do the work they were doing."

I was in a doctor's office today, and seasoned professional, who said "I had no clue, just popped into my mind in graduate school." Her assistant said "I was 5. I took care of my pets and dolls." The assistant is more aware of her idee fixe than her boss is.

I had a successful banker say "I had to be the person handling the cash in Monopoly. I dreamt about that cash often." I once asked an FBI agent the same. She said, "When I was in preschool." I asked what happened then, she said "I kept lists on everyone. What clothes they wore, what kinds of cars their parents drove. Everything."

"What do you want to be when you grow up?"

Some already know in the womb. Some already know prior to being in the womb as we've seen in this research. And then when they get here, these little notes of memory ring in their lifetime – throughout their lifetime, tapping them on the shoulder.

"Don't forget, you wanted to be a musician. Always play the instrument, don't give it up."

Once we allow that professionalism is something unattainable to most – or having a paying career in something they love to do, they can let that part of it go and play the instrument.

I found some artwork my father had painted in his 20's. I could recognize his drawings a mile away – the way he used a pencil, attention to detail. But he hadn't picked up a brush or pencil to paint for pleasure since he started work as a paid architect at Holabird and Root in Chicago.

So I begged him, bought him watercolors and soon enough he began to send me small pieces. I love them. Because I can see his frequency in them.

Portrait of "Pig" by Ro Martini, Circa 1941.

As his son, I can see my father in this drawing. I can see him in the blueprints he did for buildings around the world. The King Saud University in Riyadh. The "Porsche Plant" in Northfield, Illinois, now a Toyota Dealership. Even when sitting in a room that he designed, I can feel him.

Two examples mentioned in "Architecture of the Afterlife" – the lobby of the La Fonda Hotel in Santa Fe. I had a suddenly feeling about him and called him from the payphone. I asked if he was okay, he asked why I was asking. I said "I'm in La Fonda and thought of you." He said "We worked on that redesign when I was with Holabird and Root. I redid some of the interior." I had "experienced" his frequency.

The other was in Luana Ander's house. I was sitting in the new bedroom of her home, and looking out the window, and something – the way the light came through the window, the feeling of the room – I thought of him. I said "Who designed this room?" She said "Charlie. Remember, I asked him to." I remembered my dad saying he was doing "some drawings for Luana" and of course assumed that was sketching – but in architecture parlance it's blueprints.

Thought of him, felt his frequency in the room he'd designed before knowing who had designed the room.

I was fortunate enough to record my mother playing the piano – she suggested it late in life, that she was afraid she couldn't play at his funeral, so she had me record his music and we played it at his funeral. Then, 7 years late, when she passed, I made sure she played at her own funeral.

Not many musicians can say that. But my mother can.

So if we take the time we can find our idee fixe.

It's in our work, it's in our life, it's in our journey. It might be in many lifetimes; it might be in many journeys. The idea of a theme that runs through who we are.

People on the flipside report classrooms and having certain concepts run over many lifetimes. Like teaching a class in "overcoming addiction" might take many forms, a life of gluttony, or using drugs, or sex, or something that is addictive, and the person learns how to master that energy.

Karma means "action" or "energy" in Sanskrit, not "sin" or "Baggage" as it's come to mean.

But a person might choose a lifetime to examine a specific quality. Courage, compassion, forgiveness. And when one takes the time to look over their lifetime, they can see the underlying themes, they can see or hear the idee fixe running through their lifetime.

When I first started this journey with the film Flipside, I found myself in front of my council during my first of six hypnotherapy sessions. And I asked my council – "Why did I choose Richard?"

And I saw and heard a number of things – the actual moment when I suggested to my friends, family, and classmates that an "outside the box" way to heal people would entail making films and helping people to access healing energy through laughter.

At the time I said off handedly, "I just wish I'd chosen a more successful filmmaker" – and the hypnotherapist laughed and so did my council. Imagine hearing laughter from two sides of the veil at the same time. I said, "But I have a feeling that will change."

It didn't change in terms of success, but it did in terms of focus. Having filmed dozens, 100 sessions, 100's of hours of footage with mediums, weekly sessions with Jennifer Shaffer and other mediums, I've accumulated 100s of hours of footage. I likely don't have the time to edit it all, but I can seek out the themes.

The idee fixes of my life if you will.

And when I was editing the film "Flipside" I suddenly realized that all of my films had a running theme of someone "pretending to be someone else" or "someone who they are not." In "You Can't Hurry Love" it's people pretending to be someone else to go on dates, in "Limit Up" it's Danitra Vance the guardian angel pretending to be a devil, in "Point of Betrayal," there's the final scene where Rod Taylor dances with the ghost of his wife, played by Dina Merrill.

Death and disguise and changing identities has always been part of my work. I can recall the first paper I wrote in grade school was about a Walter Mitty character who was a mild-mannered teacher by day and a wild man by night. The Nutty Professor was a film I pitched for a remake (and someone else did.)

The point is – I've always been attracted to the concept that someone is "not who you think they are." They are often something more, something or someone greater and they may not even be able to see it in life. They have a noble character, a noble soul and they're part of a larger network of people who are all connected.

And I realized that while editing my documentary.

Now the sequel "Hacking the Afterlife" is out on Gaia, and includes bits and pieces of ten years of filming.

In essence, the *idee fixe* of your life is reflecting on the themes of all of them.

If you're someone who spends time healing others, then that's a possibility. If you're someone who spends time challenging others, that might be a theme as well. We can all look to the mirror for examples of our own journey.

We can ask our guides and teachers, "What was I thinking when I signed up for this mess?" We can reflect upon the idea that we signed up for a difficult lifetime because perhaps we're people who like a challenge. We can observe how others sign up for what appears to be chaos, when in actuality it's someone off the bench racing into the field, or an actor running in from off stage to take over a scene from a fallen comrade.

We can observe how the theme and music of our life is reflected in our friendships on the planet – our frequency and choices are reflected in the way we navigate the planet. If you're someone who needs sand to make a pearl, then perhaps reframe why one needs so much sand in their life. If you're someone who needs total solitude to consider a thought, perhaps examine ways to do that.

If you're someone who finds themselves often at their wits end, or confused by the play they're in, take the time to take a break and observe the others in the orchestra. Sit back with your instrument, bow in hand, and don't play. Just observe. See if the symphony is going the way it should, or if you're just resisting adding your few notes.

But most of all, look around oneself to find your idee fixe. The reason you've been on the planet so many times, the things that you're here to learn. Observe that it's possible to continue the symphony once someone has left the stage, that their notes are not gone, they're accessible if one takes the time to learn how to access them.

Keep the music going. Keep the tempo up. If the music is causing trauma, then learn to meditate, learn to be able to play the instrument as one is also observing why they're in the orchestra in the first place. Allow that the other musicians that are around us are there for a reason and we chose them to be there specifically to play that role, to play that music.

And then, let the music take you. After all, it's the symphony of life. It's the symphony of love. It's the symphony of consciousness.

REPRISE: "ONCE MORE WITH FEELING"

So here we are at the beginning again. A reprise.

Anthy, Luana in the streets of Roma.

People ask about the research with regard to previous lifetimes, current lifetimes. I often say "Think of it as playing a piano again. Some of the notes are out of tune, some of them are in tune – but all that falls away when someone plays with enthusiasm. Try to connect to the instrument you're playing.

Then we have the music of one's life – the musical notes of language, of showing children that those notes refer to objects. Then we have the people who are still connected to the flipside, children up to the age of 8 who can still recall previous lifetimes, can see loved ones not on the planet. They may call them imaginary friends, but they're friends none the less.

Guardians.

Then we have the various instruments of our lifetimes – the instruments that join us onstage that make up our band. The drums that keep a steady beat if possible, the bass that gives us a through line. The guitar that helps us solo through – the violins that keep our emotions just underneath, the timpani that accompanies our thunder, the keyboard that is… well you get the idea.

Think of music as a wave of consciousness.

The notes already exist. They wash over us, then out to sea.

We choose our lifetimes to learn specific pieces – some are dramatic, some are comedic, some are long and drawn out, some are short and sweet.

Each piece adds up to the symphony of who we are.

We are connected to everyone else the same way that notes are connected to the strings. The same way that the keys, black and white, all go together. They all exist side by side, and then along comes a musician to play them, move them, make them sing with each other.

We tap into the music of the universe every time we open our eyes. We tape into the music of our world as we navigate our day, hearing frequencies that carry orders, emotion, happiness, pain, sorry.

We might turn on a television and listen to other frequencies that evoke sadness, trauma or pain – or we might tap into something that is about compassion, courage and love. All frequencies.

We are in the midst of creating this epic symphony. The symphony of our lives. If one looks at Beethoven not as this "artist" who "lived his life" but just as the notes, the millions of notes that he played, the millions of notes that he wrote, that exist for all time. That each note is an echo of him, each note is tethered to his frequency, his memory and when we play his music, we connect to him directly.

The same goes for Shakespeare – every actor who speaks his words is channeling his spirit, his essence, his "higher self." And by experiencing that in a theater, we connect to who or what Will was. Same goes for musicians creating music, performing original pieces, or performing the notes of a composer. They're tapping into the essence of who that person is.

The same metaphor applies to all of us – every gesture we make, every note of our speech, our conversing, our expressing ourselves is part of the symphony of who we are.

So how do we tap into the symphony that we've written for ourselves?

We can use hypnotherapy, mediumship or meditation to bypass those filters on the brain, the organ that functions as a receiver, that filters those frequencies out that are not conducive to life. We can bypass those filters willfully, by accident when we have an NDE, OBE, perhaps using LSD or some other hallucinogen. Or when we use meditation or hypnotherapy to physically bypass those filters. Or even when someone like me asks simple questions about one's life and journey. A person taps into the record of their lifetimes and access that information.

There is no delete key in the brain. Every breath, heartbeat is recorded – every thought, action, deed – goes into the library. We can call it akashic, or etheric (which is what akashic means, literally "invisible") and when we want to know something about a previous lifetime, we can get out our library card and request it... actually no library card is required, but it's fun to think so.

So, if one wants to know what the theme or idee fixe of their lifetime is, start with the earliest thoughts. What was your "first conscious thought you'd be doing the kind of work you're doing now?" I've asked dozens of people – about half of them have some kind of childhood memory of doing the thing they're doing now. The FBI agent who said, "In preschool I kept lists of everyone." The doctor's assistant who said, "At age 5, I became serious about treating and healing my dolls and animals." The banker who said, "You couldn't play Monopoly enough with me, and I always, always had to be the banker, the one with the money."

One can get a glimpse of the theme of their lifetime by the people they've met who they felt like they'd known "before" or "forever." Sometimes it's a pal, sometimes it's a mate, and by examining that experience – slowing down the moment to recall the exact moment when they "felt in love" – that reveals something that is outside of time. The life planning session where they discussed these future events.

We can learn about our journey by examining the kinds of things that we focus on. Are we people who focus on sadness, or lugubriousness, on trauma? Are we people who focus on laughter, comedy and lightheartedness? Are we people who focus on the drama or the comedy? It doesn't matter which one focuses on, but we can scan the entirety of our lives to see the themes involved. The musical notes of who we were and who we have become.

We might change instruments. We might change paths. We might adjust, alter, change the path we are on – but the musician stays the same.

In the book "Architecture of the Afterlife" I focused on my father's influence in my life, being an architect who saw things in terms of structure. In this book, I've focused on music and musicians, and how my mother's playing concert piano every day of my life, helped me to focus on frequency, how things are connected to each other, how certain melodies repeat, how some people can harmonize with each other without realizing it, how some people feel like they're playing the same instrument at the same time.

Having spent ten years filming people under hypnosis, comparing what they've said with thousands of clinical case studies, having spent over six years filming mediums speaking directly to people on the other side, having filmed 100 cases of people accessing the flipside directly, half without hypnosis, I'm sharing what the footage has taught me.

That we are all connected. That we are all notes on the same keyboard. That we are all just walking each other home. That we have nothing to fear from the music, and we have everything to gain from the knowledge that we chose to be here, chose to play this tune and chose to play with these other musicians that are in our lives.

And now, cue the finale of Beethoven's Ninth, as I couldn't have said it any better.

Beethoven's Ninth is considered by some to be the greatest composition of one of the greatest composers of all time. The fact that he was completely, irrevocably deaf when he wrote it doesn't mean he didn't hear it.

I was introduced to the Ninth in college as part of my Humanities program. As I listened incessantly, I started to hear another story – the story of humanity. That the four movements of this symphony depicted four stages of mankind. Birth, Youth, Middle Age, Death.

The first movement; I. "Allegro ma non troppo, un poco maestoso."

Happy, but not too happy; a little bit triumphant.

The first movement of the 9th is a bit like life; some have likened to an expression of the Big Bang; order coming out of chaos. Some point to the sun rise, others point to the light coming into darkness, the birth of the planet, the dawn of consciousness. There are many themes stated – themes that are echoed throughout the symphony.

But use it as a metaphor. How does the world come into existence? Like light coming up over the horizon. Like light coming out of darkness. People in the research report there have been many "big bangs" in this universe – expansion and contraction. That there are many "big bangs" in other universes. But if one sits back, puts on the first movement of Beethoven's Ninth, they'll hear a musical "Big Bang" come out of a primordial darkness.

And then from that comes matter, comes elements, etc. Consciousness is already in existence, it doesn't arise from something else, of course it's observing this latest "Big Bang" and helping to direct it. And eventually – step outside of time to conceive of it – the planets form, they're seeded by the folks who need a place to live, to inhabit, and eventually we show up there in life form – could be our planet, might have been Mars in the past, might be an alternate Earth in another realm... but we choose to arrive there. We make that choice.

It's repeated throughout the research. We bring a portion of our conscious mind to a lifetime – we do so with the help and guidance of teachers, guides, classmates and friends. And we do our best to have an adventure, to learn things, to share things, to teach things – and when the curtain falls on that vacation, that drama, that match out in the playing field – we return home and share all the humiliations, joy and experiences.

In stories, the end of the first act is when the audience knows what the hero needs to do, but the hero has yet to learn it.

II. Molto vivace – Presto.

In a brisk, spirited manner. Lots of spirit. "As if by magic."

The second movement of the Ninth might be thought of as humans growing up or becoming human. The animation of the human being. All of the characteristics of emotion and pathos. "Ritmo di tre battute" ("rhythm of three beats"), and one beat every four measures with the direction "Ritmo di quattro battute" ("rhythm of four beats").

Love, passion, the early part of a human's journey. When hearts beat fastest in love or war. This is when a human finds their passion, their reason to be on the planet. Could be war, could be love, could be teaching, or learning. Could be disastrous, could be life affirming.

But that also applies to the journey of souls, or to the journey we all take. Reportedly we are "created" by bringing together two parts of conscious energy initially, could be a male/female kind of ration, and as the "conscious energy" grows, people tend to their flock, look over those growing young beings.

A bit like the film "Soul" by Pixar where young starlings are watched over by "Jerry's" and given option for what they're going to be. The film is more documentary than fiction in that regard – literally is echoing what has been reported by many.

After we get to a point where we are ready to "incarnate" – we are assigned a "Jerry" – sorry, that's from the film, we are assigned a "guide." In my case my guide told me during my second hypnotherapy session with Scott De Tamble, that "after all of his lifetimes, his graduation gift was me."

And my guide then described a process of discussing with me – the junior candidate – what I was after, what I thought would be an interesting portrait. And he showed me (as I recount in "It's a Wonderful Afterlife") this blank canvas and said "each lifetime is like more paint on the canvas." And after a difficult journey, or a fantastic journey, the two of us might sit back and say, "Needs more red over here." Or "It's missing some blue. Let's plan a lifetime where we learn more about peacefulness, or the passivity of existence. More "blue."

And then another journey. Sometimes one's guide will agree to accompany a person on their journey – play the role of grandfather for example, or some teacher who helps the person get over a difficult area of learning. That's reported.

And then at the end of all of my lifetimes – at the end of my "second movement" I get a chance to see a portrait of a person that comes into view with clarity. All the journeys and lifetimes have turned into this giant portrait of a journey.

But as we get towards the end of the journey, we often have a second act event, or a way of "reflection" upon the journey – just like in storytelling, just like in life.

The third movement III. Adagio molto e cantabile, Andante moderato. Tempo Primo – Andante Moderato – Adagio – Lo Stesso Tempo.

Very slowly and songlike; then a moderate pace. Then back to the original tempo, then a moderate pace. Then slow; the same pace.

The third movement is our chance to reflect on the journey. We've gone through the difficulties of the second act, and now are able to move into the third act of our life. Not everyone makes it this far, but for those who do – doesn't matter how many years they might have on the planet, as it's related to story, they learn the most in this act.

It might be after losing a loved one, no matter what age, that their loved ones say, "I realize now that towards the end of his or her journey, they seemed to be aware that it was coming to an end." "They said goodbye the night before the accident, as if they knew somehow that they wouldn't be around." "I think they did the thing that they needed to do and went home."

In Shakespeare's observation of human behavior, it's after the pomp and circumstance that one begins to slow down to reflect on the themes of one's lifetime. Like the recap of life Will Shakespeare gives us in "As You Like It."

"All the world's a stage, and all the men and women merely players; they have their exits and their entrances, and one man in his time plays many parts, his acts being seven ages.

1. At first, the infant, mewling and puking in the nurse's arms. Then the whining schoolboy, with his satchel and shining morning face, creeping like snail unwillingly to school.

2. And then the lover, sighing like furnace, with a woeful ballad made to his mistress' eyebrow. Then a soldier, full of strange oaths and bearded like the pard, jealous in honor, sudden and quick in quarrel, seeking the bubble reputation even in the cannon's mouth.

3. And then the justice, in fair round belly with good capon lined, with eyes severe and beard of formal cut, full of wise saws and modern instances; and so, he plays his part. The sixth age shifts into the lean and slippered pantaloon, with spectacles on nose and pouch on side; his youthful hose, well saved, a world too wide for his shrunk shank, and his big manly voice, turning again toward childish treble, pipes and whistles in his sound. Last scene of all, that ends this strange eventful history, is second childishness and mere oblivion, Sans teeth, sans eyes, sans taste, sans everything."

And then what? What comes next Will?

We go home.

It's true in each lifetime. Each journey has a beginning, middle and end. It might be thought of as "four acts" – beginning, middle, end and "after." Because as we've heard consistently, life doesn't end.

We are like caterpillars in our journey, and if lucky we make it to the chrysalis stage. But that too is just a stage, because at the end of the chrysalis stage we emerge from the physical, crawling life, and into the flight life. The ability to move at the speed of the wind, in our case, the ability to move at the speed of thought. Nothing has ended – it's only transformed.

Same goes for the journey of someone's conscious energy. After all of our lifetimes, after we've learned as much as we can, after we've taught as many as we can, after we've experienced and loved everyone we can, we move on to the next stage. It might be a guide for someone else, it might be a teacher, it might be someone serving on councils – there are many of those, and they often serve on many councils.

There is a myriad of things to do after we've learned the lessons incarnating – it's not as if we are "liberated" from incarnating, because it's a choice. We can come back if we want to – but at some point, we realize we've learned as much as we can from the process, and those who asked us to help in the past have moved on as well. And for us – we too might as well move on to the next act of our journey.

The Fourth Movement. *"After."*

IV. Presto; Allegro molto assai (alla marcia); Andante maestoso; Allegro energico, sempre ben marcato.

As if by magic; happy and very fast. (Like a march) Quickly with triumph, happy and energetic, always well marked, a strong accent.

It's the moment for us to return home.

The Finale. Summa Theologica.

And then, in Beethoven's own words, words that **Beethoven personally added** to Schiller's poem at the end of the Ninth Symphony and at the beginning of the chorale:

"Oh friends, not these sounds! Let us instead strike up more pleasing and more joyful ones! Joy! Joy!"

He added that to this poem. Just what did Ludwig mean by *"not these sounds?"*

Could he have meant, "These sounds of dying, of passing over, these sounds of war and chaos and things coming to an end... of instruments clashing and coming to the end of what they've been playing?

Because that's not the end, we think it's the end, but our whole life we've been listening to symphonies from the flipside, from the great beyond, from the ethers of the distant galaxies, and we know that it all doesn't end with thunder or a cacophony of drums, fire or flash.

There is more. It's something quite profound. And there's not many human words we can put to the experience of "unconditional love" – but it is consistent and it's throughout the research that people experience this feeling, this profound emotion once they've left their earthly bounds.

It's "Joy."

And those are the words that Beethoven added to Schiller's poem. **JOY! JOY!** *(Freude! Freude!)*

It's a shift. We have gone from this world, of notes and drums and crashing cymbals to a feeling of "Joy." Beethoven knew it. He'd known it his whole life. That music is, comes from "beyond the spheres." That life doesn't end on the final note of breath – that the afterlife begins with Joy.

This reminds me what my father said to me the night after he passed.

I had flown home to Chicago for his funeral, the day he passed, and I was in bed in the home he'd designed and built when I awoke to feel his strong hand on my shoulder.

I immediately, before thinking he was no longer on the planet, said his name. I was aware he was standing behind me with his hand on my shoulder. "Dad." And he said in my ear, clearly in his voice;

"I'm experiencing indescribable joy."

I'm suggesting that Beethoven in his silence, also experienced Joy and that's what he was writing about when it came to his last opus. He heard "Joy."

Not "You are so dumb" (the comment he made when asked about the first notes of the Fifth symphony. A play on words – "I am so dumb" because he'd lost his hearing by then, but also "a comment on the inequity of the experience" – as in "Oh my God, I can't believe I've lost my hearing." "You are so dumb!" But also, that he can repeat himself, write it down, and get others to play it for him. We all are so dumb. Because we haven't a clue how things *work*.

The joy of music. The joy of creation. The joy of life.

Enjoy.

Encore: "Let It Be"

Luana in Rockefeller Plaza

Recently, Carlos Santana was interviewed by Anderson Cooper during the "Homecoming Concert" in August 2021. Anderson asked Carlos about performing live, coming out of the pandemic and his new album, *"Miracles and Blessings."*

Carlos Santana: It's wonderful to be able to connect with people's hearts (again). The message is that we can transmogrify (*transform in a surprising and magical manner*) fear and darkness, we can coexist with unity and harmony, accept our own totality, accept our own light and create miracles and blessings.

People are thirsty; we're bringing living water to people with a sound resonance vibration. We are at the right time and right place to present to them another frequency, different than fear darkness and separation – which is what we've been dealing with for years.

Most people have crystallized their intentions during this period – and the questions is, "Can you prioritize why am I on this planet?" There's an opportunity for a lot more equilibrium, balance and competence.

From my point of view, time is an illusion. From where I am, I discard time and gravity. You just have to spend more time with your heart and less time up here (points to his hat).

Because that's what's happening with everybody. We've been bamboozled – we were imbued before we came out of the womb with heavenly powers which means we can create miracles and blessing. The program we've been given is for us to believe we're a wretched sinner unworthy of our own life. (Laughs) I don't think so – *"Keep those beliefs to yourself, man."*

I believe I am made of the same essence that God is – look it up in the Bible – we're "In god's image." God is only good – anything that's less than that… there's a lot of Godzilla energy in the Bible – with jealousy, if he doesn't like something, he would flood it.

That's not God. God is love. Just like you update your phone and your laptop – we need to update the Bible and the Constitution.

Gratitude is very powerful, when you say the word, even before you say it… We're at the place where we can program your whole molecular structure to say "Today I'm only going to only contemplate and entertain thoughts that are inspiring and elevating – anything else I'm going to say "No, that's going to put me in a misery ditch. I'll be sad, lonely, depressed – that's boring. I don't want to be boring. I want to be effulgent. (*Shining forth brilliantly; radiant.*)

I love to see people cry and laugh and dance at the same time – my metaphor is like when we see a wet shaggy dog shake off the water, he creates a rainbow next to the sun. That water he shakes off, we can ward off fear, we ward off lack of self-worth.

I love all the things that I've learned from people I love from John Coltrane, Mohandas Gandhi, Martin Luther King, Dolores Huerta, Harry Belafonte – I love who I'm becoming. I'm learning from those who have impeccable integrity on a very high level. It's fun to be Carlos now. What I focus on, is for the highest good for all people, impeccable integrity – if you're not with that, catch the next train, because this one's leaving." *Carlos Santana.*

*****

Here's another flipside class conversation. This was with John Lennon and is from "Backstage Pass to the Flipside."

Jennifer and I are having a conversation, and in this case, John has shown up in our café. Jennifer has said "John Lennon is here" and me, trying not to be too thrilled over the fact that five minutes earlier I had "asked aloud" for his participation, try to interview him without thinking this might actually be him.

Rich: Okay, that's good. John, we asked you to come forward today, my apologies for interrupting you.

Jennifer: He's saying very dryly; "The VIP line is getting longer (for this class.)"

Is there anything you want me to tell your family or friends?

He wants to say something to Paul McCartney. About the carpool karaoke thing.

> (Note: James Corden did a brilliant "Carpool Karaoke" with Paul, where they sang songs together and visited Penny Lane in Liverpool. Corden broke down in tears at one point, remembering the first time his grandfather played him the song.)[37]

With James Corden? (To Jennifer) Have you seen it?

(Jennifer aside) I heard about it but haven't seen it. John says, "He was there in the car with them." That he "helped Paul write a song;" there's a song Paul wrote recently, and John said, "He's going to continue to do that, help him to write music."

The karaoke bit was amazing; Paul went to the house he used to live in and walked through the rooms where he used to write and sing with John. He's helping Paul to write, now?

He says, "It's a new song, but it's based on an old song." He's saying, "There's an old song that John recorded that never got released," but he wants it to come out. Then he showed me "Hey Jude."

That was written by Paul for John's son; he used Jude instead of Julian.

(Jennifer aside) Oh, I didn't know that. It feels like it's a song that would be for Paul's kids, like "Hey Jude" was for John's son. He says, "He wants Paul to know that he

---

[37] If you only watch one "Carpool Karaoke" watch this one: https://www.youtube.com/watch?v=QjvzCTqkBDQ

was there with him in the car... Paul knows he was, because he had "the chills" while he was in the car."

Paul told the story behind "Let it Be" – the song refers to his mother Mary McCartney.

(Jennifer aside) Really? I thought it was about Jesus's mother Mary.

Everyone did. "When I find myself in times of trouble, Mother Mary comes to me" referred his mom. When he was stressed about money, he had this dream that his mom, who passed when he was a kid, came to him and told him everything was going to be okay. To just "let it be." He said it gave him such peace and comfort he remembered it when he woke up, said "Wait a second, what did she say?" John, do you know Mary?

He says, "They're hanging out."

Can she say something to Paul?

He said, "She talks to him all the time!" Hang on, "Hey Jude" keeps coming up – he's trying to tell me something. I didn't know that song was about his son Julian, by the way. (Jennifer listens) He's showing me you. He says, "Whatever it is that you said to his son got through to him."

(Note: As I've noted, Julian is in the film Cannes Man, which I took over directing. The day he was in the film, I wasn't directing, but later took over the film to finish it. The following year we showed it in Cannes, I ran into Julian, and he invited me to hang out with him and some friends. We wound up in Monte Carlo singing "Sweet Home Chicago" in a pub, and later, he had me sleep on the couch of his home in Eze.

The following morning, not too many hours after our last night, hung over, I was rudely awakened from the couch with someone shouting in my hear "Who the f*ck are you?" I mean – I heard it clear as a bell and it knocked me off the couch. I got up, rubbed my eyes, realized no one was in the living room.

Then I recognized the voice. I didn't tell Julian, I had no clue about this research then – but later, later Julian's friend Paul Allen came through to tell him to "look for black feathers as well" I mentioned it to him in an email. (Julian's charity is named White Feather after his father telling him that if he could communicate from the other side, it would be in the form of a white feather.) I'm repeating stories that have been told in my books, but it gives context for what's to follow.)

In a good way, I hope.

Yes, in the same way that vision of his mother Mary did for Paul. John is saying "Thank you."

Well, when I think of all the decades I've sung or played their tunes, I often think, "This must be what it's like for people who saw Beethoven." I am grateful to be alive at a time when the Beatles were playing, and I got to hear and play their music. So, thank you, maestro.

(Jennifer aside) No one would do this, what we're doing. Talking to the flipside.

Well, no one is ever going to believe it.

We're not here to make people believe.

Funny, I said to my skeptical friend last night, "Thank you for giving me something for the book – you're such a skeptic I realized I don't have to make everybody believe in this research. I just have to focus on the details we can verify, to help those who need to hear it. Not everyone signs up to know how the play ends; they're not meant to hear "Just let it be."

If we had everyone agreeing with us, we probably wouldn't like it anyway. Who would sign up for this job by the way – "Hey, let's talk to people no longer on the planet?"

*Well obviously, **you** signed up for it. And thank you for doing so. That's it, thanks class. Thanks, Luana, John, everyone. Bill Paxton.*

I had no idea you gambled with Billy. He said to me, "Why didn't you have the connection (to the flipside) when you guys gambled together in Cannes? He lost his shirt!"

Very funny. He did, but then so did I. A nice book end. Thanks Billy. Thanks class. Catch you on the flipside.

*****

Harry Houdini famously debunked mediums and psychics a century ago. But why did he do that?

Because he was one himself. He had an experience where he heard the voice of his deceased mother. He was in the midst of a trick in the East River in Manhattan, escaping while "under the ice" and he lost direction, couldn't find the hole in the ice. His life about to end from drowning, he heard the voice of his mother guide him to the hole in the ice.

He then tried to contact his mother using the mediums and psychics of the day. None could. But Harry could and did. He is the only one who knows the tone and timbre of his mother's voice. He currently knows her voice because he's on the flipside with her. (And he can answer questions one might have about that experience by asking him directly.)

His mother gave him "new information." Something he didn't know (where the hole in the ice was) but she did. In the same form, Paul McCartney heard new information from his deceased mother.

In the episode of "Carpool Karaoke" with James Corden, Paul said he wrote "Let it Be" when he was "having financial worries" and his mom came to him in a dream to let him know "everything was going to be fine, not to worry." He said he heard her say to him the words "just let it be."

James Corden wept as they sang it together, said "I remember my grandfather playing the song for me... I wish he was here to see this." Paul said matter of factly, "He is."[38]

Recently, in the miniseries "One Strange Rock" astronaut Jerry Linenger said his father came to visit him several times while he was on the international space station. He said he could "see him out of the corner of his eye" and the impression he got was that his father stopped by to "tell him how proud of him he was."[39]

It's important to repeat this for those suffering from depression, loneliness; we are never, ever alone.

---

[38] The best ever: https://youtu.be/QjvzCTqkBDQ

[39] "One Strange Rock" episode "Survival."

We have guides and loved ones watching over us always. They're always accessible. They know what we are going through and sometimes they can "get through the clutter" to give you a direct message to save your life.

When I did the first of six hypnotherapy sessions, I never thought I could be hypnotized, didn't "believe" other worldly events could be accessible or I would "get anywhere." But after 4 hours of hypnosis, I was experiencing a conversation with "spiritual beings" I'd known forever.

As the session was ending, I asked them "Is there a message I can bring back?"

I heard **"Just let go."** Let go of anger, let go of fear, resentment, let go of everything holding you back from being who you are, from being who you want to be.

"Just let go" is a bit like **"Let it be."**

So, thank you Mary McCartney for giving us your son *and* giving your son these lyrics: "When I find myself in times of trouble, Mother Mary comes to me *(from the flipside)* **speaking words of wisdom, let it be**. And in my hour of darkness, **she is standing right in front of me** *(clearly, he saw her in this vision)* **speaking words of wisdom**, let it be. Whisper words of wisdom, let it be." [40]

Recently, in an interview with Paul about his new book "Lyrics" he noted that the name of his band "Wings" came as a result of a dream or vision of an angel he had when his daughter was in the ICU after her birth. Apparently, Paul is a medium, yet never talks about it.

---

[40] Written by Paul McCartney and John Lennon. Photo from Hulu.

*****

Paul also did a music documentary with Rick Rubin. ("McCartney 1, 2, 3" on Hulu)

What makes it unique is that they listen to the songs with all of the stems, different tracks and then isolate various parts. We get to hear Paul make a mistake ("that's why we don't dig into the mixes!") or get to hear the genesis of various songs by isolating the tracks.

It's a fascinating look into music.

He also speaks of his relationship with John Lennon and George Harrison. Plays the lick from "Linking" a tune, he and George wrote at age 14.

At one point, he repeats something he's said before, that the reason he and John started writing songs together is because they "ran out of playing covers, and because other bands were playing the same covers, he and John began to write."

Allow me to expand on that for a moment.

Based on the research, based on the idea that people on the flipside plan their lifetimes, sketch out the story points prior to coming here, I'd offer that since they started writing songs before they appeared on stage, it's something that they've always known.

The idee fixe of one's life.

We can examine why we chose our lifetimes, and how the things that spurred us along the way become the things we repeat throughout the lifetime, like repeating music in various songs. Taking bits and pieces of information from our youth and carrying it forward.

It's an unusual moment when he speaks of breaking up with John – it's clear he thought he and John would be together forever as writing partners. He'd never considered that wouldn't be the case. But even then, when we observe our lifetimes from a different lens, and in light of the interviews with John and George, they can see in perspective why things occurred.

Why breaking up was something that needed to occur ten years before John would no longer be on the planet. Not a conscious decision, but as noted, he said in the flipside interviews "He'd always knew his life would be short." It's not like we come to the planet knowing the method of how we might depart – but we do often report having a sense or knowing that it's going to happen earlier than expected.

As Dave Schultz, the Olympian murdered by John Dupont told his father Phillip at age five – "Dad, can you keep a secret? I asked my council if I could come here to teach a lesson in love, they agreed – but I won't be here very long."

His father forgot about that secret until he gave the eulogy for his son's funeral.

His son knew, his son reported that he knew – and yet it was forgotten until it occurred.

People have a sense of the score of their lifetime – they've put the notes together, put together the charts, have a sense of who and what they're going to become and why. Or if the journey is short or long.

But some unusual revelations in this documentary with Paul. Never learned to write music. Still doesn't write music. Many great musicians like him never learned to read or write a note yet made some of the greatest music ever.

Michael Jackson. Eric Clapton. Eddie Van Halen. Robert Johnson. Elvis Presley. Taylor Swift. Bob Weir. Bob Dylan. Jimi Hendrix. Stevie Wonder. Lionel Richie. Stevie Ray Vaughan. Danny Elfman. Django Reinhardt. Dave Brubeck. *None of the Beatles learned to write music.*

I saw Ringo recently on Jimmy Kimmel. Jimmy pointed out that he was such a fan he couldn't quite believe the good fortune he had to be alive when the Beatles played. I felt the same way, and recall making the comment somewhere, "I can't believe I had the good fortune to be alive when the Beatles were making music." It must have been how some folks have felt when their favorite composer was alive and was able to hear their new music with fresh ears.

Yes none of the Beatles learned to read or write music. They could not "sight read" the way *my mom could sight read.*

After seeing the film "Shine" about the pianist who spent his life mastering the Rachmaninoff Concerto #3 ("Perhaps the most difficult piece ever written for piano, Rachmaninoff's third piano concerto is 40 minutes of finger-twisting madness" *The Washington Post*) I took my mother down to an old sheet music store on Wabash Avenue in Chicago. It had mountains of scores, and we bought the score for that Piano concerto. (Sergei Rachmaninoff's Piano Concerto No. 3 in D minor, Op. 30, 1909)

Takes about 30 minutes to drive back our suburban home in Northbrook, Illinois. On the way, I asked if she'd ever played it. She said "No." And then, on the way home, she opened it up and read the score.

The way one is reading this book, or listening to this book, she took the sheet music with its myriad of notes and staffs and signatures and time – for an entire orchestra - and read it like a book, on the way home in the car.

When we got back home, she sat in the living room at her Baldwin piano and played it.

Not haltingly. Not one note every five seconds. Played the score. Might have stopped to turn the page, but that was it. Played it as if she had "already heard it."

I told this story to a fellow who had played the Rach #3 at Carnegie Hall. He said, "No way. It took me ten years to play in public in one sitting." I shrugged. "I don't know man; she sat down and played the whole thing. In forty minutes."

I think the guy called me crazy, a fool, a liar – I don't recall, it was an odd conversation between two people at a party in a loft in Manhattan. "You're lying." *"I swear to God."* "There's no f*cking way." *"Way. She played it man."* "Get out of here." *"I'm not going."* Etc.

Mom could sight read because she knew the language. She spoke that language. More fluent in piano than I am in Italian. (I've lived in Rome, am fluent in gestures as well). But it's this thing we have of assuming our experience is someone else's. She had bypassed the filters that people have at seeing a score of sheet music, into the world where it was sound to her – music to her ears. She could see and hear the notes without playing them.

And she still can from the flipside.

She came through recently to talk about this book. We were doing our podcast and she told Jennifer to tell me, "Don't worry if the ideas bounce around. Don't worry that they don't all add up. Just ask us questions."

It's a funny thing to hear – we all have our muse, but rarely does the muse show up and say **"Hey! Get back to work! We've got a book to finish!"**

In Hulu's *"McCartney 1, 2, 3"* Paul points out that the last note of John's song "A Day in the Life" reverberates "forever," out into the ether, the harmonics on top of the harmonics. A note that travels through time.

Paul spoke about the song *Yesterday*.

He spoke of how the song came to him, fully in a dream. Woke up, mentioned it to his girlfriend, played it on the piano. He didn't write music, so he didn't write it down. Threw in some fake lyrics for "Yesterday" – *"Scrambled eggs. Oh, my baby how I love your legs..."* but went around asking people where the song was from.

He figured George Martin would know, or John might know it – neither did, both encouraged Paul to write it.

"*Yesterday,*" like *"Let it Be"* came in a dream to Paul. Fully formed. Like getting lottery numbers. The most played song in the history of music. In *"Yesterday"* he had the melody, but the words came to him later. In *"Let it Be"* he had the words from his mother, and later came the music.

Meant to be that "Let it Be." "Yesterday" is alive because we carry all of our yesterdays within our conscious mind. Some argue that all the tomorrows are there too, or the "likely idea of them." "Yesterday" was meant to be.

I've heard that Paul is in touch with John and George on the flipside – how could he not be? Why would they not be in touch with him? The idea is that others need to realize that we are always in touch with our classmates, teachers, guides – song writing buddies. Play writing buddies. We just need to bypass the filters. And many musicians already have altered filters. It's worth pointing out, based on the research, that he and John knew prior to coming to the planet, prior to showing up in Liverpool they would be writing together.

Further, when Paul was talking about the breakup of the band, he pointed out he was *heartbroken*. He had never considered he wouldn't be writing music with John, never considered he wouldn't be part of the greatest band on the planet. He was clearly in pain recounting those years of anguish, retiring to the highlands of Scotland where he and Linda found each other. Built another life. On an "Angel's Wings."

But there's a flipside element to this as well.

We do have a higher portion of ourselves "back home." John in his interviews from the flipside, said that he knew that he wasn't going to have a long life. He may not have known the process of returning home but was aware of the likelihood.

The band splitting up may have been something to soften the inevitable blow of what was to occur a decade later.

That is, our higher self is aware of events in the not so distant future, likely outcomes, and that even though John found his muse, the two of them creating "Imagine" perhaps the most iconic description of the flipside ever written, the person he was supposed to be with during the next phase of his life, aware that there were lessons to be learned, another son to be born (Sean) aware on some level that he was moving into the third act of his life.

And by splitting up the band or agreeing that it was obviously time to split up over money issues – was a favor to the others to help them to find their own path.

Because it gave his pal ten years to figure out how to navigate the rest of it on his own, without his writing partner, with whom he was destined to write some of the greatest love songs, greatest ballads of all time. A gift given with love. All part of that same frequency of love.

I'll close with these lyrics, written by John and Yoko. It's the best description of the flipside I've heard put into music.

"Imagine there's no heaven, it's easy if you try, No hell below us, above us, only sky. Imagine all the people... living for today... Imagine there's no countries; it isn't hard to do. Nothing to kill or die for, and no religion, too. Imagine all the people, living life in peace..." (Words and Music by John Lennon and Yoko Ono)

People report on the flipside, we return home when the curtain falls. That's not opinion, theory or wishful thinking – it's just in the data. No library cards to get in the pearly gates. There's no hierarchy. "All religions point to the same garden." Where people experience unconditional love, even if they've never experienced love on the planet. That experience is the experience of being in touch with the connectivity of all things, of all beings. Like diving into a pool of consciousness, realizing that we are all connected to each other.

And all hearing a symphony of joy. As Elvis noted in his interview, what he experienced crossing over to the flipside was... *joy.*

It is not the end. The Journey is the adventure and we are all just walking each other home.

Luana during her Broadway debut

Finally, a fan said after listening to a recent podcast, asked our moderator on the flipside for some assistance. "Dear Mr. Martini, I hope to find you well. I'll try to keep it short.

Whilst driving to work yesterday (I'm a teacher now, I teach Dutch in a Dutch secondary school), I listened to your podcast, last week's to be precise, and I could anticipate all of the answers Miss Anders gave to your questions.

Of course, that's amazing in itself, but I decided to ask her if she wanted to help me out. One of the classes I teach is especially challenging and they broke me last Tuesday, so I was afraid of going back in with them.

Miss Anders told me she'd help me "together with the kid", meaning my most important and beloved guide, then she touched my head, so that I'd know where she was.

The lesson went better thanks to her. She wanted me to write to you, I don't know why, and she made me listen twice to your talk "Going home" at IANDS. (Available on YouTube via Richard Martini MartiniZone) I tried to file it away, but the pull is strong, like it would mean something to you or that you'd need to know this. But I could be wrong.

Either way, my motto is to never leave things unsaid. Thank you again for your work, it does so much good. Have a nice day from my side of the globe and a good evening on yours."

Recently, during our podcast, "Hacking the Afterlife" Luana mentioned something Jennifer and I had never heard before. She said "**There is no veil**. The veil is a human construct."

Pretty startling comment. Luana is saying that the "illusion" that there is a veil between the afterlife and life on the planet is inaccurate. We choose to believe there is a veil rather than observing one. That the "filters" that are on our brain that prevent us from accessing this information can be bypassed, and once they are bypassing, the "veil" disappears.

I'll give Robin Williams the last word. Last night I had a dream where I was discussing this topic with him. He said, "I am the light at the end of the tunnel."

I remembered that he had a tunnel named after him which leads from Sausalito to the Golden Gate(s).

Literally, *the light at the end of the tunnel.*

"Love love."

Author, Luana and Dave Patlak

About the Author

Dedicated to Anthy. Thanks for letting me choose you.

To my wife and kids who have put up with me and "the flipside research" for so long. To Sherry for playing the piano, to Olivia for playing guitar and her singing voice, to RJ for playing Hans Zimmer scores on the piano after hearing them once.

To Mrs. Helfrich, my first piano teacher. To that teacher who taught me how to transpose written guitar chords to piano – I forget your name but have never forgotten the technique and have taught it to many. To Abbie Adams for being the vocalist who inspired me to join a band, to Bruce Haring who got us together to become a band later in life that played the House of Blues and other venues.

To Bob Shaye who heard me playing in a club one night and put me on his yacht for the millennium cruise where I played for or accompanied Penny Marshall, Francis and Ellie Coppola, Renny Harlin, Toby Emmerich, Richard Perry who sang Johnny Cash tunes while I played.

To the late owner of Monteverde in Odeon who gave me a gig playing at his restaurant in Paris whenever I stopped by. To the clubs in Mumbai, Stockholm, Paris, Dublin, NY, LA, NOLA, Chicago where I got to sit in or rock an audience. I'd ask the bartender for "free drinks for me and my pals if they liked what I played." Many unpaid bar tabs at the Martinez in Cannes.

To Joel Gotler, my agent who plays the blues harp. Played a track on my first film. Still plays gigs in the valley. To Duncan Clark who once took a punch meant for me by an angry pianist at La Chunga bar in Cannes. Jim Deck for his guitars and joie de vivre. To Charles Grodin who looked at me playing the piano and said, "Really?" To Francis Coppola who accompanied on standup bass at his home in Napa while playing rock standards during Thanksgiving dinners with Luana. To Don Everly who sat in and sang "Knocking on

Heaven's Door" with me and Zappa saxman Craig Cole. To Paul Simon for *being Paul.*

To my brothers who all had musical talents in varying degrees, Jeff on bongos, Rob on classical guitar, Chaz on electric. Even dad with his violin. I came from a house of music, and it was normal for everyone to perform during holidays. To the great tunes from Mom and Aunt Macie on dueling pianos, Aunt Martha who sang along, to Aunt Catherine. To their mother Mimi who could croon with the best of them, I recall her kicking a heel over the keyboard when I played boogie woogie. To my musical muses over many lifetimes, Ludwig, Hector, Mose, Muddy, BB, Ray, Tom, John, George… what a treat to meet you via your music in this life. To be able to hear you in my head when I say your name.

To Jennifer Shaffer, Luana Anders for putting me in touch with the flipside. To my father Romeo Charles Martini, a Chicago based Architect who taught me how to read a blueprint, to my mom Anthy, a concert pianist who taught me that practice makes perfect, and home is where the heart is. We'll catch you on the reprise.

Hear her play at AnthyMartini.com

Author's Bio:

Chicago native, author and award-winning filmmaker Richard Martini has written and/or directed 9 award winning theatrical feature films. "Flipside" was his debut non-fiction book on a topic. The documentaries "Flipside" and "Talking to Bill Paxton" "Hacking the Afterlife" are distributed by Gaia TV and Amazon Prime. This is his Ninth Book.

Has written for "Variety" "Premiere" and "Inc.com" His books include "Flipside: A Tourist's Guide to the Afterlife" "It's a Wonderful Afterlife: Further Adventures in the Flipside volumes one and two" "Hacking the Afterlife" have all have been to #1 in their genres in kindle at Amazon after his appearances on "Coast to Coast" radio with George Noory.

"Backstage Pass to the Flipside: Talking to the Afterlife with Jennifer Shaffer 3" and "Architecture of the Afterlife" are available online or via major online book outlets.

For more information: *RichMartini.com - MartiniZone.com* on YouTube. Podcast: *HackingTheAfterlife.com*

Author's photo by Grammy award winning Russ Titelman.

For momly

www.ingramcontent.com/pod-product-compliance
Lightning Source LLC
Chambersburg PA
CBHW070417010526
44118CB00014B/1792